SECON

Te

SUPER MINDS

Lucy Frino · Melanie Williams
with Herbert Puchta · Peter Lewis-Jones · Günter Gerngross

CAMBRIDGE
UNIVERSITY PRESS

Thanks and acknowledgements

Acknowledgements

The authors and publishers acknowledge the following sources of copyright material and are grateful for the permissions granted. While every effort has been made, it has not always been possible to identify the sources of all the material used, or to trace all copyright holders. If any omissions are brought to our notice, we will be happy to include the appropriate acknowledgements on reprinting and in the next update to the digital edition, as applicable.

Photography and illustrations

The photographs and illustrations in the teaching notes are reused from the Student's Book.

The photographs and illustrations in the Introduction are reused from the Student's Book, Workbook, Practice Book, Flashcards, Presentation Plus and Practice Extra.

Contents

Map of the course iv

Introduction
Welcome to *Super Minds Second Edition* vii
The thinking course, revisited viii
The Cambridge Life Competencies Framework x
Cognitive control functions xii
Unit walkthrough xiii
Components overview xvi

Teaching notes
Friends TB4
1 At school TB10
2 Let's play TB22
3 Pet show TB34
4 Lunchtime TB46
5 Free time TB58
6 The old house TB70
7 Get dressed TB82
8 The robot TB94
9 At the beach TB106

Language focus key TB118
Audioscripts and videoscripts TB119

Map of the course

Friends (pages 4–9)

Vocabulary	Language focus	Story
Greetings Numbers *one* to *ten* Colours	*What's your name? I'm (Thunder).* *How old are you? I'm (seven).* *Flash's bag is …*	*Meet the Super Friends* **Value** Making friends

▶ Song: Sing the alphabet

1 At school (pages 10–21)

How do we learn?

Vocabulary	Language focus	Story	Skills	Think and learn
Classroom objects: *ruler, pen, book, rubber, pencil case, pencil, desk, notebook, bag, paper*	*What's this?* *It's a (pencil).* *Is it a (pen)?* *Yes, it is. / No, it isn't.* *Open your book, please.* *Pass me a (ruler), please.* *Sit at your desk, please.*	*Watch out, Flash!* **Value** Helping each other **Phonics** The letter sound *a*	• Listening • Speaking, reading and writing	**Science:** Senses **Project:** Make a senses book.

▶ Song: What's this? What's this? ▶ Creativity: Create that! ▶ Revision: Think back

2 Let's play (pages 22–33)

What do toys look like?

Vocabulary	Language focus	Story	Skills	Think and learn
Toys: *computer game, kite, plane, bike, doll, monster, train, go-kart, car, ball*	*What's his/her name?* *His/Her name's (Ben/Sue).* *What's his/her favourite toy?* *His/Her favourite toy's his/her ball.* *How old is he/she?* *He's/She's (seven).* *It's a (new kite).* *It's an (ugly monster).*	*The go-kart race* **Value** Fair play **Phonics** The letter sound *e*	• Reading • Listening, speaking and writing	**Maths:** 2D shapes **Project:** Design a toy.

▶ Song: Come and see ▶ Creativity: Do that! ▶ Revision: Group check

3 Pet show (pages 34–45)

What do animals need?

Vocabulary	Language focus	Story	Skills	Think and learn
Animals: *donkey, elephant, spider, cat, rat, frog, duck, lizard, dog*	*The (lizard)'s in/on/under the (bag).* *I like / I don't like (dogs).*	*The spider* **Value** Being brave **Phonics** The letter sound *i*	• Listening and speaking • Reading, speaking and writing	**Environmental studies:** Nature **Project:** Make a spider's web.

▶ Song: There's a pond ▶ Creativity: Create that! ▶ Revision: Think back

4 Lunchtime (pages 46–57)

Where does food come from?

Vocabulary	Language focus	Story	Skills	Think and learn
Food: *apple, banana, cake, pizza, sausage, cheese sandwich, fish, chicken, peas, steak, carrots*	*I've got / haven't got a (sandwich).* *Have we got any (cheese)?* *Yes, we have. / No, we haven't.*	*The pizza* **Value** Waiting your turn **Phonics** The letter sound *o*	• Listening and writing • Reading and speaking	**Science:** Food **Project:** Write a story about a fruit.

▶ Song: The magic tree ▶ Creativity: Do that! ▶ Revision: Group check

5 Free time (pages 58–69)

Which activities do we do?

Vocabulary	Language focus	Story	Skills	Think and learn
Days of the week: *Monday, Tuesday, Wednesday, Thursday, Friday, Saturday, Sunday*	*I (play football) on (Saturdays).* *Do you (watch TV) at the weekend?* *Yes, I do. / No, I don't.*	*We're lost!* **Value** Asking for help when you need it **Phonics** The letter sound *u*	• Listening and speaking • Reading and writing	**Physical education:** Activities **Project:** Make a poster.

▶ Song: I'm bored. I'm bored. ▶ Creativity: Create that! ▶ Revision: Think back

6 The old house (pages 70–81)

How are houses different?

Vocabulary	Language focus	Story	Skills	Think and learn
The home: *bedroom, bathroom, living room, kitchen, hall, stairs, cellar, dining room*	*There's a (monster).* *There are (four cats).* *Is there a (plane)? Yes, there is.* *Are there any (rats)? No, there aren't.* *How many (cars) are there?* *There are (four cars).*	*At the house* **Value** Looking after your friends **Phonics** The letter sound *h*	• Listening and writing • Reading and speaking	**Geography:** Homes **Project:** Design a house.

▶ Song: We live in different homes ▶ Creativity: Do that! ▶ Revision: Group check

7 Get dressed (pages 82–93)

How do clothes look different?

Vocabulary	Language focus	Story	Skills	Think and learn
Clothes: *sweater, skirt, shorts, trousers, jacket, socks, jeans, shoes, baseball cap, T-shirt*	*Do you like this (hat) / these (shoes)?* *Yes, I do. / No, I don't.* *(Olivia)'s wearing (a red sweater).* *Is he/she wearing (a blue T-shirt)?* *Yes, he/she is. / No, he/ she isn't.*	*The cap* **Value** Saying sorry **Phonics** The letter sounds *sp* and *st*	• Reading • Speaking, listening and writing	**Art and design:** Patterns **Project:** Design a T-shirt.

▶ Song: You look good ▶ Creativity: Create that! ▶ Revision: Think back

8 The robot (pages 94–105)

How can we move?

Vocabulary	Language focus	Story	Skills	Think and learn
The body: *arm, hand, knee, fingers, leg, foot, toes, head*	*I can/can't (stand on one leg). He/She can/can't (skip). Can you (swim)? Yes, I can. / No, I can't.*	*The problem* **Value** Teamwork **Phonics** The letter sound *g*	• Listening and speaking • Reading and writing	**Physical education:** Movements **Project:** Make a dance.
▶ Song: Help!		▶ Creativity: Do that!		▶ Revision: Group check

9 At the beach (pages 106–117)

Where can we go on holiday?

Vocabulary	Language focus	Story	Skills	Think and learn
Holidays: *paint a picture, listen to music, catch a fish, take a photo, eat ice cream, play the guitar, read a book, make a sandcastle, look for shells*	*Let's (play the guitar). Good idea. Where's the (blue book)? It's in the (green bag). Where are the (orange books)? They're in the (black bag).*	*The top of the hill* **Value** Modesty **Phonics** The letter sounds *ee* and *ea*	• Listening and speaking • Reading, listening and writing	**Geography:** Landscapes **Project:** Write a diary for a perfect holiday.
▶ Song: *You and me*		▶ Creativity: Create that!		▶ Revision: Think back

Key to teaching notes icons

- Cambridge Life Competencies Framework
- Cognitive control functions
- Stickers
- Story
- Values

In the teaching notes, these two icons use the colours shown here in order to help contrast the two areas for teachers. For students, both kinds of icon use one colour.

Welcome to SUPER MINDS SECOND EDITION

Rediscover *Super Minds!*

Welcome to *Super Minds 2nd Edition*, a thoroughly updated and enhanced new edition of a much-loved English course from this renowned author team.

Accompany your students on exciting adventures with the intrepid characters, as they enjoy creative projects, authentic CLIL content, and the flexibility of the extensive skills practice, whilst working towards B1 level on the Common European Framework of Reference for Languages (CEFR).

Aligned to the Cambridge Life Competencies Framework, *Super Minds 2nd Edition* has a particular focus on developing Critical and Creative Thinking skills. In addition, throughout the course, students will develop their working memory, inhibitory control and cognitive flexibility, three key cognitive control functions for young learners. Together with the universal values introduced in each story, these skills help create curious and successful lifelong learners, and socially responsible individuals.

Super Minds 2nd Edition is supported by a comprehensive digital package in *Cambridge One*, a new-generation learning environment, including big-screen quality animated videos for the classroom, Practice Extra with digital activities for home or lab learning, together with comprehensive data views, rewards, and the capacity to assign homework digitally.

Super Minds 2nd Edition is a course that combines the very best of rich classroom experience with contemporary pedagogical research.

Super Minds 2nd Edition: The thinking course, revisited

***Super Minds* is much loved by millions of learners of English in over 70 countries. Since its publication we have carried out extensive research to find out what teachers and learners love about *Super Minds*, and what could be updated and made even better.**

While this new and improved 2nd Edition of *Super Minds* maintains its easy-to-use, comprehensive language syllabus and unit structure, the experience of teaching and learning with the course is thoroughly refreshed and contemporary.

What have we kept?

The things teachers and learners love:

- relatable characters who enjoy exciting adventures
- fun and catchy songs and chants which aid engagement in the classroom and at home
- interactive and engaging projects and activities
- authentic CLIL content and extensive skills practice
- a comprehensive language syllabus.

What have we improved?

***Super Minds 2nd Edition* represents a significant update. Here's how *Super Minds 2nd Edition* has changed:**

1 New design

- The characters and stories throughout the course have been transformed with new contemporary illustrations: today's students will find them as relatable as ever and be charmed by their adventures.
- Higher levels have been designed to reflect the increased sophistication of today's pre-teens.
- A full-colour Workbook gives learners further practice and consolidates learning.

2 Fresh and updated content

- Exciting new animated story videos and song videos from Starter to Level 4, as well as animated *Language focus* videos at all levels.
- New *Think and learn* CLIL content and videos linked to topics students will be studying in their first language.
- Creative and Critical Thinking strands have been updated and developed in line with the Cambridge Life Competencies Framework. Activities are mapped to the Framework and explained in the Teacher's Book.
- Activities designed to enhance cognitive control functions which will lead to more successful language learning.
- New *Big Questions* at the beginning of every unit give students a gradual introduction to Enquiry-Based Learning.

3 Enhanced digital support

- Extensive digital support for teachers and students is accessed through our new learning environment, *Cambridge One*.
- Presentation Plus gives easy access to resources in the classroom, including the new animated videos.
- Practice Extra provides extra digital activities for students in a carefully tailored environment designed specifically for Primary learners. It includes interactive games to review language and *Brain Break* activities to aid motivation and help recharge the brain.

Presentation Plus

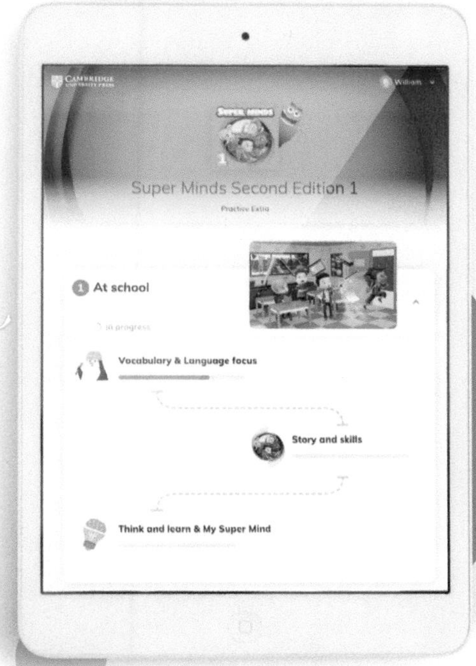

Practice Extra

The Cambridge Life Competencies Framework

Our world is changing fast and we need to prepare our students with the skills and experiences that go beyond learning an additional language.

Our job as Primary educators is complex. How do we prepare our students for a future which may be dramatically different from the present? Experts say there are some key skills which will be essential for the citizens of tomorrow: working together with people from around the world, thinking creatively to solve problems, analysing sources more critically, communicating our views effectively, and maintaining a positive mindset in an increasingly complex world.

The Cambridge Life Competencies Framework supports teachers in this challenging area – we understand that the engaging and collaborative nature of the language classroom is the perfect place to develop and embed these key qualities.

Competency

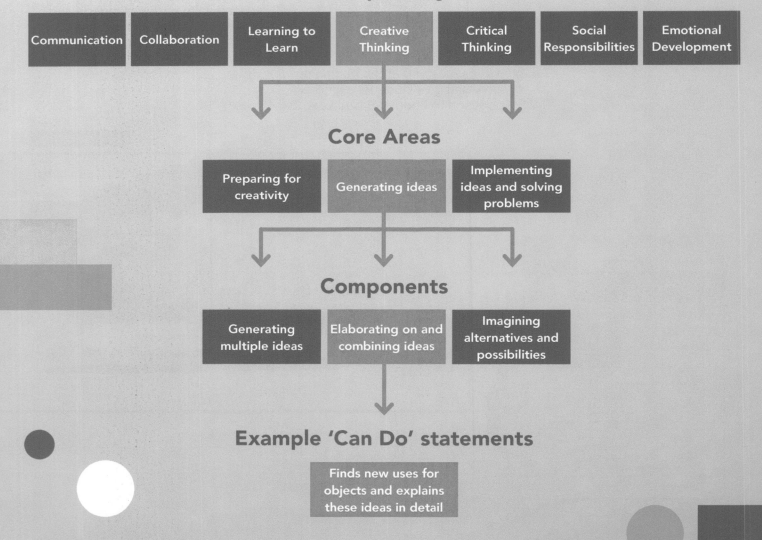

Communication | Collaboration | Learning to Learn | Creative Thinking | Critical Thinking | Social Responsibilities | Emotional Development

Core Areas

Preparing for creativity | Generating ideas | Implementing ideas and solving problems

Components

Generating multiple ideas | Elaborating on and combining ideas | Imagining alternatives and possibilities

Example 'Can Do' statements

Finds new uses for objects and explains these ideas in detail

Super Minds 2nd Edition and the Cambridge Life Competencies Framework

The Cambridge Life Competencies Framework underpins the Critical and Creative Thinking strands of *Super Minds 2nd Edition*, helping to create curious and successful lifelong learners.

Critical Thinking

This activity from Unit 4 of the Student's Book helps learners understand and analyse links between ideas by comparing different factual and fictional information.

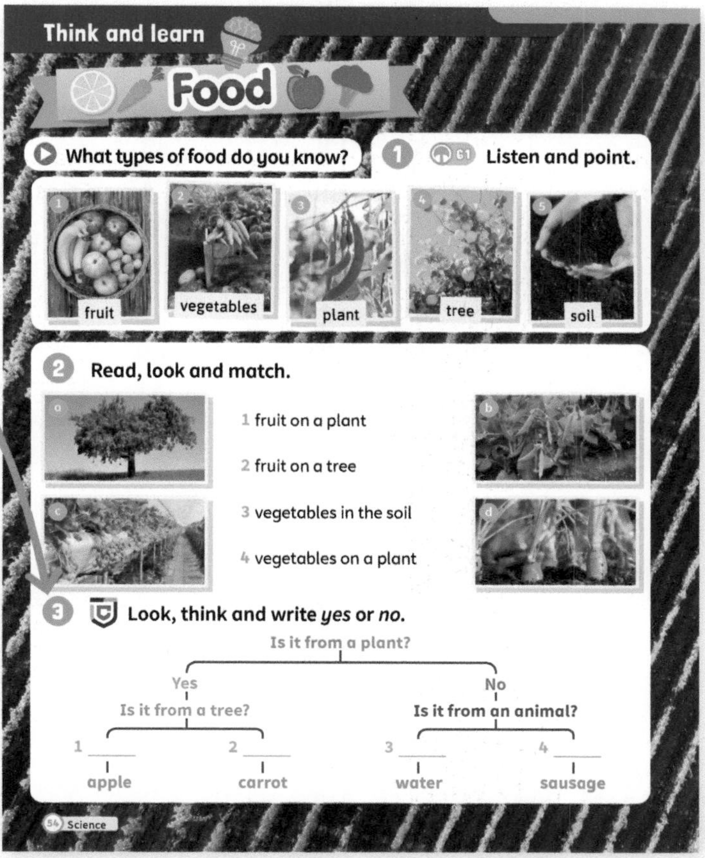

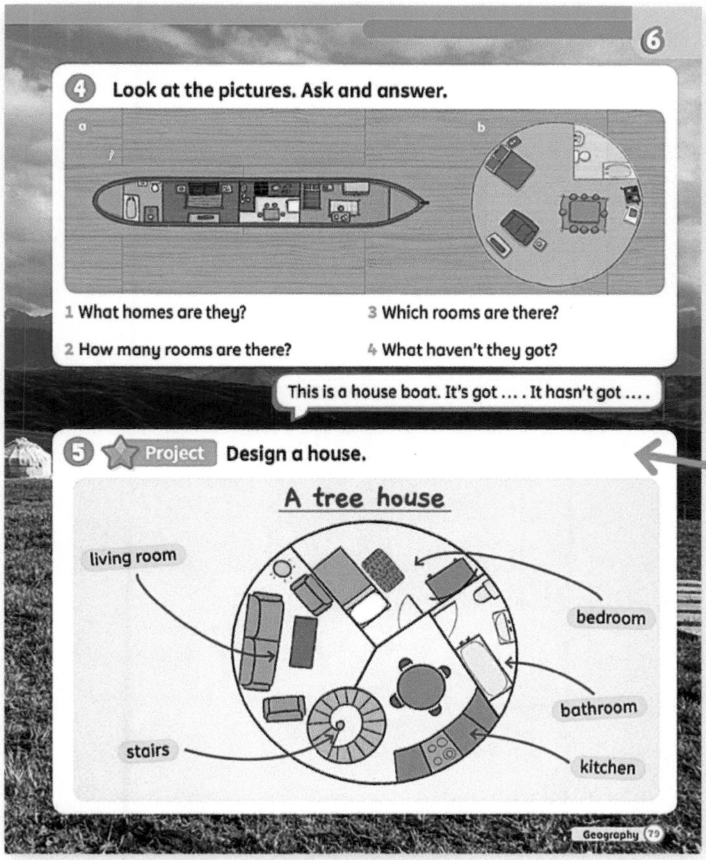

Creative Thinking

This project in Unit 6 of the Student's Book helps learners develop Creative Thinking skills by creating new content and imagining alternatives and possibilities.

For more information about the *Cambridge Life Competencies Framework*, go to languageresearch.cambridge.org/clc

Cognitive control functions

Successful language learning requires our learners to be in control of their own learning and of themselves. To do this, they need to:

- set goals
- organise learning over time
- focus attention to be able to stay on task
- adapt behaviour in order to overcome challenges and reach goals.

To manage these behaviours successfully, the brain uses **cognitive control functions** which determine students' success in learning and have a significant influence on their future success and wellbeing.

Activities in *Super Minds 2nd Edition* have been designed to enhance the **three core areas** of learners' cognitive control functions:

Working memory

is the ability to hold information in mind so that certain tasks can be completed.

This activity in Unit 1 of the Workbook helps to improve learners' working memory.

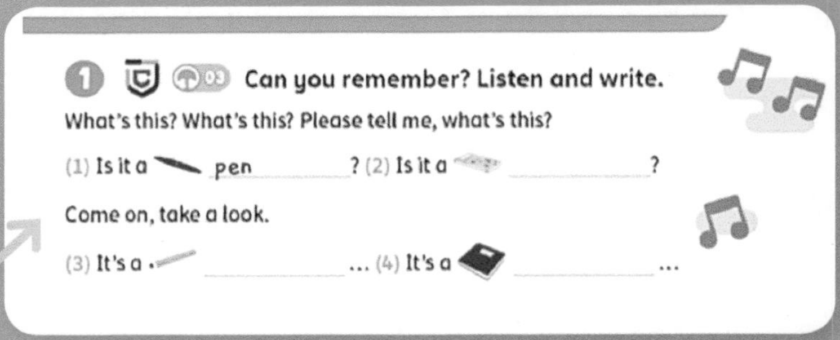
1 Can you remember? Listen and write.
What's this? What's this? Please tell me, what's this?
(1) Is it a pen ? (2) Is it a ?
Come on, take a look.
(3) It's a ... (4) It's a ...

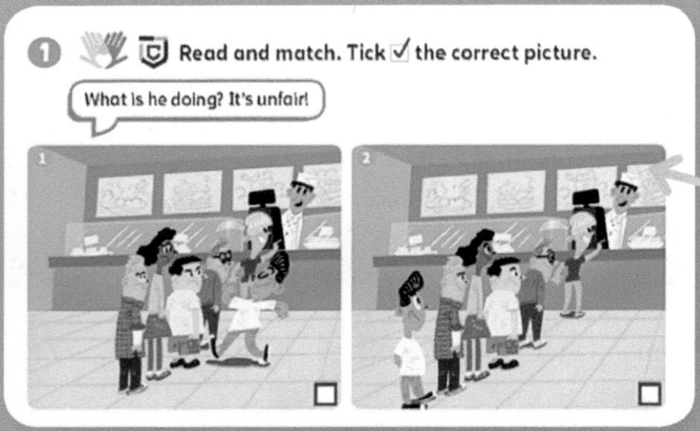
1 Read and match. Tick the correct picture.
What is he doing? It's unfair!
1
2

Inhibitory control

refers to the abilities to focus attention and control our emotional and behavioural responses.

This activity in Unit 4 of the Workbook helps to improve learners' inhibitory control.

Cognitive flexibility

is needed for solving problems, and enables students to look at issues from different viewpoints, to think 'outside the box' and to adapt to changing conditions.

This project in Unit 4 of the Student's Book helps to improve learners' cognitive flexibility.

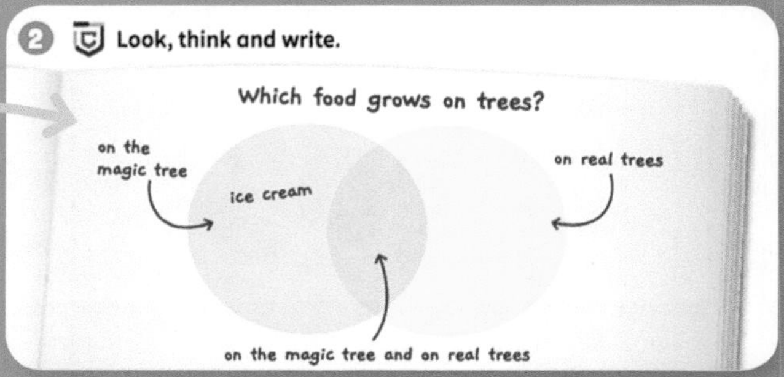
2 Look, think and write.
Which food grows on trees?
on the magic tree
ice cream
on real trees
on the magic tree and on real trees

Unit walkthrough

Key vocabulary

is presented in an opening illustration which features the *Super Minds* characters and sets the scene for the main story of the unit. Full-colour digital or printed flashcard sets help learners practise vocabulary.

The Big Question

is a new feature that gives a gradual introduction to Enquiry-Based Learning. Each *Big Question* is directly related to the unit topic and is explored throughout the unit with further ideas for exploitation available in the Teacher's Book.

Fun and informative songs

practising and extending the vocabulary and language of the unit feature throughout *Super Minds 2nd Edition*. Karaoke song videos can be found in Presentation Plus and the teacher and learner resource areas in *Cambridge One*.

Contextualised language

is presented in new 2nd Edition story-based animated *Language focus* videos, featuring the entertaining character Penny the penguin. Each unit has two animated videos which can be accessed through Presentation Plus and the teacher and learner resource areas in *Cambridge One*.

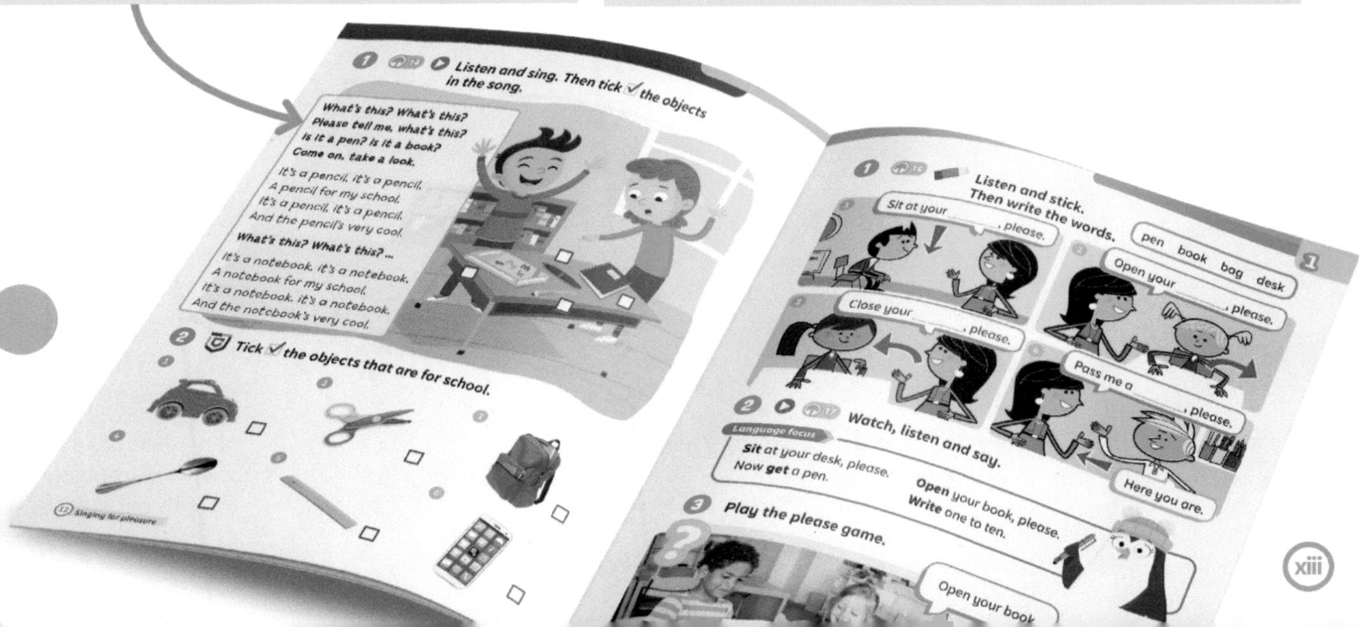

Episodic adventure stories

linked to the unit theme run throughout each level and feature the classic *Super Minds* characters.

Brand new big-screen quality animated story videos

are a new feature of the 2nd Edition, and can be accessed through Presentation Plus and the teacher and learner resource areas in *Cambridge One*.

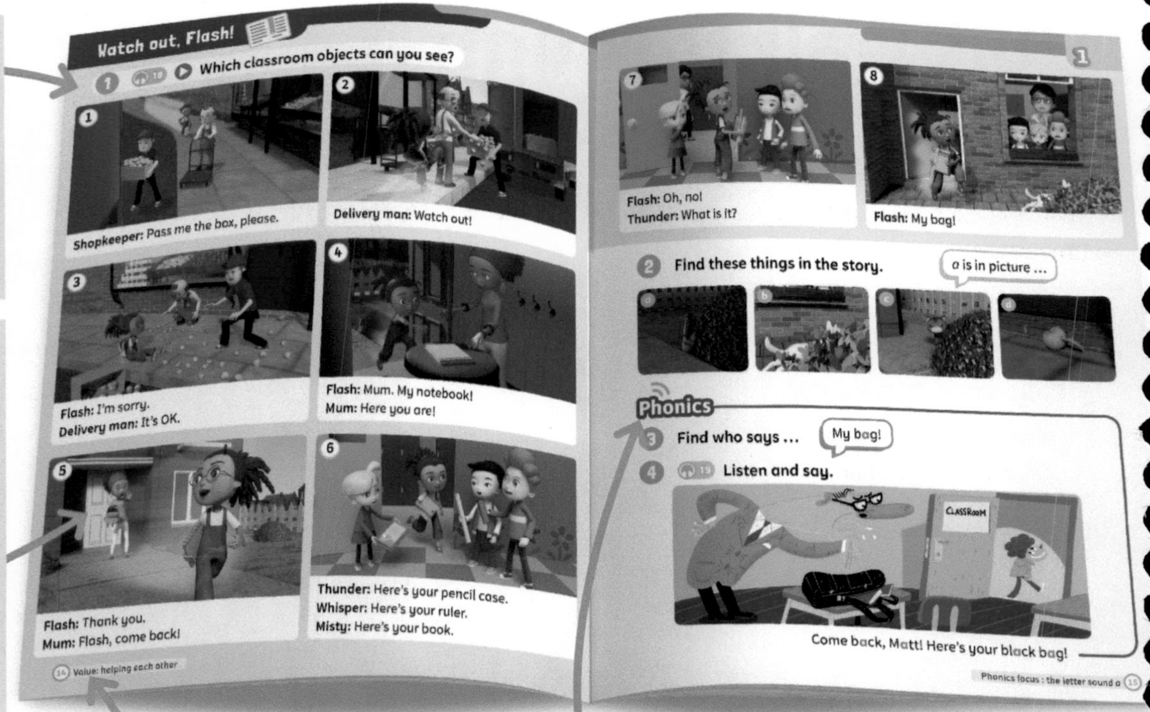

Universal values

are introduced with each story and supported with extension activities in the Teacher's Book. Thinking about values and applying them when interacting with others is a key life competency and helps build socially responsible individuals.

Phonics

in each unit link to the story. Further phonics practice can be found in the corresponding pages of the Workbook.

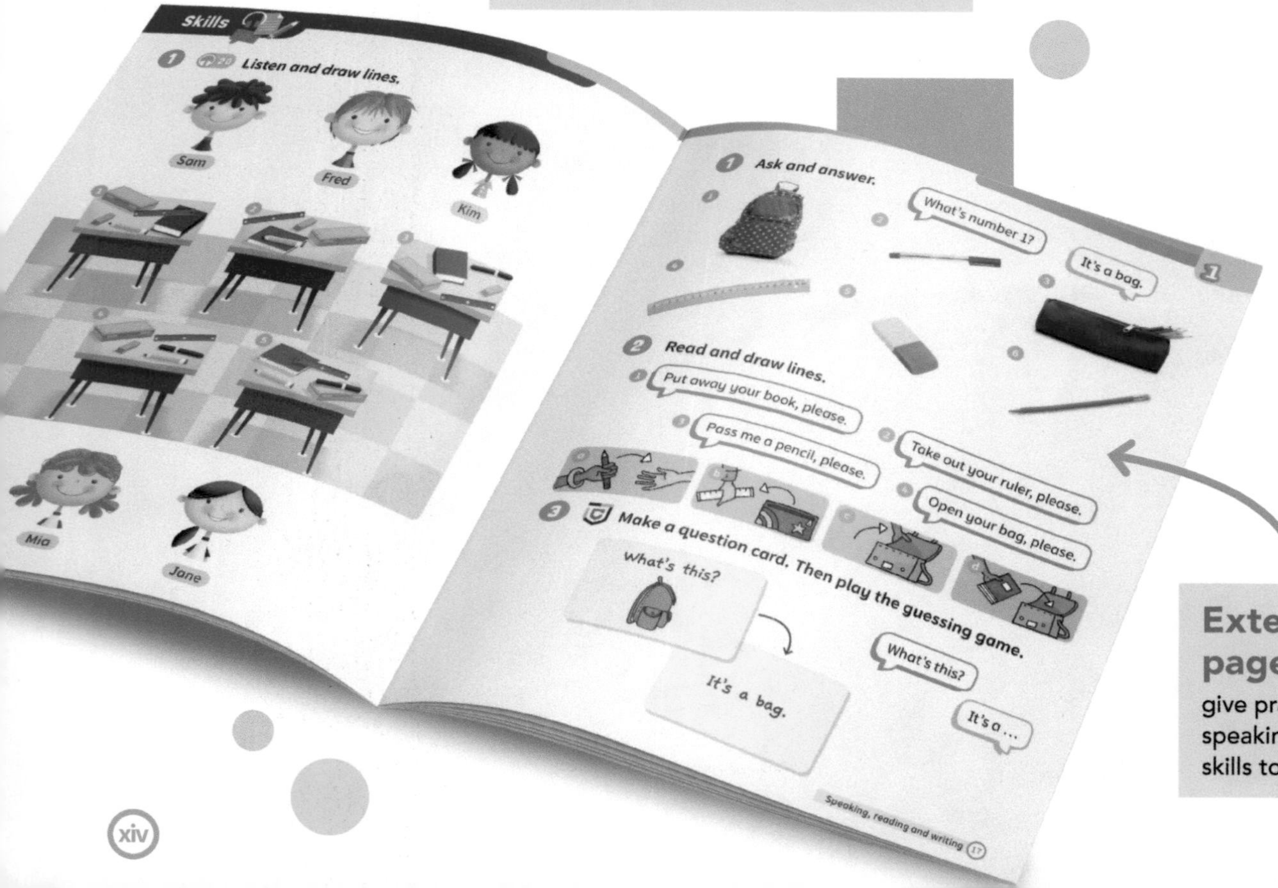

Extensive Skills pages

give practice of listening, speaking, reading and writing skills to extend learning.

Think and learn CLIL projects

integrate content and language, with students learning about other curriculum subjects in English so that their English is expansive. The CLIL syllabus has been specially designed to cover similar topics to those that students will be encountering in their first language at the same stage.

Brand new documentary-style videos

present the topic and the vocabulary of the CLIL pages.

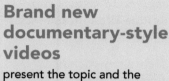

Project

Each *Think and learn* spread culminates in a project that can be carried out in class or set as homework.

Create that! and *Do that!*

offer further opportunities for students to develop their creativity as well as practise their listening skills.

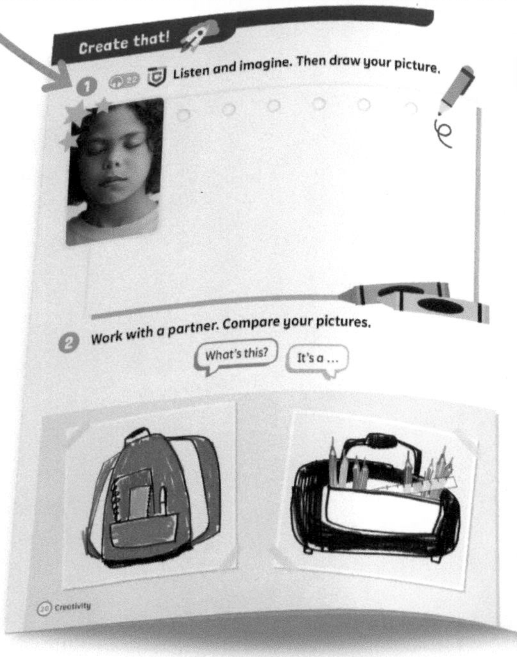

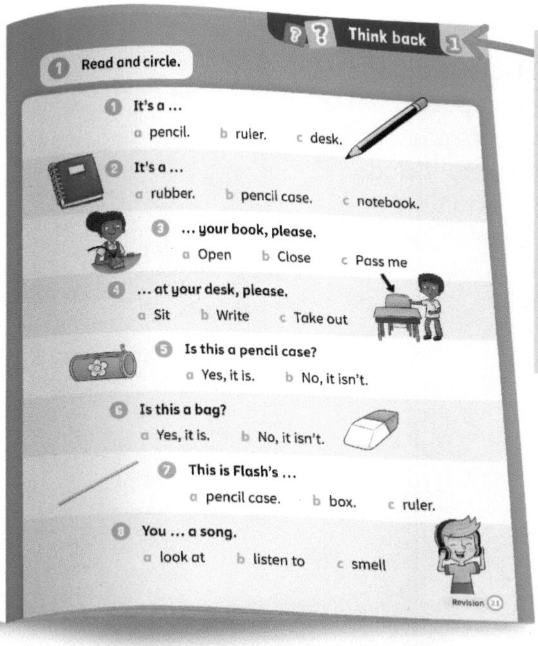

Think back and *Group check*

review pages consolidate learning and alternately promote independent and collaborative learning.

Components overview

Student's components

The **Student's Book** contains 10 units, each with a fun and relevant topic for learners and its own vocabulary and language focus. The back of the Student's Book also contains an additional *Language focus* section for each unit, and two pages of colourful stickers to practise language and skills in corresponding activities throughout the book.

The **Workbook**, now full-colour for the 2nd Edition, correlates page by page with the Student's Book, making it easy to use both books in class. The Workbook also includes a code for students to access the Digital Pack, including Practice Extra.

Student's Book

Workbook

The **Super Practice Book** is an additional and optional component for students that practises both language and skills, with teacher and parent notes also available. This component has been updated for the 2nd Edition to include speaking and listening in addition to reading and writing pages.

Teacher's components

The **Teacher's Book** features the Student's Book pages interleaved on each spread, ensuring that your classroom experience is as smooth as possible. It includes activity-by-activity mapping to Critical and Creative Thinking in the Cambridge Life Competencies Framework, as well as to cognitive control functions.

Flashcards help learners practise key vocabulary from the unit, with an illustration or photo on one side and target language on the other. Digital flashcards are available for all levels, with the option of a set of printed flashcards for each level from Starter to Level 4.

Flashcards

Poster packs are available, with five vibrant posters for each level, providing teachers with an eye-catching, engaging resource for language practice. The posters focus on key language from the Student's Book, and include extra words from the corresponding Young Learners English syllabus to extend students' vocabulary. Accompanying activity notes offer a variety of interactive, engaging activities to fully exploit the posters.

Super Practice Book

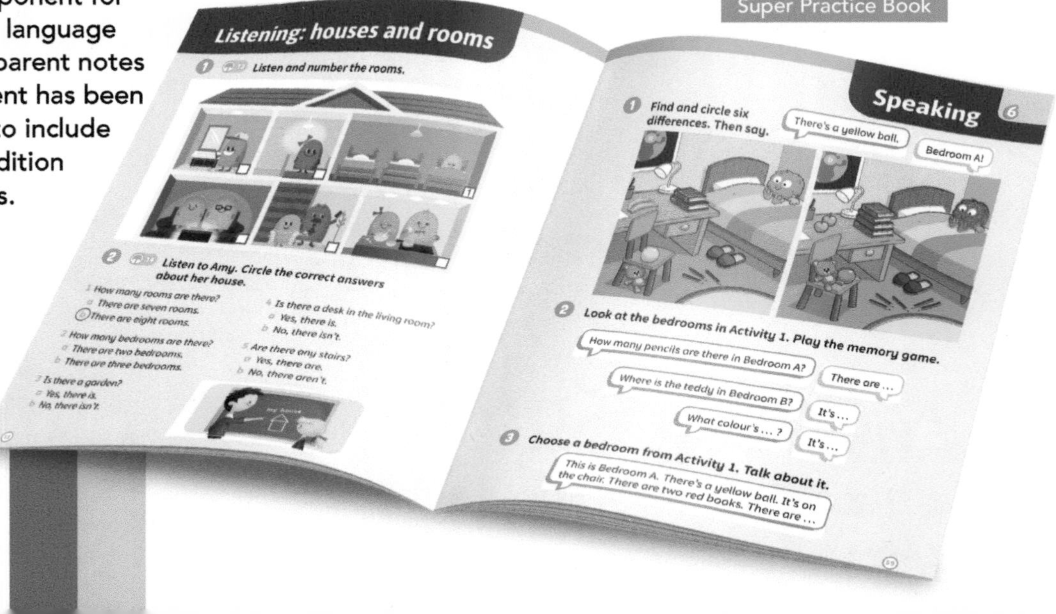

Digital components

***Super Minds 2nd Edition* is supported by a comprehensive digital package for the teacher and the student. It is designed to be flexible and offers rich support for the classroom, while offering age-appropriate additional support for students, whether in the classroom or at home.**

The digital package can be found all in one place in our new learning environment *Cambridge One*, ensuring the digital experience is smooth and intuitive. Teachers can access the content using the unique code found on the inside front cover of this Teacher's Book. Students will find their access code on the inside front cover of their Workbook.

The *Super Minds 2nd Edition* digital package contains the following components.

For teachers:

Presentation Plus provides page-faithful reproductions of the Student's Book and Workbook, and includes:

- hotspots to audio and video content and interactive reproductions of activities
- interactive games and digital flashcards
- quick and easy access to the Teacher's Book notes corresponding to the Student's Book or Workbook page.

Teacher Resources include:

- a wide range of downloadable photocopiable activities
- teacher's notes, parent's notes and answer keys for the Super Practice Book
- downloadable, printable tests for Starter Level
- access to all the course audio and video.

Test Generator provides the option of ready-made or customisable tests at different levels of challenge for Levels 1 to 6.

For students:

Practice Extra includes:

- online activities which consolidate the classroom learning, including animations and interactive games to engage students
- *Brain Breaks* activities designed to aid motivation and help recharge the brain.

Learner Resources provides students with access to the wealth of audio-visual content that *Super Minds 2nd Edition* has to offer.

Portfolio provides students with the opportunity to evidence their project work.

Presentation Plus

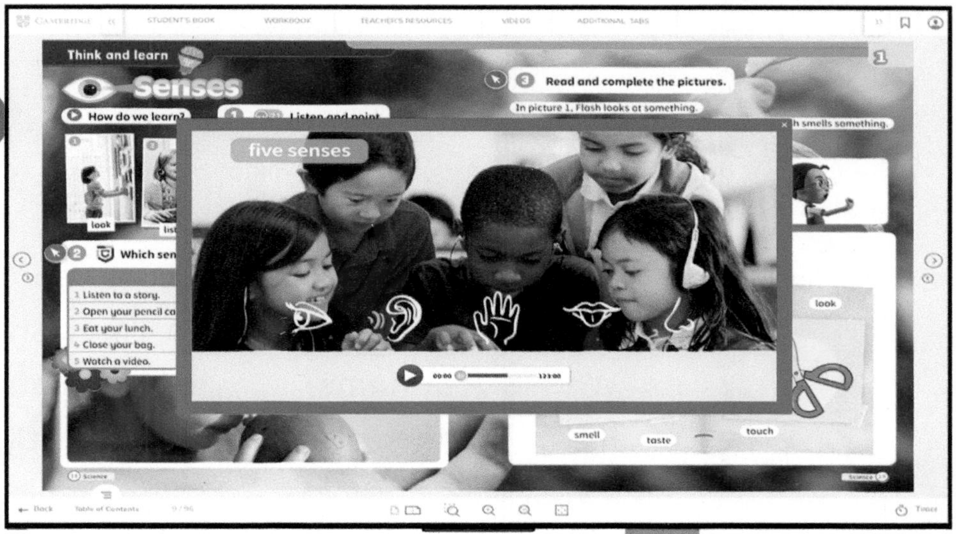

Practice Extra

Friends

1 01 **Listen and look. Then listen and say the words.**

2 02 **Listen and chant.**

Hi, I'm Whisper.
What's your name?
Hi, I'm Thunder.
What a nice name!

Hi, I'm Flash.
What's your name?
Hi, I'm Misty.
What a nice name!

Learning outcomes:
- to name and talk about characters
- to practise greetings and introductions
- to say a chant

New language: *Hi, What's your name? I'm* (name), *What a nice name!* character names

Cognitive control functions: Working memory

Materials: flashcards 1–4 (characters), music, pieces of card (optional)

Warm-up

Aim: to review *Hello* and *Hi*
- Wave to the class and say *Hello*. Encourage students to wave back and say *Hello*. Repeat, but this time say *Hi*.
- Greet a student with *Hello,* (name). Prompt the rest of the class to wave at him/her and say *Hello,* (name). Repeat with different students, alternating between *Hello* and *Hi*.
- Students practise saying *Hello* to one another in pairs.
- Do a mingling activity. Ask students to stand up and walk around. Play some music. When you pause the music, students stop walking and say *Hello!* to their nearest classmate.

1 01 SB p4 **Listen and look. Then listen and say the words.**

Aim: to introduce the names of the characters
- Students look at the picture in their Student's Books. Point to the name labels. Ask the students why they start with capital letters. Elicit that they are names. Say *Look at the names. Listen.*
- Play the recording. Students point to the character names when they hear them.

For script see TB p119.

- Play the second part of the recording. Students repeat the names.
- Point to the character names/ pictures in turn or show the character flashcards. Students say the names.
- Students practise pointing and naming in pairs.

2 02 SB p4 **Listen and chant.**

Aim: to present *Hi, What's your name? I'm* (name).
- Play the recording. Students listen and follow the chant in their Student's Books.

For chant script see SB p4.

- Play the recording again, pausing after each line for students to repeat. Make sure they understand the meaning of *What a nice name!*
- Practise the chant as a class. Show the character flashcards as prompts.
- Invite four students to come to the front. Give each one a character name. They perform the chant for the class, each saying two lines. Repeat with different groups of four students.

Practice

Aim: to personalise and practise the new language
- Invite a pair of students to the front.
- Prompt them to do the chant, using their own names instead of *Whisper, Thunder,* etc. They each say their name twice.
- Repeat with two more pairs of students.
- Make pairs. Students practise the chant, using their own names, taking turns to start.

1 WB p4 **Read and match. Colour the circles.**

Aim: to review colours and character names

Key: 2 b, 3 a, 4 c

Ending the lesson

Aim: to review key language from the lesson
- Repeat the mingling activity from the Warm-up. Students walk around as music plays. When the music stops, students make a pair with the nearest student. They take turns to introduce themselves using *Hi, I'm* (name). *What's your name?*

Stronger students: Students can respond *What a nice name!*

Extension activity

Aim: to make a name label and practise language from the lesson
- Hand a piece of card to each student. Show them how to fold it in half lengthways and write their name on it.
- Students stand the card on their desks. Call a volunteer to the front of the class. He/She says *Hello,* (name) to as many students as possible, reading the names on the cards.
- Ask students to turn their cards around and see if the student can remember the names.

Learning outcomes:
- to count from *one* to *ten*
- to talk about how old you are

New language: *one, two, three, four, five, six, seven, eight, nine, ten, How old are you? I'm* (age).

Recycled language: *What's your name? I'm* (name).

Flashcards: 5–14 (numbers *one* to *ten*)

Warm-up

Aim: to review giving and asking names
- Say to a student *Hi! What's your name?* The student responds *Hi! I'm* (name).
- Encourage the student to ask his/her neighbour *What's your name?* and the second student to reply *I'm …* Continue around the class.

1 03 SB p5 Listen and point to the numbers.

Aim: to present and practise numbers *one* to *ten*
- Teach the numbers using the flashcards.
- Give students time to look at the picture in their Student's Book.
- Play the recording. Students listen and point to the numbers.

For script see SB p5.

- Say one of the numbers. Students point to the correct child in the picture. Repeat several times.
- Say a series of numbers between *one* and *ten*. Students write the figures in their notebooks.
- Write the answers on the board for students to check.

2 04 SB p5 How old are the Super Friends? Listen and write.

Aim: to practise the written form of numbers *one* to *ten*
- Revise the characters' names using the picture. Check students understand how the speech bubbles work (i.e. that each character is saying his/her age and students have to write the number they hear, or the number word).
- Play the recording. Give students thinking and writing time.

For script see TB p119.

- Students check in pairs.
- Play the recording again. Check answers with the class.

Key: Misty: 6/six, Whisper: 8/eight, Flash: 8/eight, Thunder: 7/seven

3 SB p5 Ask and answer.

Aim: to present and practise *How old are you? I'm* (age).
- Ask different students *How old are you?* and prompt them to respond *I'm* (age). Practise pronunciation of the question.
- Students practise the question and answer in open pairs.
- Point to the conversation in the Student's Book. Read the questions and choose a confident student to read the answers.
- Demonstrate the conversation, with real names and ages, with the student.
- Students practise in pairs or groups of four, giving their real names and ages. Change pairings/groups several times.

1 WB p5 Look and match.

Aim: to practise reading numbers *one* to *ten* (as words)

Key: b three 3, c ten 10, d eight 8, e nine 9, f one 1, g four 4, h five 5, i two 2, j six 6

2 WB p5 Write the number words.

Aim: to practise spelling of numbers *one* to *ten*

Key: b one, c six, d two, e seven, f nine, g eight, h four, i ten, j five

3 WB p5 Look. Then write about you.

Aim: to review language from the lesson

Ending the lesson

Aim: to review numbers *one* to *ten*
- Use the flashcards to review the numbers.
- Show the flashcards at random. Students say the number.
- Invite ten students to the front and hand out the flashcards at random.
- Students quickly arrange themselves in order (one to ten).
- Ask the class to check the order by calling out the numbers together.

Extension activity

Aim: to review numbers *one* to *ten*
- Each student writes numbers *1* to *10* in any order in their notebook, without showing anyone.
- Put students into pairs. Student A dictates his/her numbers while Student B writes. Then they swap roles. They check answers by comparing with their original list.

Stronger students: Students write number words, rather than figures.

1 03 Listen and point to the numbers.

2 04 How old are the Super Friends? Listen and write.

3 Ask and answer.

What's your name?
I'm Carlos.
How old are you?
I'm six.

1 05 Listen and sing.

A B C D E
F G H I J
Hey! Sing with me!
K L M N O
P Q R S T
Sing with me.
U V W X Y Z
We can sing the alphabet!
We can sing the alphabet!

2 Play the alphabet game.

What's after 'N'?

'O'.

What's before 'W'?

'V'.

Learning outcomes:
- to sing a song
- to practise saying the letters of the alphabet

New language: *Sing with me, We can sing the alphabet, What's before/after ('N')?*

Critical thinking: Solves simple puzzles (e.g. word puzzles)

Cognitive control functions (WB): Working memory

Materials: alphabet cards: one for each letter of the alphabet (write the capital letter on one side and the lower case letter on the other)

Warm-up

Aim: to raise awareness of the alphabet
- Call to the front four students whose names start with the first four letters of the alphabet. If this sequence is not possible, any four-letter sequence in the alphabet will do, e.g. *D, E, F, G*.
- Stand the students in alphabetical order according to the first letters of their names. Say their names, repeating the first letter, e.g. *Anna, A; Ben, B*.
- Tell students the lesson is about the alphabet.

1 05 06 SB p6 Listen and sing.

Aim: to present and practise the letters of the alphabet
- Teach the letter names in English, using the alphabet cards or writing letters on the board.
- Point to each letter in turn, saying the name for students to repeat.
- Repeat two or three times, focusing on vowels and unusual letters such as *J, K, Q* and *Y*.
- Play the audio (05). Students follow the song in their Student's Books.

For song lyrics see SB p6.

- Play the audio again, in sections. Students repeat.
- Play the song video, pausing for students to repeat.
- Use the karaoke version of the audio (06) or video for students to sing in groups.

2 SB p6 Play the alphabet game.

Aim: to give students further practice saying the alphabet
- Stick the alphabet cards (capital letters) on the board or write the alphabet from start to finish. Point to letters and say, e.g. *B is after A. C is after B. D is after C.* Ask *What's after D?* Ask similar questions about different letters. Present *before* and *What's before ...?* in the same way.
- Students work in pairs. They ask and answer about the letters, using the alphabet in their Student's Books.
- Monitor to check pronunciation. Also ask *What's after/before ...?*
- Ask volunteers to come to the board and write the lower case letters next to / below the capitals.

Extra support: Students copy out the alphabet (capitals and lower case) in their notebooks.

1 01 WB p6 Can you remember? Listen and write.

Aim: to practise capital letters

For song lyrics see SB p6.

Key: G, Q, T, X

Ending the lesson

Aim: to review the letters of the alphabet
- Hand out the alphabet cards at random to a number of students. For smaller classes, use only some of the cards, but make sure they are sequential (e.g. *A* to *M*, or *N* to *Z*).
- Invite the students with cards to arrange themselves in alphabetical order at the front. Prompt by asking, e.g. *What's before 'F'? What's after 'F'?* Encourage students to use the same questions (in English) to complete the task.
- Do the activity once with the lower case and again with the capital letters.

Extension activity

Aim: to practise the alphabet sequence
- Make groups of six students.
- Students arrange themselves in alphabetical order, according to the first letter of their names. Encourage them to ask *What's your name?* and *What's before/after ...?* as they decide where to stand.
- Ask each group to check that another group is in the correct order.
- Put students into new groups of six and repeat.

Learning outcomes:
- to recognise and say some colours
- to talk about possession using *'s*

New language: *yellow, red, orange, purple, green, blue, balloon, bag, (Flash)'s bag is (green).*

Recycled language: character names

Materials: coloured pens or pencils

Warm-up

Aim: to review the letters of the alphabet
- Sing the alphabet song from SB p6 again with the students.

1 07 SB p7 Listen and point to the balloons.

Aim: to present the colours
- Use the pictures in the Student's Book to present the colours.
- Point to each balloon in turn and say the colour.
- Students repeat.
- Play the recording. Students listen and point. Repeat.

For script see SB p7.

- In pairs, students take turns to point to the balloons and say the colours.

2 08 SB p7 Listen and match.

Aim: to practise recognising the colour words, and to present *'s* for talking about possession
- Revise the characters' names and teach *bag*, using the pictures.
- Say, e.g. *Point to the green bag.* Repeat for the different colours.
- Play the recording. Students draw a line from each character to their bag.

For script see TB p119.

- Play the recording again for students to check. They compare answers in pairs.
- Check answers with the class.
- Ask, e.g. *What colour is Flash's bag?* Students reply in chorus, e.g. *Green.* Write an example sentence, e.g. *Flash's bag is green*, on the board and point out the way *'s* is used to say that something belongs to someone.

Key: 1 c, 2 a, 3 d, 4 b

3 SB p7 Look at Activity 2. Make sentences.

Aim: to practise talking about possession with *'s*
- Make sentences about the students' bags, e.g. *Carlo's bag is yellow.*
- Point to the first character in Activity 2 and the prompt in the speech bubble in Activity 3. Elicit the complete sentence.
- Students practise making sentences about the bags in pairs. Monitor. Encourage students to talk about the colour of their classmates' bags in the same way.

Key: Flash's bag is green. Thunder's bag is blue. Misty's bag is purple. Whisper's bag is red.

1 WB p7 Colour the words.

Aim: to practise reading the colours

Key: Students colour according to the given words.

2 WB p7 Write your name. Then draw a picture of you.

Aim: to personalise the new language

Ending the lesson

Aim: to review spelling of the colours
- Write the six colours in jumbled letter order on the board.
- Students work in pairs to unjumble them.
- Students then put the colours in alphabetical order: *blue, green, orange, purple, red, yellow.*

Extension activity

Aim: to find the colours in the classroom
- Say, e.g. *Find a blue bag.* Demonstrate by pointing to / touching someone's bag of the correct colour and say (Name)*'s bag is blue*.
- Repeat with different colours. Students can move around the room to find the bags, or do this from their seats. Encourage the students to make a sentence with *'s* when they find the bag.
- Students can also play in pairs.

1 07 **Listen and point to the balloons.**

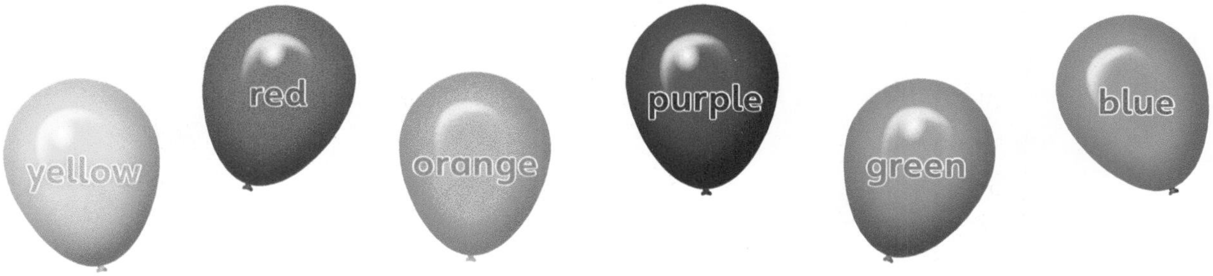

2 08 **Listen and match.**

1

2

3

4

a

b

c

d

3 **Look at Activity 2. Make sentences.**

Flash's bag is …

Meet the Super Friends

1 09 What is the cat's name?

1

Misty, Whisper and Flash: Wow!

2

Flash: Look at me!
Thunder, Misty and Whisper: Cool!

3

Misty: My turn. Look!

4

Thunder, Whisper and Flash: Misty?

5

Misty: What about you, Whisper?
Whisper: I speak to animals.

6

Whisper: What's your name, cat?
Cat: I'm Tabby.

Learning outcomes:
- to listen to, read, watch and act out a picture story
- to review language from the unit

New language: *What is the cat's name? Wow! Look at me, My turn, What about you? I speak to animals, Cool, cat, power*

Recycled language: character names, *What's your name? How old are you? I'm* (name/age).

Value: making friends

Materials: cat mask and blanket for each group of five students (optional)

Warm-up

Aim: to review *What's your name? How old are you?*
- Say, e.g. *Hello, Jim* to a student, not using his/her real name.
- When the student looks confused, ask, e.g. *Are you Jim? No? What's your name?*
- Repeat with other students, each time using the wrong name.
- Do the same with *How old are you?*, guessing the wrong ages, and encouraging students to reply, e.g. *I'm seven.*

Meet the Super Friends

1 09 ▶ SB pp8–9 **What is the cat's name?**

Aim: to present a picture story
- Review the names of the four Super Friends and teach *cat* using the pictures in the Student's Book.
- Read the title of the story and elicit the meaning of the question.
- Point to the captions of the story and make sure students realise that the words in bold are the names of the speakers and the words after the colon are what they say.
- Play the audio. Students listen and read to find the name of the cat (*Tabby*).

For script see SB pp8–9.

- Play the *Super Friends* video. Then play the video again, pausing to check comprehension. Point to Flash running and ask *Who's this?*
- Repeat for the other Super Friends. Teach the word *(super) power* and ask students to mime and/or explain the superpower of each Super Friend.
- At the end of the story ask *How old is the cat?* (*Four*)

1 02 WB p8 **Who says it? Listen and tick ☑.**

Aim: to review phrases from the story

For script see TB p119.

Key: 1 Flash (1st picture), 2 Whisper (2nd picture), 3 Cat (2nd picture)

2 WB p8 **Match the Super Friends with the powers.**

Aim: to review the story

Key: 2 d, 3 c, 4 a

Ending the lesson

Aim: to practise the story
- Put students into groups of five.
- Students each take a role of one of the characters (including the cat). The student playing the cat could wear a cat mask, and the student playing Misty could use a blanket to act disappearing, if available.
- Play the recording. Students repeat in role.
- Students practise the role play in their groups.
- Volunteer groups role play for the class. Encourage them to try to emulate the expression and intonation from the recording.

Note: Students can mime the powers in the story, i.e. lifting something heavy, running very fast, becoming invisible, and reading the cat's mind.

Extension activity

Aim: to review phrases from the story
- Call out phrases from the story in turn, e.g. *Look at me!*
- Students say who is speaking.

Learning outcomes:
- to interpret deeper meaning from a story
- to review language from the story and the unit

Recycled language: vocabulary and grammar from the unit

Value: making friends

Creative thinking (WB): Creates texts that express personal interests, emotions, or identity

Flashcards: 5–14 (numbers *one* to *ten*)

Warm-up

Aim: to review the story
- Mime running very fast. Elicit from students who in the story can do this.
- Repeat for the powers of the other Super Friends.
- Students take turns to come to the front and mime a superpower. The class says the name of the correct Super Friend.

2 SB p9 Read and number the pictures.

Aim: to practise phrases from the story and discuss the value of making friends
- Play the recording of the story with Student's Books closed.
- Students try to do the activity in pairs.
- Pairs check with other pairs.
- Check answers with the class. Students say the names of the characters as a response.
- Focus on the parts of the story where the characters ask each other (and the cat) questions.
- Elicit why we ask a new person we meet about themselves (to get to know them). Talk about how finding out about someone else is a good way to make friends. Ask students how they met their friends, what they have in common and why friends are important.

Note: This discussion will probably need to take place in L1.

Key: 2, 5, 1, 4, 3

1 WB p9 Write and circle.

Aim: to enable students to assess their own learning

Key: 2 green, 3 purple

2 WB p9 Write the letters.

Aim: to review letters of the alphabet

Key: 2 F, 3 J, 4 N, 5 Q, 6 S

3 WB p9 Read. Then draw and write.

Aim: to enable students to personalise the topic

Optional: Put students into groups of four. They take turns to show the picture they drew and read their sentences to the group. Students can copy their pictures and descriptions onto a piece of paper. The pages can be put together to make a class book, called 'This is our class'.

Ending the lesson

Picture dictionary

Aim: to review numbers *one* to *ten* and colours
- Students look at the Picture dictionary page for numbers 1–10 (WB p118).
- In pairs, they take turns to point to a number and say the word.

Key: two, three, four, five, six, seven, eight, nine, ten

Extension activity

Aim: to review the letters of the alphabet
- Spell out some of the words from the unit, e.g. *B A G.*
- Students say the word, e.g. *bag,* and find it on a page of the unit.
- Repeat for *cat*, colours, etc.

Stronger students: Students can play this game in pairs.

Thunder: Wow! How old are you?
Cat: Meow.

Whisper: No! Listen to me.

Whisper: How old are you?
Cat: I'm four.

Thunder, Misty and Flash: Cool.

2 Read and number the pictures

1 Look at me.
2 My turn. Look!
3 I'm Tabby.
4 How old are you?
5 No! Listen to me.

1 At school

1 10 **Listen and look. Then listen and say the words.**

BIG QUESTION How do we learn?

2 11 **Listen and chant.**

Flash, Flash, please come back!
Flash, Flash, please come back!

Your ruler, your pen,
Your paper, your book,
Your pencil,
And your pencil case.

Flash, Flash, close your bag!
Flash, Flash, close your bag!

Your ruler, your pen,
Your paper, your book,
Your pencil,
And your pencil case.

Learning outcomes:
- to name and talk about classroom objects
- to say a chant

BIG QUESTION to start to think about the Big Question *How do we learn?*

New language: *ruler, pen, book, rubber, pencil case, pencil, desk, notebook, bag, paper, Come back, Close your bag*

Recycled language: colours

Cognitive control functions: Working memory

Flashcards: 15–24 (classroom objects)

Warm-up

Aim: to review colours
- Play a true/false game to review colours. Point to items and make true or false sentences about colour. Students stand up only when a sentence is true (e.g. point to something green and say *It's red* – students don't stand).

Presentation

Aim: to present classroom objects
- Hold up each flashcard in turn. Say the word for the class to repeat. Do this three or four times.
- Hold up each flashcard for students to say the word without your help. They can point to the item if it is nearby.
- Stick the flashcards on the board or around the room (next to or on the appropriate object, if possible).

1 10 SB p10 **Listen and look. Then listen and say the words.**

Aim: to practise classroom objects
- Students look at the picture in their Student's Books. Elicit the names of the characters.
- Play the recording. Students point to the objects and words when they hear them.

For script see TB p119.

- Play the recording again. Students repeat the words.
- Students practise pointing and naming in pairs. They also say the colours of the items.

BIG QUESTION How do we learn?

Aim: to encourage students to find out about how we learn
- Read the Big Question. Ask students to think about what they usually do in class, e.g. *We listen. We sing.*
- In pairs, students think about other ways they learn. Accept any reasonable suggestions for activities (not always in the classroom) which help learning, e.g. listening to others, asking questions.
- Elicit and discuss ideas as a class. **Note:** Some of the discussion will need to be in your students' first language (L1).

2 11 SB p10 **Listen and chant.**

Aim: to give students further practice saying the classroom words
- Play the recording. Students listen and follow the chant in their Student's Books.

For chant script see SB p10.

- Play the recording again, pausing after each verse for students to repeat. Do the chant as a class and then in groups.
- Students put the objects from the chant on their desks. They do the chant again, holding up the relevant objects. They can add actions for *please come back* and *close your bag*.

Practice

Aim: to personalise and practise the new language
- Students close their Student's Books.
- In pairs, they take turns to name the classroom objects on their desks from SB Activity 2.

1 WB p10 **Look and match.**

Aim: to practise matching words with pictures

Key: 2 g, 3 f, 4 e, 5 j, 6 b, 7 d, 8 a, 9 c, 10 i

2 WB p10 **Look and colour.**

Aim: to review colours and classroom objects

Key: 2 green ruler, 3 purple rubber, 4 orange pencil case, 5 yellow bag, 6 blue notebook

Ending the lesson

Aim: to review key language from the lesson
- Display the flashcards. Point to flashcards at random for students to say the words.

Extension activity

Aim: to review colours and classroom items
- Students look at the picture in their Student's Books for one minute and try to memorise it. Then they close their books. Say, e.g. *It's red.* Students say the name of the item from memory.
- Students can also play this game in pairs.

Learning outcomes:
- to ask and answer about classroom objects
- to play a game

New language: *What's this? It's a (ruler). Is it a (ruler)? Yes, it is, No, it isn't.*

Recycled language: classroom objects

Flashcards: 15–24 (classroom objects)

Warm-up

Aim: to review classroom objects
- Stick the flashcards on the board (picture side). Write the wrong word under each one, e.g. write *pen* below the ruler.
- Invite students to come up and swap two flashcards so that the word and picture match, until they all match.

1 12 SB p11 Listen and number the pictures.

Aim: to present *What's this? It's a (ruler). Is it a (ruler)? Yes, it is. No, it isn't.*
- Give students time to look at the pictures in their Student's Books. Say one of the items in the pictures, e.g. *It's a pencil case.* Students point to the correct picture.
- Play the recording. Students listen and number.

For script see TB p119.

- Students check in pairs.
- Play the recording again. Check answers with the class.

Key (from left to right): 2, 3, 4, 1

2 13 SB p11 Watch, listen and say.

Aim: to focus students on grammatical form
- Point to the picture of the penguin and say *This is Penny. Penny the penguin*. Write the name on the board. Students practise saying *Penny the penguin*.
- Play the *Penny the penguin* video. Students watch and listen, then watch and read. Check understanding of the grammar.
- Play the audio. Students follow in their Student's Book and join in.

For script see SB p12.

- Students practise the questions and answers in pairs (one holding a ruler, one asking the questions). Then they swap roles.

3 SB p11 Play the guessing game.

Aim: to give students practice with questions and answers
- Point to the first picture and ask *What's this? Is it a pen?* Students answer with their own ideas. Encourage them to ask questions to guess in the same way.
- In pairs, students take turns to ask and answer about the rest of the pictures.
- Elicit guesses and confirm what each item is.

Key: 1 desk, 2 pen, 3 ruler, 4 paper

1 WB p11 Look and write.

Aim: to review classroom objects

Key: 2 it, 3 isn't, 4 is

2 WB p11 Read and tick ✓.

Aim: to practise the new grammar

Key: 2 Yes, it is. 3 Yes, it is. 4 No, it isn't.

Ending the lesson

Aim: to review new language from the lesson
- Start drawing something, e.g. a bag, on the board and ask *What's this?*
- Draw slowly, pausing often for students to guess. Encourage them to ask full questions, e.g. *Is it a book?* and answer them with *Yes, it is* or *No, it isn't*.
- Repeat, drawing different items. After several rounds with the whole class, students can play the same game in pairs, taking turns to draw items.

Extension activity

Aim: to play a game to practise the new grammar
- Hold a flashcard so that students can't see the whole picture. Ask *What's this?* The students guess (*It's a …* or *Is it a …?*) Make the game competitive by scoring a point for each incorrect guess.
- Repeat with different flashcards.
- Students can play in pairs, drawing a picture and then covering part of it so their partner can't see and asking *What's this?*

1 12 Listen and number the pictures.

What's this?
It's a ruler.

What's this?
Is it a pencil?
No, it isn't. It's a pen.

What's this?
Is it a pencil case?
Yes, it is.

What's this?
Is it a rubber?
Yes, it is.

2 13 Watch, listen and say.

Language focus

What's this?

Is it a pencil? — No, **it isn't**.

Is it a ruler? — Yes, **it is**.

3 Play the guessing game.

What's this?

Is it a … ?

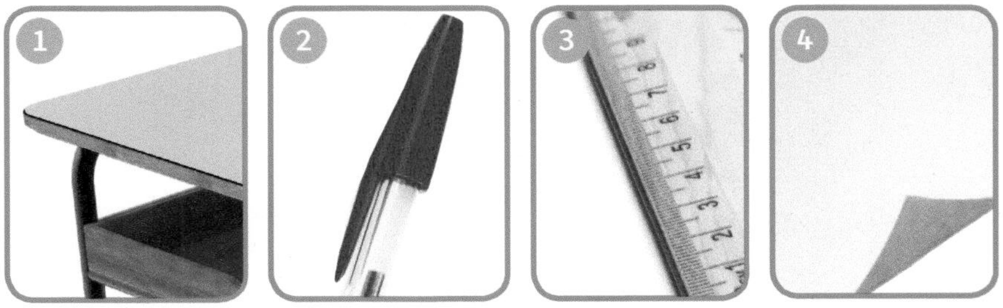
1
2
3
4

1 14 Listen and sing. Then tick ☑ the objects in the song.

What's this? What's this?
Please tell me, what's this?
Is it a pen? Is it a book?
Come on, take a look.

It's a pencil, it's a pencil,
A pencil for my school.
It's a pencil, it's a pencil,
And the pencil's very cool.

What's this? What's this? ...

It's a notebook, it's a notebook,
A notebook for my school.
It's a notebook, it's a notebook,
And the notebook's very cool.

2 Tick ☑ the objects that are for school.

1

☐

2

☐

3

☐

4

☐

5
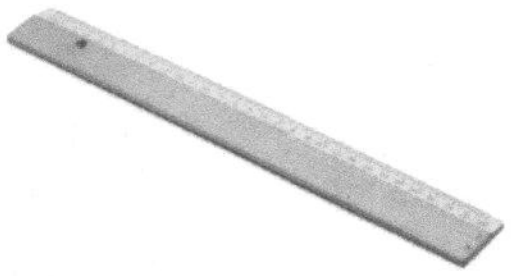
☐

6

☐

Learning outcomes:
- to sing a song
- to practise asking and answering questions about classroom objects

New language: *Please tell me, Come on, Take a look, for my school, Cool*

Recycled language: classroom objects, *What's this? It's a …*

Cognitive control functions: Cognitive flexibility

Cognitive control functions (WB): Working memory

Flashcards: 15–24 (classroom objects)

Warm-up

Aim: to review classroom objects, and questions and answers
- Flash each flashcard very quickly in front of the class and ask *What's this?*
- Students respond (*It's a …*) or guess (*Is it a …?*)

1 14 ▶ 15 SB p12 **Listen and sing. Then tick ✓ the objects in the song.**

Aim: to sing a song with the class, and practise listening for specific details
- Students look at the picture. Elicit what they can see on the desk. Say *These are for school.*
- Pre-teach *tell me*, e.g. say to different students *Tell me a number. Tell me your name.* Use mime to teach *take a look* and *cool.*
- Play the audio (14). Students follow the song in their Student's Books.

For song lyrics see SB p12.

- Play the audio again for students to tick the objects they hear. Check answers.
- Play the song video, pausing after each verse for students to repeat.
- When students have learnt the song, use the karaoke version of the audio (15) or video to practise the song with the whole class and then in groups.

Key: Students tick the pencil and the notebook.

Practice

Aim: to practise the language from the song with real classroom objects
- Put classroom objects not in the song at the front of the class, e.g. a pencil case, a pen, a ruler, a rubber and a bag.
- Hold up one item and sing the chorus (*What's this? What's this?* etc.)
- Students sing the answer, using the song as a model, e.g. *It's a ruler, it's a ruler, A ruler for my school.*
- Repeat with different items.

2 SB p12 **Tick ✓ the objects that are for school.**

Aim: to practise recognition skills
- Point to the first picture and ask *Is it for school?* Students say *No, it isn't.* Explain that they only tick the things that are for school.
- Students look, think and tick. They compare answers in pairs.
- Check with the class.

Stronger students: Teach the names of items 1, 4, 5 and 6.

Key: Students tick pictures 2 (scissors), 3 (bag) and 5 (ruler). Some students might think that a spoon and a phone are also for school – accept any reasonable explanations.

1 03 WB p12 **Can you remember? Listen and write.**

Aim: to practise the song

For song lyrics see SB p12.

Key: 2 book, 3 pencil, 4 notebook

2 WB p12 **Look and write.**

Aim: to practise reading questions and writing short answers

Key: 2 it is. 3 Yes, it is. 4 No, it isn't. 5 Yes, it is. 6 No, it isn't.

Ending the lesson

Aim: to review key language from the lesson
- Stick flashcards of the items in the song on the board in order (pen, book, pencil, notebook).
- Play the song from SB Activity 1 again. Students join in, pointing to the flashcards.

Extension activity

Aim: to practise the spelling of classroom objects
- Students close their Student's Books.
- Write words for classroom objects on the board with letters missing for students to complete in pairs. Elicit answers by getting students to spell the words aloud in English.

Learning outcomes:
- to give and respond to classroom instructions
- to play a game

New language: imperatives: *Sit (at your desk), Open your (bag), Close your (book), Pass me a (pen), Get a (pen), Write (one to ten), please, Here you are*

Recycled language: classroom objects

Materials: Unit 1 stickers, scissors

Warm-up

Aim: to review classroom objects

- Hold up or point to different classroom objects. Ask *What's this? Write the word.* Students write the words in their notebooks.
- Students check answers and spelling in pairs before the class check. Students use the English letter names when they give their answers.

Stronger students: Students can write a sentence with *It's a …* for each item.

1 16 SB p13 Listen and stick. Then write the words.

Aim: to present imperatives

- Give students time to look at the pictures. Explain that a classroom object is missing in each one. Ask them to guess which it might be for each picture.
- Students find their stickers and cut them out together with the backing paper.
- Play the recording. Students listen and choose the correct stickers.

For script see TB p119.

- Students check in pairs.
- Play the recording again. Check answers with the class.
- Students stick the stickers on the pictures and write the words.
- Read and mime each instruction. Students copy the action as you give the instruction. Repeat two or three times.

Key: 1 desk, 2 bag, 3 book, 4 pen

2 17 SB p13 Watch, listen and say.

Aim: to focus students on grammatical form

- Play the *Penny the penguin* video. Students watch and listen, then watch and read. Check understanding of the grammar and make sure they realise that *please* makes an instruction polite.
- Play the audio. Students follow in their Student's Book. They join in and do a mime in response to each imperative.

For script see SB p13.

- Students practise the sentences in pairs.
- Give different instructions for students to mime the actions, e.g. *Pass me a notebook, please. Open your pencil case.*

3 SB p13 Play the please game.

Aim: to give students practice with giving and following instructions

- Give different instructions. When you say *please* after an instruction, students do it. When you don't say *please*, students don't do it.
- Give instructions quickly one after the other, practising the imperatives and different classroom objects. You can make the game competitive by telling students they are 'out' if they carry out an instruction incorrectly (or do something when you haven't said *please*). Stop after about five minutes and declare those who are still 'in' the winners.

1 WB p13 Write the words.

Aim: to give students practice in writing imperatives

Key: 2 get, 3 Open, 4 Write

2 WB p13 Look and number the pictures.

Aim: to give students practice with reading and matching

Key: b 3, c 1, d 2, e 6, f 5

Ending the lesson

Aim: to practise key language from the lesson

- A volunteer student comes to the front of the class and gives instructions for the class to follow.

Stronger students: The volunteer can lead a please game, rather than giving simple instructions.

Extension activity

Aim: to give students further practice with imperatives

- Play the chain game. Put students into small groups. One student gives an instruction to the student on his/her left. The student carries out the instruction and then gives a new instruction to the student on his/her left.
- If students repeat an instruction or make a mistake, the game changes direction.

1 16 Listen and stick. Then write the words.

pen book bag desk

1
Sit at your ________, please.
2
Open your ________, please.
3
Close your ________, please.
4
Pass me a ________, please.
Here you are.

2 17 Watch, listen and say.

Language focus

Sit at your desk, please.
Now **get** a pen.
Open your book, please.
Write one to ten.

3 Play the please game.

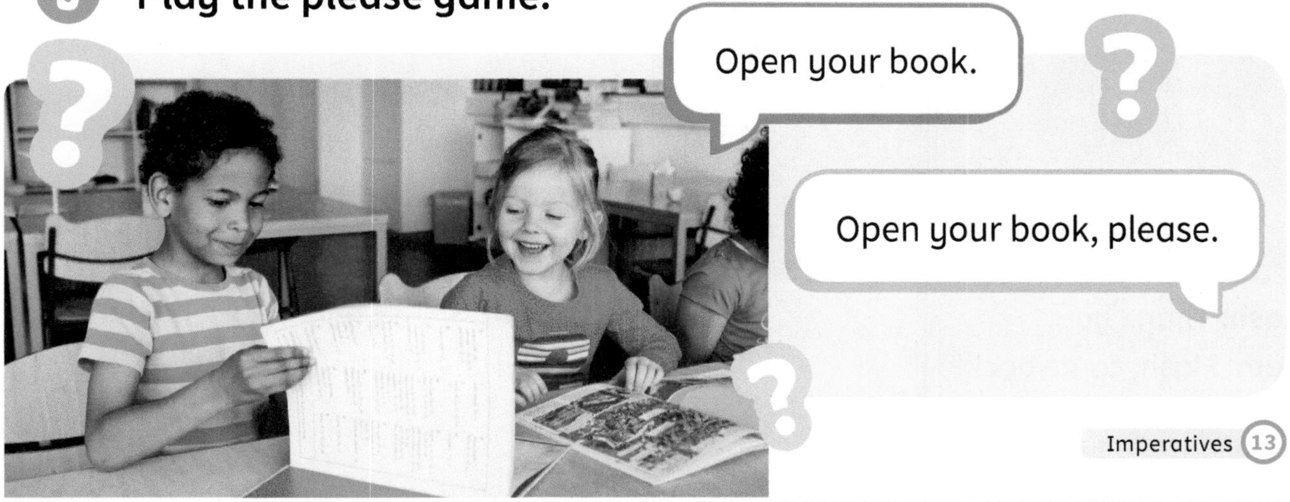
Open your book.
Open your book, please.

Watch out, Flash!

1 18 Which classroom objects can you see?

Shopkeeper: Pass me the box, please.

Delivery man: Watch out!

Flash: I'm sorry.
Delivery man: It's OK.

Flash: Mum. My notebook!
Mum: Here you are!

Flash: Thank you.
Mum: Flash, come back!

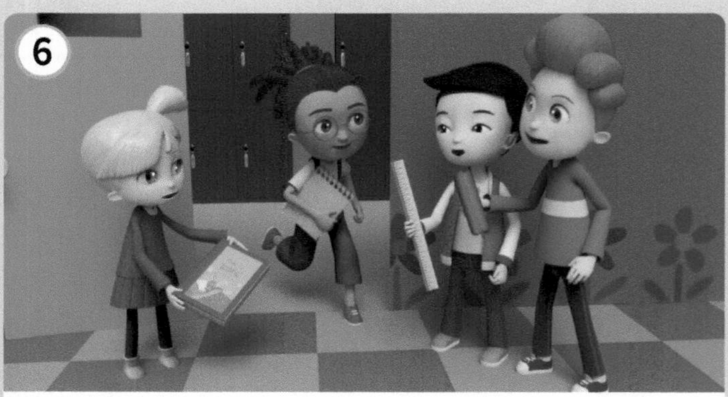

Thunder: Here's your pencil case.
Whisper: Here's your ruler.
Misty: Here's your book.

Learning outcomes:
- to listen to, read, watch and act out a picture story
- to review language from the unit

New language: *box, Watch out, I'm sorry, It's OK, Mum, Here you are, Thank you, Come back, Here's (your pencil case)*

Recycled language: classroom objects, imperatives

Value: helping each other

Critical thinking (WB):
Identifies characters, setting, plots and theme in a story
Sorts and classifies objects and activities according to key features (e.g. types of animal or transport)

Materials: flashcards 15–24 (classroom objects), a box and peaches/balls and classroom objects for each group of seven students (optional)

Warm-up

Aim: to review the characters and the story
- Elicit the names of the four Super Friends (*Misty, Flash, Whisper, Thunder*) and ask individual students to mime their special powers. Ask students who their favourite character is.

Watch out, Flash!

1 18 SB pp14–15 Which classroom objects can you see?

Aim: to present a picture story
- Elicit which characters are in the pictures. Teach *box* using the first picture.
- Stick the flashcards on the board and review the words. Ask *Which classroom objects can you see in the story?* Point to the second frame and elicit *bag*. Give the students time to look for the items in the rest of the pictures, but do not confirm answers.
- Remind students that the names of the speakers in the story are on the left and explain *shopkeeper* and *delivery man*, using the pictures.
- Play the audio. Students look and listen for the classroom objects.

For script see SB pp14–15.

- Check answers or call students to the front to tick the correct flashcards.
- Play the whole *Super Friends* video. Play the video again, pausing to check comprehension. Make sure students realise that Flash leaves her bag at her house, e.g. ask *Where's the bag?* and then ask why her mum says *Flash, come back!* (*because she's forgotten her bag*).
- Talk with the class about the value (helping each other). Ask who helps Flash in the story (*her mum and her friends*) and if they can find another example of helping (*the shopkeeper helps the delivery man pick up the fruit*).

Key: A bag, a notebook, a pencil case, a ruler and a book.

1 04 WB p14 Who says it? Listen and tick ✓.

Aim: to review phrases from the story

For script see TB p119.

Key: 1 Flash (1st picture), 2 Flash (2nd picture), 3 Man (1st picture)

2 WB p14 Look and tick ✓ or cross ✗.

Aim: to review the storyline

Key: 2 ✓ 3 ✓ 4 ✗ 5 ✓

3 WB p14 Who says it? Match.

Aim: to check comprehension of key phrases

Key: 2 a, 3 d, 4 b

Ending the lesson

Aim: to practise the story
- Put students into groups of seven. They each take a role of one of the characters.
- Play the recording. Students repeat in role.
- Students practise the role play in their groups. They can use props (a box, peaches or balls, and the classroom items: a bag, a notebook, a pencil case, a ruler and a book).
- Groups role play for the class.

Extension activity

Aim: to review phrases from the story
- Students close their Student's Books.
- Write scenes from the story on the board, with lines in the wrong order, e.g. *Pass me the box, please. / I'm sorry. / Watch out! / It's OK.*
- In pairs, students order the lines. Encourage pairs to read the corrected scenes with expression, or act them.

Learning outcomes:
- to interpret deeper meaning from a story
- to practise saying the short vowel sound /æ/, as in *bag*
- to review language from the story and the unit

New language: *black*

Recycled language: classroom objects, *cat*

Phonics focus: Your students will be able to identify and say the letter sound /æ/ in the sound sentence.

Value: helping each other

Critical thinking (WB): Makes predictions and estimations from given information

Warm-up

Aim: to review phrases from the story
- Go around the class. Pick up several objects and pass them to students, saying, e.g. *Here's your pencil case.* Students respond *Thank you.*
- Students practise this language in groups of four.

2 SB p15 Find these things in the story.

Aim: to focus on detail in the story
- Give students time to re-read the story as you play the recording.
- Students do the activity individually and then check in pairs.
- Check with the class, encouraging students to use the language in the speech bubble.

Key: a is in picture 4, b is in picture 8, c is in picture 5, d is in picture 3.

3 SB p15 Find who says …

Aim: to present the letter sound /æ/
- Write *bag* on the board, using a red pen for the *a*. Separate out the three phonemes in the word and say each one separately (*b – a – g*) before saying the whole word.
- Students repeat *My bag!* after you and find the phrase in the story (picture 8).

Key: Flash

4 19 SB p15 Listen and say.

Aim: to practise the sound /æ/, a short vowel sound
- Play the recording. Students look at the picture, read and repeat.

For script see TB p119.

- Check understanding of *black* by asking students to point to other black items in the classroom. Explain that *Matt* is a shortened version of the name *Matthew*.
- Repeat the sentences as a class without the recording. Say them loudly, slowly, quickly, whisper them, etc.
- Students take turns to repeat in pairs.

1 WB p15 Who says what? Write numbers.

Aim: to focus students on the value of helping each other

Key: a 3, 2, b 1

2 05 WB p15 Write and match. Listen and say.

Aim: to give further practice reading and saying words with the letter sound /æ/

For script see TB p119.

Key: 2 A fat rat – d, 3 A black hat – c, 4 A black bag – a

Ending the lesson

Aim: to review and write decodable words with the letter sound /æ/
- Dictate the sound sentences while students write. They compare their sentences with a partner before checking in the Student's Book.
- Have a spelling test. Individually or in pairs, students write words from the unit which include the letter sound /æ/ as you read them out: *thank, Flash, back, bag, black, cat.*

  Note: In British English received pronunciation, *pass* (see story frame 1) is pronounced /pɑːs/ with a long 'a' sound: /ɑː/. In some areas of Britain the 'a' in *pass* is pronounced with a short 'a' sound: /æ/.

Extension activity

Aim: to discuss the value of helping each other
- Focus on the parts of the story where the characters help each other.
- Elicit from students why this value is important and elicit examples of when students have helped people.

  Note: This discussion will probably need to take place in L1.

7

Flash: Oh, no!
Thunder: What is it?

8

Flash: My bag!

2 Find these things in the story.

a is in picture …

a

b

c

d

Phonics

3 Find who says …

My bag!

4 19 Listen and say.

Come back, Matt! Here's your black bag!

Skills

1 20 **Listen and draw lines.**

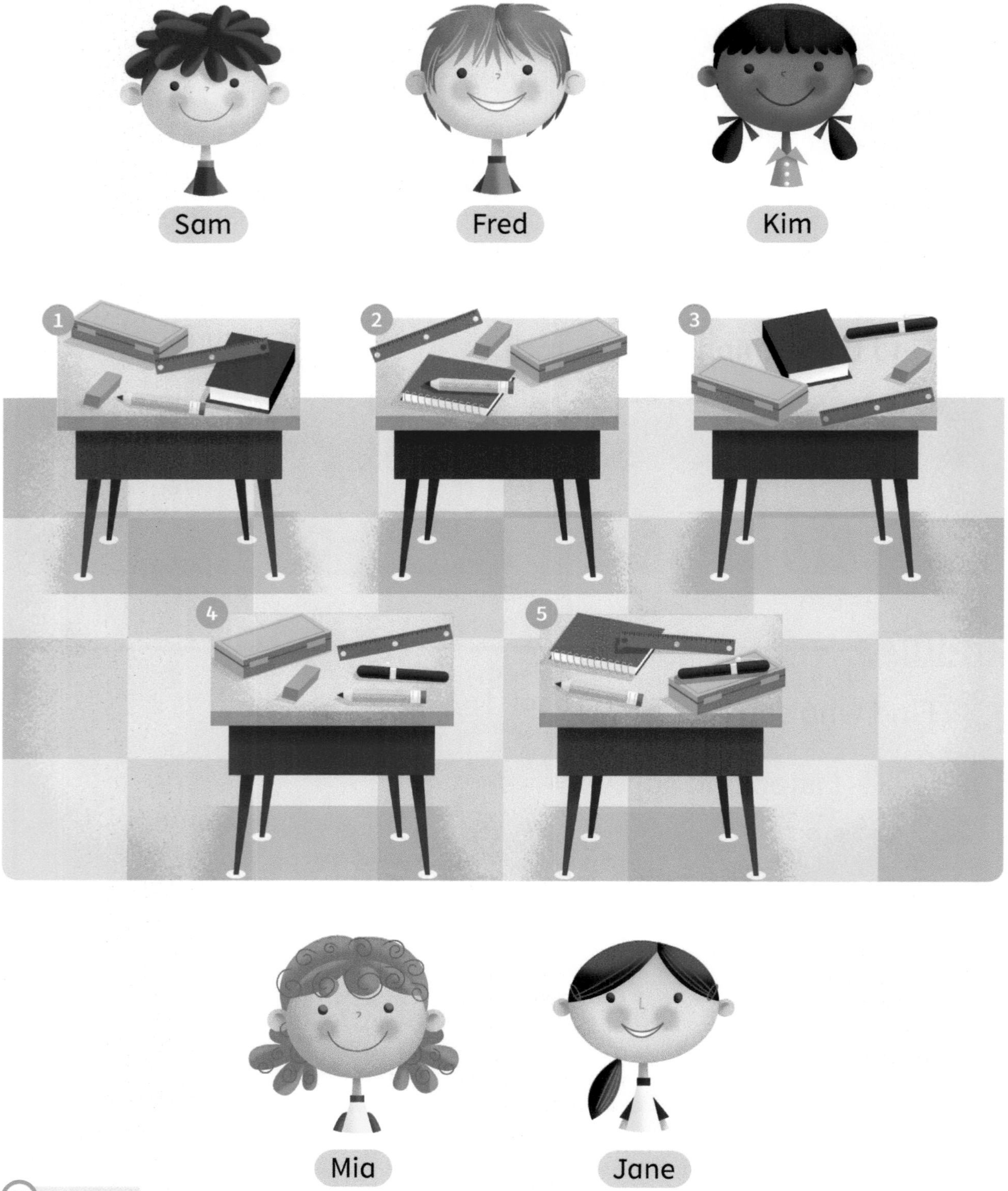

Learning outcomes:
- to listen for specific information
- to read for specific information
- to review classroom objects using *This is my … There's a …*

New language: *Sam, Fred, Kim, Mia, Jane, This is (my desk), There's a (bag).*

Recycled language: classroom objects

Flashcards: 15–24 (classroom objects)

Warm-up

Aim: to review classroom objects
- Display the flashcards on the board. Elicit what the objects are.
- Draw one of the objects in a corner of the board, hiding it so students cannot see.
- Students have three guesses. They ask, e.g. *Is it a bag?* Respond with short answers (*No, it isn't. / Yes, it is.*) The student who guesses does the next drawing.
- Repeat four or five times.

1 20 SB p16 Listen and draw lines.

Aim: to practise listening for specific information
- Read out the names of the five children in the pictures. Say *Point to (Jane).* Students listen and point to practise recognising and reading the names before they listen.
- Tell students to look carefully at the objects on the desks.
- Make sure students know what to do. Read the instructions aloud.
- Play the recording through without stopping.

For script see TB p119.
- Give students time to check their answers with a partner.
- Play the recording through again without stopping.
- Check with the class.
- Describe one of the desks in the pictures using *There's …* Students point to the correct desk and say the name.

Stronger students: Students can do the same activity in pairs (taking turns to describe the items on one of the desks).

Key: 1 Fred, 2 Kim, 3 Jane, 4 Mia, 5 Sam

1 WB p16 Look and read. Tick ☑ or cross ☒.

Exam skills

Aim: to practise reading for specific information (scanning)

Key: 3 ☒ 4 ☒ 5 ☑ 6 ☑

Ending the lesson

Aim: to give students listening practice, and to review vocabulary
- Draw a simple picture of a desk with items on it, but keep your picture hidden from the class.
- Say *Listen.* Describe the picture you have drawn, using gesture to help with meaning, e.g. *In my picture there's a desk. On the desk there's a pencil case, a book and a ruler. And there's a cat!*
- Say *Now listen and draw!* Repeat the description, pausing to give students time to draw. If you have time, you can add colours and let students mark each item with the correct colour (e.g. *The pencil case is red.*)
- Show your original picture for the class to compare their drawings.
- Ask a volunteer to repeat the description of the picture, pointing to the items in their version.

Stronger students: Check the colours, e.g. *What colour's the pencil case?*
- Students can colour the picture at home.

Extension activity

Aim: to give students writing practice
- Students place several objects of their choice on their desks.
- They draw a picture of their desks, with the objects, in their notebooks.
- They write sentences about their picture. Write a model text about your own desk on the board for guidance, e.g. *This is my desk. There's a notebook, a pen, a pencil, a rubber and a ruler.*
- Monitor and check spelling and that students are using commas to separate the items in their list.

Learning outcomes:

- to ask and answer about pictures
- to read for specific information
- to use *What's this? It's a ...* in a game

New language: *What's number (1)? Put away your (book), Take out your (ruler).*

Recycled language: classroom objects, colours, numbers, imperatives, *It's a (bag).*

Creative thinking: Creates content for peers to use in class activities

Creative thinking (WB): Uses own ideas for doing creative activities like retelling stories

Materials: piece of A4 card for each student (and one for yourself)

Warm-up

Aim: to review imperatives

- Give students simple instructions, e.g. *Sit at your desk, please,* building up to more complicated ones, e.g. *Pass your friend a black pen, please.* Students do the actions.

1 SB p17 Ask and answer.

Aim: to give students practice in asking and answering questions

- Students take turns to ask and answer about the pictures in pairs.
- Check and give further practice using open pairs.

Key: 2 a pen, 3 a pencil case, 4 a ruler, 5 a rubber, 6 a pencil

2 SB p17 Read and draw lines.

Aim: to practise reading for specific information (scanning)

- Present *Take out your (ruler)* and *Put away your (ruler)* by demonstrating.
- Students practise the new instructions in pairs, using classroom items.

Stronger students: Students can add colours, e.g. *Take out your green pencil. Put away your blue pen.*

- Read the instructions aloud and do the first one as an example.
- Students complete the activity individually.
- Students compare answers with their friends. Then check with the class. Students mime the answers.

Key: 1 d, 2 b, 3 a, 4 c

3 SB p17 Make a question card. Then play the guessing game.

Aim: to give students practice in reading, writing and speaking

- Draw a picture of a 'close-up' of a classroom object on a card. Write the question *What's this?*
- Write the answer on the back of the card (e.g. *It's a ruler*), but don't show this side to the class.
- Show the picture side of the card and ask *What's this*? Students guess. Show the answer and read the sentence when they guess.
- Students make their own cards. Circulate and check spelling.
- Students work in groups and take turns to show the picture on their card and ask *What's this?*

1 06 WB p17 Listen and number.

Aim: to practise listening for specific information

For script see TB p119.

Key: 2 ruler, 3 pencil case, 4 notebook, 5 rubber, 6 book, 7 bag, 8 pen

2 WB p17 Draw and write about your pencil case.

Aim: to practise writing and to personalise the language

Ending the lesson

Aim: to practise listening and to play a memory game

- Call six students to the front with their cards from SB Activity 3. They each show the picture and read the sentence on the back. The class repeats. Make sure there are at least four different objects.
- Give the class a minute to memorise the cards. Then ask the volunteers to hide them.
- Students who are not holding the cards try to repeat the items in order, e.g. *It's a pencil case. It's a notebook. It's a bag*. The volunteers holding the cards respond with *Yes, it is* or *No, it isn't.*
- Repeat the game with different volunteers – this time eight or ten.

Extension activity

Aim: to practise word order of instructions

- Write classroom instructions on the board with the word order jumbled, e.g. *book, please. / away your / Put*
- Students put the words in the correct order.

1 Ask and answer.

What's number 1?

It's a bag.

1

2

3

4
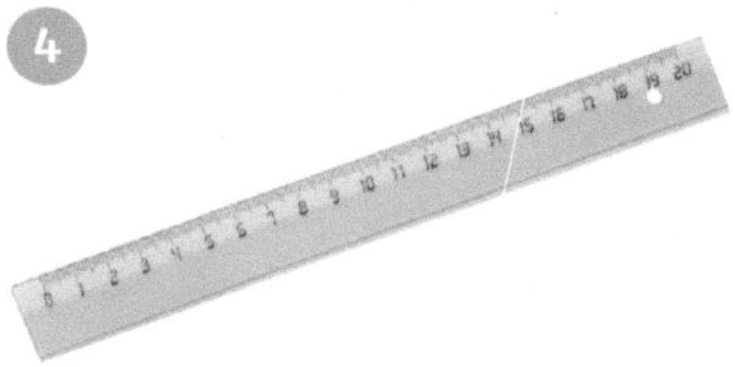

5

6

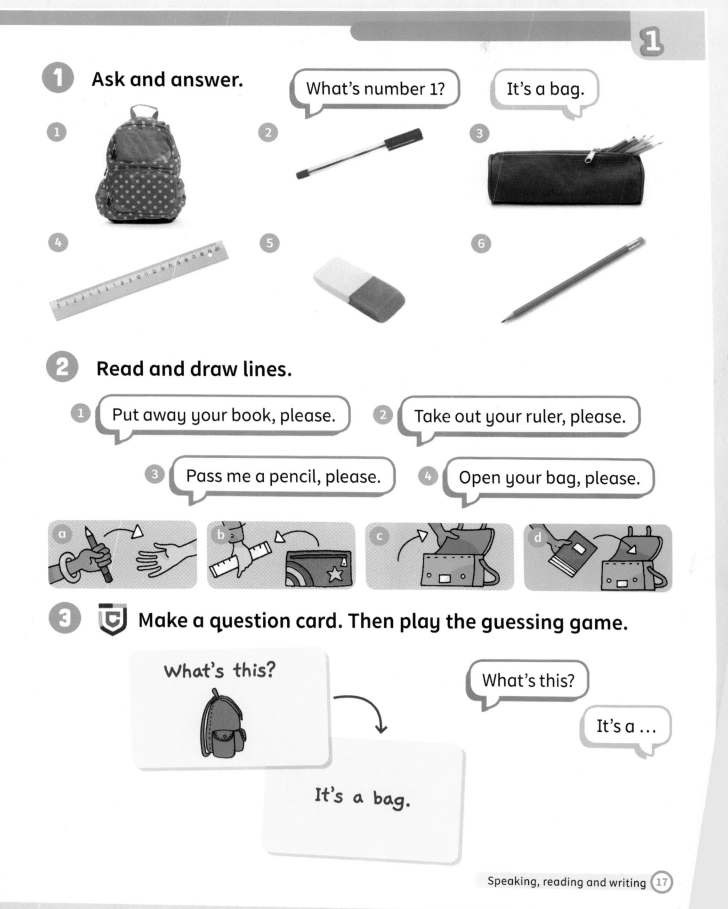

2 Read and draw lines.

1 Put away your book, please.

2 Take out your ruler, please.

3 Pass me a pencil, please.

4 Open your bag, please.

3 Make a question card. Then play the guessing game.

What's this?

It's a …

Senses

How do we learn?

1 21 Listen and point.

1

2

3

4

5

2 Which senses do you use? Read and tick ✓.

	look	listen	smell	taste	touch
1 Listen to a story.					
2 Open your pencil case.					
3 Eat your lunch.					
4 Close your bag.					
5 Watch a video.					

Learning outcomes:

- to integrate other areas of the curriculum through English: Science
- to identify senses and how we use them to learn

BIG QUESTION to explore the Big Question *How do we learn?*

New language: *senses, look, listen, smell, taste, touch, story, Eat your lunch, Watch a video.*

Recycled language: classroom objects

Critical thinking: Uses pre-defined categories to analyse familiar concepts

Critical thinking (WB): Demonstrates understanding of links between new ideas

Materials: items to look at, listen to, smell and/or taste (e.g. fruit, salt, sugar) and touch (e.g. toys of different materials) (optional)

Note: Before the Extension activity, check if any students have allergies.

Warm-up

Aim: to introduce the idea of using senses to learn

- Write the Big Question *How do we learn?* on the board.
- Brainstorm verbs from instructions in the Student's Book (e.g. *watch, listen, write, sing, make, play*) and write them around the question on the board.
- Focus on one activity, e.g. *sing*, and encourage students to think about what we need to do to learn a song (we need to listen). Students can answer in L1.

SB p18 How do we learn?

Aim: to raise students' awareness of the five senses

- With Student's Books closed, play the video.

For videoscript see TB p119.

- Ask students what they remember. They can use L1 to tell you about the computer, fruit, flower, etc.
- Ask students to watch again and answer *Which senses do you use?* Play the video again and elicit answers (students can answer in English and L1).

1 21 SB p18 Listen and point.

Aim: to present words to describe senses

- Play the recording. Students listen and point to the photos.

For script see SB p18.

- Play the recording again. Students repeat.

2 SB p18 Which senses do you use? Read and tick ✓.

Aim: to practise words to describe senses

- Read the instruction aloud and make sure students know how to read the table. Do the first row (*Listen to a story*), copying the table on the board if necessary. Make sure students know they can tick more than one column.
- Read tasks 1 to 5 and check understanding of *story* and *Eat your lunch.*
- In small groups, students complete the activity, discussing the rest of the tasks (2 to 5) and ticking the columns.
- Elicit answers. Talk about which tasks apply to what the child is doing in the photo (*smell the mango, look at the mango, touch the mango*).

Key:

	look	listen	smell	taste	touch
1 Listen to a story.		✓			
2 Open your pencil case.	✓				✓
3 Eat your lunch.	✓		✓	✓	✓
4 Close your bag.	✓				✓
5 Watch a video.	✓	✓			

1 WB p18 Look and write.

Aim: to give practice identifying senses

Key: 2 see, 3 touch, 4 listen, 5 taste

2 WB p18 Look and match.

Aim: to encourage students to make use of their own experience and knowledge

Key: 2 e, 3 a, 4 c, 5 d

Ending the lesson

Aim: to review what students have learnt in the lesson

- Elicit what students learnt today and write it on the board, e.g. *Today I've learnt about how we use our senses to learn.* Students copy in their notebooks.

Extension activity

Aim: to review language from the lesson

- Ask *How do we learn about the world? Which senses do we use?*
- Hand out items for students to look at, touch, smell, listen to and perhaps taste. Ask different students *Which senses?*

Learning outcomes:
- to extend the focus on Science through English
- to complete a project

New language: *something*

Recycled language: *senses, look, listen, touch, taste, smell*

Creative thinking: Combines newly learnt material with own ideas

Critical thinking (WB): Makes predictions and estimations from given information

Creative thinking (WB): Chooses options to create something new

Cognitive control functions: Cognitive flexibility

Materials: coloured pens or pencils, A4 paper (one piece for each student), five medium-sized boxes or trays, and items to explore the senses from the previous lesson (optional), digital or print portfolios

Note: If you are doing the Extension activity, check if any students have allergies.

Warm-up

Aim: to review words to describe senses
- Elicit words to describe senses from the previous lesson, and write them on the board.
- Agree on an action for each sense word (e.g. raising your hands to your ears for *listen*). Practise saying the words while doing the actions with the class.
- Say a sense word. Students do the correct action. They can play the same game in pairs.

3 SB p19 Read and complete the pictures.

Aim: to practise reading and the new senses vocabulary
- Read the instruction for Activity 3 and make sure students know they need to draw in the missing parts of the pictures. Explain the meaning of *something*.
- Students complete the activity individually, and then compare their pictures in pairs.
- Circulate and check answers.

Key: Students draw: 1 something to look at, 2 something to smell, 3 something to taste

4 Project SB p19 Make a senses book.

Aim: to enable students to apply what they have learnt about the senses
- Tell students they are going to make a senses book. Give each student a piece of A4 paper.
- Students fold the two short edges of the paper together to create a spread with two pages.
- Students decide on two things they would like to include. They don't have to know the words in English, but they should be things that use the senses, e.g. items of food, animals, classroom objects, toys.
- Students draw a picture on each page of their spread and write around each picture the sense words associated with this item.
- Help students put together their spreads to make a book, in small groups.
- Write *My senses book* on the board. Groups copy the phrase onto the cover page of their book. Fast finishers can decorate the covers.
- Alternatively, students could create their senses book digitally and save it to their digital portfolios.

3 WB p19 Look and write.

Aim: to give students practice in identifying situations in which different senses are used

Key: 1 Listen, 2 Look, 3 Taste

4 WB p19 Choose and draw.

Aim: to give students practice in categorising and personalising the topic

Lesson review

- Write on the board: *Today I've …*
- Elicit what students did today, e.g. *practised senses vocabulary, and made a senses book.*
- Write it on the board. Students copy it into their notebooks.

Extension activity

Aim: to make 'sense stations'
- Arrange a row of medium-sized boxes or trays in a corner of the classroom. Label them *look, listen, smell, taste, touch.*
- Hand out food items (fruit, salt, herbs, etc.), toys or materials and ask students which sense station they would like to put them in. Some items can be placed in more than one station.
- Students visit the sense stations and use their senses to explore the items there. Encourage them to use the language from the lesson. They can also add items from outside the classroom or from home.

3 Read and complete the pictures.

In picture 1, Flash looks at something.

In picture 2, Flash smells something.

In picture 3, Flash tastes something.

4 Project Make a senses book.

look listen touch taste smell

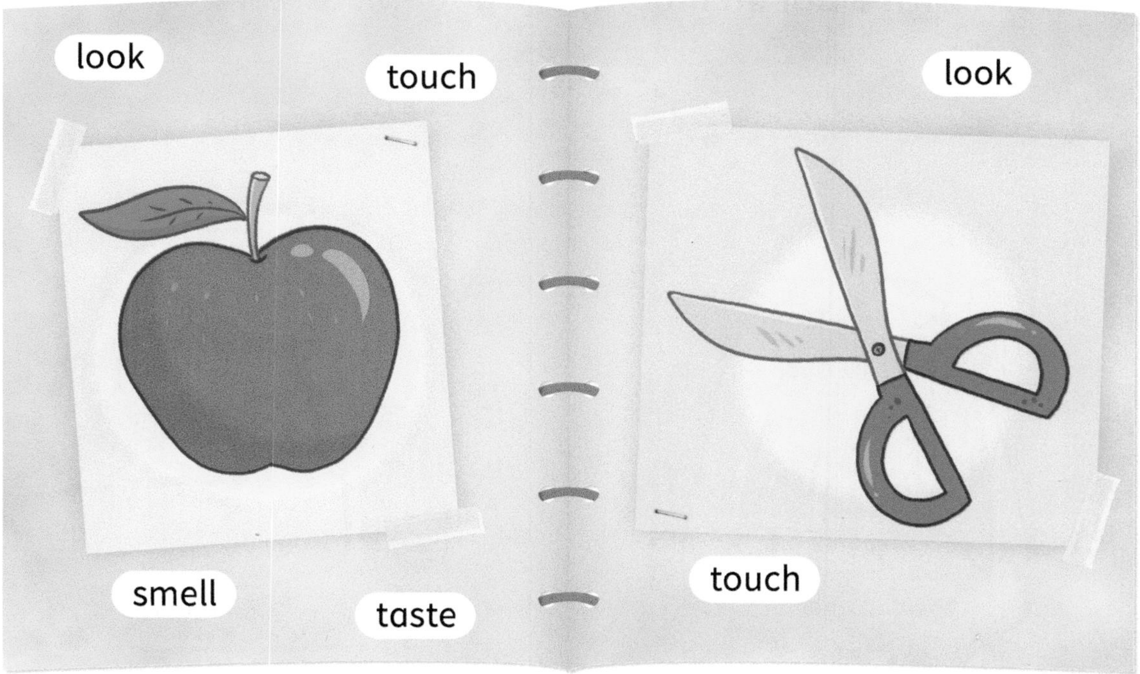

Create that!

1 22 **Listen and imagine. Then draw your picture.**

2 **Work with a partner. Compare your pictures.**

What's this?

It's a …

Learning outcomes:
- to listen, imagine and draw to demonstrate meaning
- to describe classroom objects

New language: *eyes* (*Close your eyes*), *Imagine, Penny has, for you, What colour is it? What's in the bag? Is there a (book)? Draw the picture.*

Recycled language: classroom objects, colours, imperatives

Creative thinking: Chooses options to create something new

Creative thinking (WB): Uses different media to make and describe his/her own designs

Cognitive control functions: Inhibitory control

Materials: coloured pens or pencils; For the WB making activity: toilet-roll tube, scissors, cardboard, glue, magazines

Warm-up

Aim: to review classroom objects and instructions
- Put the class into two teams, numbered 1 and 2 or named after colours.
- Give the teams instructions in turn, e.g. *Team 1, stand up. Team 2, open your pencil case. Team 1, sit down. Team 2, take out your pencil. Team 1, close your eyes*. Students mime or do the correct action. Once they have got the idea, make it more difficult by varying the groups (e.g. give two instructions to Team 1, one to Team 2, and so on).
- You can make the game competitive by telling students they are 'out' if they do the wrong action. The team with the most students left 'in' at the end wins.

Stronger students: Play with more than two teams to make it even more challenging (students have to listen very carefully).

1 22 SB p20 Listen and imagine. Then draw your picture.

Aim: to give students practice in listening and following instructions
- Explain the activity. Make sure students have coloured pens or pencils and that they know the meaning of *imagine* and *draw*.
- Play the recording for students to follow instructions.

For script see TB p120.

- Play the recording again before students draw, if necessary.
- Circulate as they draw their pictures, asking *What colour is your bag? What's in your bag?* Praise students for using their imagination and for their originality.

2 SB p20 Work with a partner. Compare your pictures.

Aim: to practise speaking
- Draw a picture of a bag on the board with different items inside it. Use colours if possible. Talk about the picture using *It's …* (e.g. *It's a bag. It's green. Look inside. It's a ruler. It's red. It's my notebook. What's this? It's a cat! In my bag!*)
- Students work in pairs. They show each other their pictures and describe. Encourage them to say as much as they can.

1 WB p20 Make a pencil holder.

Aim: to enable students to follow a set of instructions to make a pencil holder

Ending the lesson

Aim: to give students further practice in giving and responding to instructions
- Students put their empty pencil holders from the WB activity on their desks, together with a selection of classroom items.
- Give instructions for them to listen and follow, e.g. *Put three pencils, one pen and a ruler in your pencil holder. Now take out your ruler and a red pencil.*
- Students repeat the activity in pairs, taking turns to give instructions.

Extension activity

Aim: to review colours and classroom items

Aim: to give students practice in writing instructions
- Students work in pairs. They write a set of three instructions, similar to those in the Warm-up, to give to another pair. Write prompts on the board to help, e.g. *Close … Open … Take … Pass me …*
- Pairs swap instructions, read them silently and then act them out.

Learning outcomes:
- to review language from the unit by doing a quiz
- to reflect on learning

BIG QUESTION to think about how the unit has helped them talk about the Big Question *How do we learn?*

Recycled language: vocabulary and grammar from the unit, colours, the alphabet

Creative thinking (WB): Creates texts that express personal interests, emotions, or identity

Cognitive control functions (WB): Cognitive flexibility

Warm-up

Aim: to review colours
- Revise pronunciation of the alphabet, if necessary (e.g. play the alphabet song 05 from Student's Book p6).
- Write the colours (*yellow, red, orange, green, blue, purple, black*) in jumbled letter order on the board.
- Students work in pairs and write each colour correctly.
- Choose pairs to spell out each colour word and ask them to find an item of that colour in the classroom.

1 SB p21 Read and circle.

Aim: to enable students to review language from the unit by doing a quiz
- Make sure students know how to answer by circling one option for each sentence, using the picture clues. Do the first item as an example, if necessary.
- Students do the quiz in pairs. The first time, they do it without looking back through the unit.
- Pairs check their work with other pairs.
- Students then look back to check questions they did not know.
- Check answers with the class.

Key: 1 a, 2 c, 3 b, 4 a, 5 a, 6 b, 7 c, 8 b

Picture dictionary

Aim: to review vocabulary for classroom objects
- Students look at the Picture dictionary page for classroom objects (WB p119).
- In pairs, they take turns to point to one of the pictures and say the word.
- Then students write the words under the pictures.

Key: book, desk, notebook, pen, pencil, pencil case, rubber, ruler, paper

1 WB p21 Write and circle.

Aim: to enable students to assess their own learning

Key: 2 Yes, it is. 3 No, it isn't.

2 WB p21 Look and write.

BIG QUESTION **Aim:** to enable students to revisit the Big Question and consolidate learning

Key: 2 listen, 3 taste, 4 smell, 5 touch

3 WB p21 Read. Then draw and write.

Aim: to enable students to personalise the topic

Ending the lesson

Aim: to enable students to express their preferences
- Ask students what their favourite activity is from the unit (e.g. the song, chant or one of the games) and have a class vote.
- Repeat the most popular activity with the class.

Extension activity

Aim: to enable students to share what they have learnt
- Put students into groups of four.
- Each student opens their Workbook at p21.
- Students take turns to read aloud what they have written for Activity 3 and to say something about their pictures.
- Encourage students to compare what they have written and drawn.

Think back 1

1 Read and circle.

1 It's a …

a pencil. b ruler. c desk.

2 It's a …

a rubber. b pencil case. c notebook.

3 … your book, please.

a Open b Close c Pass me

4 … at your desk, please.

a Sit b Write c Take out

5 Is this a pencil case?

a Yes, it is. b No, it isn't.

6 Is this a bag?

a Yes, it is. b No, it isn't.

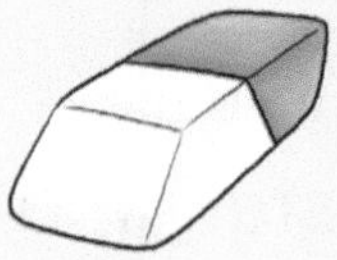

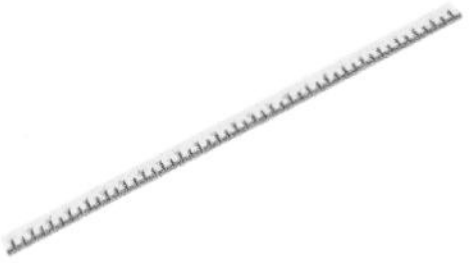

7 This is Flash's …

a pencil case. b box. c ruler.

8 You … a song.

a look at b listen to c smell

2 Let's play

1 23 **Listen and look. Then listen and say the words.**

BIG QUESTION What do toys look like?

2 24 **Listen and chant.**

Open the door, come with me.
Lots of toys for you and me.
A doll, a car, a monster and a train,
A big, big ball, a go-kart and a plane.

Open the door, come with me.
Lots of toys for you and me.
A bike, a kite, and a computer game.
A big, big ball, a go-kart and a plane.

Learning outcomes:
- to name and talk about toys
- to say a chant

BIG QUESTION to start to think about the Big Question *What do toys look like?*

New language: *pink, grey, computer game, kite, plane, bike, doll, monster, train, go-kart, car, ball, toy shop, Open the door, Come with me, Lots of toys for you and me, big, A (bike), a (kite) and a (computer game).*

Recycled language: colours, classroom objects, numbers *one* to *ten*

Cognitive control functions: Working memory

Materials: flashcards 25–34 (toys), real toys (dolls, balls, trains, cars, etc.) (optional)

Warm-up

Aim: to review colours
- Say *Find something blue.* Students take turns to find a blue item, or the whole class can stand and point. Repeat for the other colours. Teach *pink* and *grey* using things in the classroom.
- Point to objects and ask different students *What colour is it? Is it (blue)? What colour is your bag / pencil case / notebook?*

Presentation

Aim: to present toys
- Hold up each flashcard in turn. Say the word for the class to repeat. Do this three or four times.
- Hold up each flashcard for students to say the word without help.
- Stick the flashcards on the board.

1 23 SB p22 Listen and look. Then listen and say the words.

Aim: to practise toys
- Students look at the picture in their Student's Books.
- Elicit who they can see (the four Super Friends) and where they are. Teach *toy shop*.
- Play the recording. Students point to the toys and words when they hear them.

For script see TB p120.

- Play the recording again. Students repeat the words.
- Students practise pointing and naming in pairs.

BIG QUESTION What do toys look like?

Aim: to encourage students to find out what toys look like
- Read the Big Question. Ask students to think about the toys in the picture, or hand out real toys and ask, e.g. *What colour is the (train)?*

Stronger students: Students can ask and answer about the colours of the toys in pairs.
- Encourage students to think about other ways that toys look different. Accept any reasonable suggestions and encourage students to think about materials and patterns.
- Discuss ideas as a class.
  Note: Some of the discussion will need to be in your students' first language (L1).

2 24 SB p22 Listen and chant.

Aim: to give students further practice saying the toys
- Play the recording. Students listen and follow the chant in their Student's Books. Teach *big*.

For chant script see SB p22.

- Play the recording again, pausing after each verse for students to repeat. Do the chant as a class and then in groups.
- Hand out the toy flashcards at random around the class.
- Students do the chant again. The student with the relevant flashcard holds it up when they say the word.

1 WB p22 Look and number.

Aim: to give students practice reading the new words

Key: 2 b, 3 f, 4 e, 5 a, 6 d, 7 g, 8 h, 9 j, 10 c

2 WB p22 Join the dots. What is it? Write.

Aim: to review toys

Key: go-kart

Ending the lesson

Aim: to review key language from the lesson
- Display the flashcards on the board. Write a number under each one.
- Say a word, e.g. *doll*. Students write the number in their notebooks. Continue with all the toy items.

Extension activity

Aim: to practise the new vocabulary
- Students close their books.
- Display nine of the flashcards on the board and ask *What's missing?* When students guess, show them the missing card.
- Mix up the flashcards. Display eight of them and play again. Repeat with seven, six and five.

Learning outcomes:
- to ask and answer simple questions using *his, her, he, she, he's, she's*

New language: *his, her* (*What's his/her name? His/Her name's …*), *he, she* (*How old is he/she? He's/She's (eight).*), *favourite* (*What's his/her favourite toy? His/Her favourite toy's his/her …*)

Recycled language: numbers *one* to *ten*, toys

Materials: flashcards 25–34 (toys), Unit 2 stickers, scissors

Warm-up

Aim: to review toys
- Flash each flashcard very quickly in front of the class.
- Elicit the word and give the flashcard to the student who says it correctly.
- Invite ten students to come and stick the flashcards on the board, repeating the word.
- Pre-teach *favourite* and ask different students *What's your favourite toy?*

1 25 SB p23 Listen and stick.

Aim: to present *his, her, he, she, he's, she's*
- Give students time to look at the pictures. Point to each child and say his/her name. Explain that a toy is missing below each picture.
- Students find their stickers and cut them out together with the backing paper.
- Play the recording. Students listen and choose the correct stickers.

For script see TB p120.

- Students check in pairs.
- Play the recording again. Check answers with the class.
- Students stick the stickers under the pictures.
- Play the recording again with the stickers in place.

Stronger students: Ask how old each child is.

Key: 1 bike, 2 train, 3 ball, 4 kite

2 26 SB p23 Watch, listen and say.

Aim: to focus students on grammatical form
- Play the *Penny the penguin* video. Students watch and listen, then watch and read. Check understanding of the grammar.
- Play the audio. Students follow in their Student's Book and join in.

For script see SB p23.

- Students practise the questions and answers from the chant in pairs, changing the names to people they know, if they wish. Monitor and check for correct use of *he, she, his* and *her.*

3 SB p23 Ask and answer.

Aim: to give students practice asking and answering questions
- Draw two pictures, one of a boy and the other of a girl, on the board. Say *These are my friends.* Encourage students to ask questions from the grammar box about each person (e.g. *What's his name? How old is he? What's his favourite toy?*) Make sure they are choosing between *he, she, his* or *her* correctly.
- Students draw a picture of a female friend and/or a male friend. The friend(s) can be real or imaginary.
- Put students into pairs. They show each other their pictures and take turns to ask and answer about the friends. They can make up information or answer about a real person.

1 WB p23 Draw lines and write.

Aim: to practise writing the toys

Key: 2 car, 3 computer game, 4 bike

2 WB p23 Read and match.

Aim: to practise reading the new language

Key: 2 a, 3 f, 4 d, 5 b, 6 e

Ending the lesson

Aim: to review new language
- Invite a boy to come to the front and ask him to choose a toy flashcard.
- The student holds the flashcard up. Ask *What's his favourite toy? What's his name? How old is he?*
- Repeat with a girl.
- Repeat with other boys and girls. Students can also ask and answer the questions in open pairs.

Extension activity

Aim: to give students practice with word order
- Write questions and answers from the lesson on the board in jumbled word order, e.g. *his toy computer game His favourite is.*
- Students unjumble the questions and answers.

1 Listen and stick.

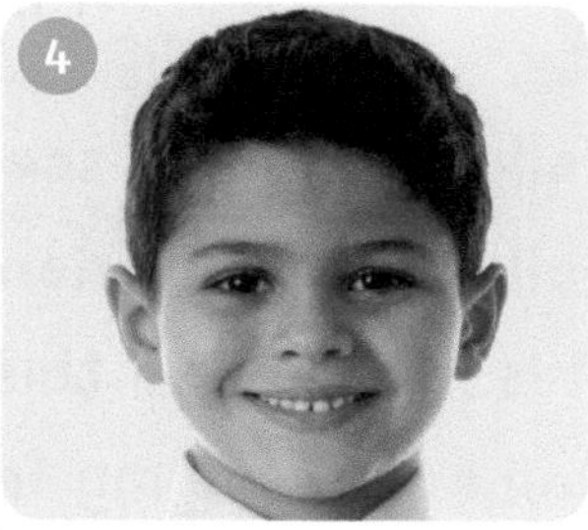

Sophie	Alex	Olivia	Mark

2 Watch, listen and say.

Language focus

What's **his** name?	What's **her** name?
His name's Ben.	**Her** name's Kate.
How old is **he**?	How old is **she**?
He's ten.	**She**'s eight.
What's **his** favourite toy?	What's **her** favourite toy?
His favourite toy's **his** train.	**Her** favourite toy's **her** plane.

3 Ask and answer.

What's his name?
BEN
How old is he?

1 27 **Listen and sing. Then draw lines to the toys in the song.**

Hello, come and see me.
Hello, meet my friends.
This is Mike and this is Jane.
Come and see my friends.

How old is he?
What's his name?
What's his favourite toy?
He's seven years old.
His name's Mike.
His favourite toy's his bike.

Hello, come and see me ...

How old is she?
What's her name?
What's her favourite toy?
She's seven years old.
Her name's Jane.
Her favourite toy's her plane.

Hello, come and see me ...

2 **Write a new verse for the song.**

She's ...
Her name's ...
Her favourite toy's ...

Learning outcomes:
- to sing a song
- to practise talking about favourite things

New language: *Come and see me, Meet (my friends), This is (Mike), (He's/She's seven) years old.*

Recycled language: toys, *What's his/her name? His/Her name is … How old is he/she? What's his/her favourite toy? His/Her favourite toy's his/her …*

Creative thinking: Substitutes words or lines to a song or poem.

Creative thinking (WB): Creates texts that express personal interests, emotions, or identity

Cognitive control functions (WB): Working memory

Materials: flashcards 25–34 (toys) or real toys

Warm-up

Aim: to review toys
- Choose a toy flashcard without showing the class, or hide a real toy in a bag. Say *This is my favourite toy. What is it? It isn't a monster. It isn't a go-kart*. Students have to guess.
- The student who guesses correctly chooses the next flashcard (or real toy).

1 27 ▶ 28 SB p24 Listen and sing. Then draw lines to the toys in the song.

Aim: to sing a song with the class and listen for details
- Students look at the picture. Elicit what toys they can see. Pre-teach *Come and see me* and *Meet my friends*.
- Play the audio (27). Students follow the song in their Student's Books.

For song lyrics see SB p24.

- Play the audio again for students to draw lines from the green dots in the song to the correct toys. Check answers.
- Play the song video, pausing after each verse for students to repeat.
- When students have learnt the song, use the karaoke version of the audio (28) or video to practise the song with the whole class and then in groups.

Key: Students draw lines to the bike and the plane.

2 SB p24 Write a new verse for the song.

Aim: to encourage students to look at language patterns
- Read the instructions and explain that students need to think about how they could change the lines from the song about the boy and girl.
- Write names on the board that rhyme with toys and elicit the rhyming words, e.g. *Elaine* (train), *Spike* (bike), *Dwight* (kite), *Paul* (ball), *Moll* (doll).
- Help students come up with a new verse using one of the names and the correct gender, e.g. *She's seven years old. Her name's Elaine. Her favourite toy's her train.* Practise the new verse using the karaoke version of the audio (28) or video.
- Put students into pairs to make up their own verses using the names on the board, or imaginary names.

1 07 WB p24 Can you remember? Listen and circle.

Aim: to check comprehension of the song

For song lyrics see SB p24.

Key: 2 his, 3 He's, 4 His, 5 she, 6 her, 7 She's, 8 Her

2 WB p24 Draw and write about you.

Aim: to enable students to personalise the language

Ending the lesson

Aim: to review key language from the lesson
- Pairs take turns to sing their new verses for the song to the class.

Extension activity

Aim: to give students practice in ranking
- Write the toys from the lesson on the board and write *1, 2, 3* next to the ones you like best (1 being your favourite).
- Students do the same individually, and then compare their answers in small groups.
- Elicit from students which their favourites are.
- Make a bar chart on the board displaying this information. Ask the class *Which is our favourite toy?*

Learning outcomes:
- to use adjectives to describe objects

New language: *a/an, small, ugly, beautiful, long, short, old, new, cold, different, It's a/an (white) (ball). The (small) (car) is different.*

Recycled language: *big*, colours, toys

Critical thinking: Sorts and classifies objects and activities according to key features

Materials: flashcards 25–34 (toys) or real toys (different colours and sizes)

Warm-up

Aim: to review toys and games
- Clap twice and say, e.g. *plane*. Students repeat.
- Clap twice more and add another toy, e.g. *plane, doll*. Students repeat.
- Continue, making a chain of toys.

1 (29) SB p25 Listen and number the pictures.

Aim: to present adjectives
- Show a toy flashcard or real toy and ask *What's this?* Students say, e.g. *It's a train*. Add a colour, e.g. *Yes. It's a green train.* Show more flashcards or toys and elicit similar sentences.
- Use real toys or draw pictures to review *big*, and teach *small, long, short, old, new, beautiful* and *ugly*. Students make sentences, e.g. *It's a small ball.*
- Point to *a* and *an* in the sentences. Explain *We use 'an' before words beginning with a, e, i, o or u (vowels).*
- Point to each picture in the Student's Book and students read the phrases. Say, e.g. *Find the old pink bike.* Students point.
- Play the recording. Students listen and number.

For script see TB p120.

- Play the recording again. Check answers.

Key: a 2, b 5, c 3, d 8, e 1, f 6, g 7, h 4

2 (30) SB p25 Watch, listen and say.

Aim: to focus students on grammatical form
- Play the *Penny the penguin* video. Students watch and listen, then watch and read. Check comprehension of *cold*.
- Point to the phrases in Activity 1 and elicit that the colour word comes after the other describing word (just before the toy/noun).
- Play the audio. Students follow in their Student's Book. They join in and do mimes.

For script see SB p25.

- Students practise the sentences in pairs.

3 SB p25 Find the different picture and say.

Aim: to practise describing toys with adjectives
- Point to the first group of pictures and elicit a phrase about each item, e.g. *A new white desk*. Ask which item is different and read the example speech bubble.
- In pairs, students find the different items.
- Accept any reasonable suggestions.

Key (possible answers): 2 The bike is different. It is green. 3 The go-kart is different. It is old. 4 The car is different. It is short.

1 WB p25 Look, read and tick ✓.

Aim: to give students practice reading adjective phrases

Key: 2 a, 3 a, 4 b

2 WB p25 Write the words in the correct order.

Aim: to practise adjective/noun order

Key: 2 a long blue train, 3 a new red bike

Ending the lesson

Aim: to practise the new adjectives using memory strategies
- Create a mime for each new adjective with the class and practise them.
- Say an adjective. Students do the mime.

Extension activity

Aim: to practise adjectives
- Ask students to draw a toy or classroom object, keeping the picture secret.
- Put students into pairs. They take turns to guess their partner's picture by making phrases with adjectives, e.g. *a new ruler.*

Stronger students: Students can also colour their picture (so their partner can guess, e.g. *A long red ruler*).

1 29 Listen and number the pictures.

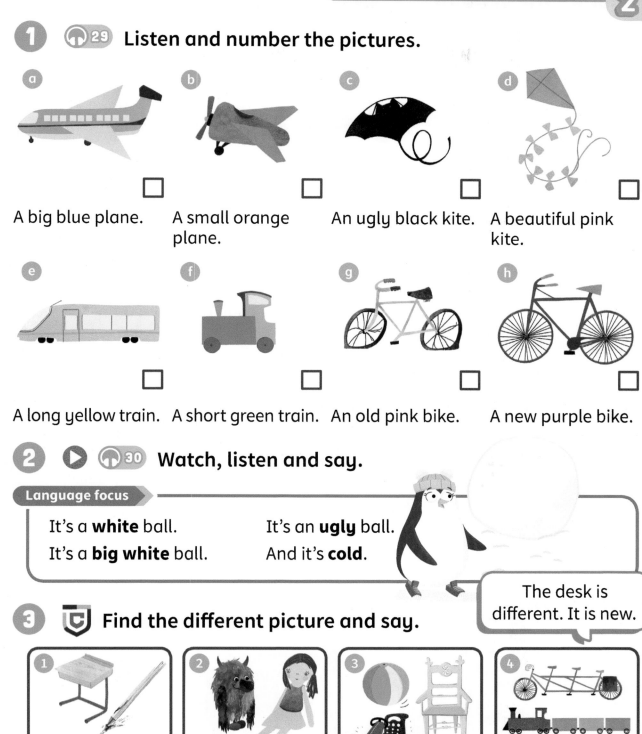

a  ☐ A big blue plane.

b  ☐ A small orange plane.

c  ☐ An ugly black kite.

d  ☐ A beautiful pink kite.

e 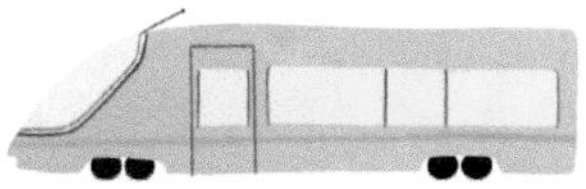 ☐ A long yellow train.

f  ☐ A short green train.

g  ☐ An old pink bike.

h  ☐ A new purple bike.

2 30 Watch, listen and say.

Language focus

It's a **white** ball.
It's a **big white** ball.
It's an **ugly** ball.
And it's **cold**.

3 Find the different picture and say.

The desk is different. It is new.

1 

2 

3 

4 

The go-kart race

1 31 Why is Misty happy?

Man: This is Ben from the Red team and this is Misty from the Green team!

Red team driver: Ha ha ha! What an ugly old go-kart!

Man: 1, 2, 3 – go!

Thunder and Whisper: Go!

Flash: Great, Misty!

Red team girl: She's first! Stop her!

Misty: Help!

Thunder: Oh, no!

Red team driver: Ha ha ha! Now I'm first!

Misty: That isn't fair!

Thunder: Just a minute.

Thunder: Hold on, Misty!

Learning outcomes:
- to listen to, read, watch and act out a picture story
- to review language from the unit

New language: *race, happy, team (the Red/Green team), What a/an (ugly old go-kart)! go, (I'm/She's/You're) first, Stop (her), That isn't fair, Just a minute, Hold on, Congratulations*

Recycled language: colours, numbers, adjectives, toys

Value: fair play

Critical thinking (WB): Sorts and classifies objects and activities according to key features

Warm-up

Aim: to give students practice with adjectives and adjective order

- Tell students to look at the pictures in SB p25 Activity 1. Say, e.g. *Find an old pink bike.* Students point. They do the same in pairs.
- Say *Look at the pictures and remember!* Give students 30 seconds to study the items. Then say *Close your books.*
- In pairs, students try to remember the pictures. They can do this in the correct order (e.g. *A big blue plane, a small orange plane, an ugly black kite*, etc.) or in any order, but they need to remember the adjectives for each item. Monitor and help, gently correcting any mistakes in adjective order.
- Choose volunteers to say a phrase they remember, or to recite all the items with the correct adjectives (in order, if possible).

The go-kart race

1 31 SB pp26–27 **Why is Misty happy?**

Aim: to review the characters, and present a picture story

- Elicit the names of the four Super Friends and ask students to mime their special powers.
- Ask what Flash said in the previous episode (*I'm sorry*).
- Elicit which characters students can see in the pictures and explain that there is a go-kart race. Check understanding of *race*. Teach *team* and *first* using the pictures.
- Check that students understand the names of the speakers in the captions: *girl, driver, man,* and that the man is announcing and starting the race at the beginning.
- Mime being happy and ask *Who's happy today?* Ask *Why is Misty happy?* Give students time to look at the pictures and guess why.
- Play the audio. Students look and listen for why Misty is happy.

For script see SB pp26–27.

- Play the whole *Super Friends* video. Then play the video again, pausing to check comprehension. Ask, e.g. *Who's in the Red team? Who's in the Green team? Who starts the race? What does he say? Who's first? Who's first now?*
- Ask students to guess what the value in the story is (fair play).

Key: Misty's happy because she wins the race.

1 08 WB p26 **Who says it? Listen and tick ✓.**

Aim: to review phrases from the story

For script see TB p120.

Key: 1 Misty (1st picture), 2 Ben (2nd picture), 3 Thunder (1st picture)

2 WB p26 **Order the pictures in the story. Write numbers.**

Aim: to review the storyline

Key: a 2, b 4, (c 1), d 6, e 5, f 3

Ending the lesson

Aim: to practise the story

- Put students in groups of six (one for each role).
- Play the recording. Students repeat in role.
- Students practise the role play in groups. Encourage them to use actions and plenty of emotion for key lines, such as *1, 2, 3 – go! Help! Oh, no! That isn't fair! Hold on* and *Congratulations!*
- Volunteer groups role play for the class.

Extension activity

Aim: to review the story

- Write *Man* and *Misty* on the board.
- Say phrases from the story, spoken by the man or Misty.
- Students call out either *Man* or *Misty*.

Learning outcomes:
- to interpret deeper meaning from a story
- to practise saying the short vowel sound /e/, as in *red*
- to review language from the story and the unit

Recycled language: language from the story, *ten, red, pen*

Phonics focus: Your students will be able to identify and say the sound /e/ and contrast it with the sound /æ/ (as in *cat*).

Value: fair play

Critical thinking (WB): Identifies characters, setting, plots and theme in a story

Warm-up

Aim: to review the story and focus on the value of fair play
- Play the audio of the story again while students follow in their books.
- Ask students to point to the parts of the story where the children try to cheat.
- Elicit why fair play is important and elicit examples of times when students have experienced unfairness. **Note:** This discussion will probably need to take place in L1.

2 SB p27 Look at the picture and tick ✓ the correct sentence.

Aim: to review the story
- Students look at the picture and read the four phrases silently.
- They tick the phrase that matches the picture, and then compare answers in pairs.
- Check with the class.

Key: 3 Hold on.

3 SB p27 Find who says ...

Aim: to present the letter sound /e/
- Write *Ben* and *red* on the board, using a red pen for the letter *e* in each word. Separate out the three phonemes in the words and say each one separately (e.g. *B – e – n*) before saying the whole word.
- Students repeat *This is Ben from the Red team* after you.
- Students find the sentence and the picture of the man in the story and point (picture 1).

Key: The man

4 32 SB p27 Listen and say.

Aim: to practise the sound /e/, a short vowel sound
- Play the recording. Students look at the picture, read and repeat.

For script see TB p120.

- Repeat the sentence as a class without the recording. Say it loudly, slowly, quickly, whisper it, etc.
- Students take turns to repeat in pairs.

1 WB p27 Who says it? Tick ✓ the correct picture.

Aim: to focus students on the value of fair play

Key: Picture 1

2 09 WB p27 Write *e* or *a*. Listen and say.

Aim: to practise reading and saying words with the letter sounds /e/ and /æ/

For script see TB p120.

Key: 2 e, 3 e, 4 a, 5 e, 6 e, 7 a, 8 a

Ending the lesson

Aim: to review language from the story
- Write key phrases from the story on the board, e.g. *Stop her! I'm first. That isn't fair! Congratulations!* Practise with the class, encouraging students to use the correct intonation.
- Divide the class into groups and assign a phrase to each group.
- Students stand up and walk around, saying their phrase to whoever they meet.

Extension activity

Aim: to review and write decodable words with the sound /e/ and distinguish this sound from /æ/
- Students close their Student's Books. Dictate the sound sentence while students write. They compare their sentences with a partner before checking in the Student's Book.
- Students write two columns in their notebooks, headed e and *a*. Say words with the two sounds, e.g. *cat, red, pen, hat, black, ten, desk, bag*. Students write each word in the correct column. You could also use the script for WB Activity 2.

7

Misty: Woah!

Red team driver: No!

8

Man: Congratulations, Misty! You're first!

Misty: Thank you!

2 Look at the picture and tick ✓ the correct sentence.

1 Congratulations! ☐
2 Help! ☐
3 Hold on. ☐
4 Just a minute. ☐

Phonics

3 Find who says … "This is Ben from the red team!"

4 32 Listen and say.

Ken and his ten red pens!

Skills

1 Look at the pictures and choose the correct words.

1

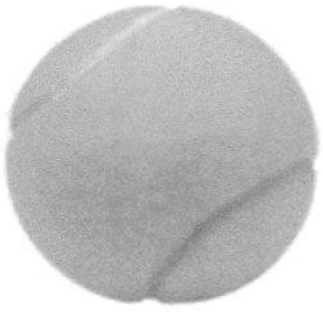

It's **a big** / **a small** ball.

2

It's **an ugly** / **a beautiful** monster.

3

It's **a long** / **a short** train.

4

It's **a small** / **a big** car.

5

It's **a beautiful** / **an ugly** doll.

6

It's **a new** / **an old** teddy.

Learning outcomes:
- to read for specific information
- to listen for specific information
- to review toys

New language: *colour it (grey), What colour? Show me (the computer game), fantastic, very good, Her favourite (number is four).*

Recycled language: toys, adjectives, colours

Critical thinking (WB): Demonstrates understanding of links between new ideas

Materials: flashcards 25–34 (toys), coloured pens or pencils

Warm-up

Aim: to review toys

- Place the flashcards in a row on the board. Draw an outline around each one.
- Elicit the word for each picture by pointing and asking *What's this?* working from left to right.
- Take one flashcard away.
- Elicit the word for each picture, working from left to right, including the missing flashcard.
- Continue in this way, removing one flashcard at a time until there are none on the board and students are reciting the words from memory.

Stronger students: Students can also say what colour the toys are (e.g. *a green monster*).

- Hand out the flashcards to ten students, who place them in the correct spaces on the board. Encourage them to help each other and give clues, e.g. *It's yellow. It's small.*

1 SB p28 Look at the pictures and choose the correct words.

Aim: to practise reading

- Tell students to look carefully at the pictures and the sentences.
- Make sure they know that they circle two words each time (*a* or *an* and the adjective). Do an example.
- Students complete the activity individually, and then compare answers.
- Check with the class. There may be some disagreement, e.g. about what is beautiful.

Key: 1 a small, 2 an ugly, 3 a long, 4 a big, 5 a beautiful, 6 an old

1 10 WB p28 Listen and colour. Exam skills

Aim: to present *Show me …* and practise listening for specific information in an exam-style task

- Make sure students have coloured pens or pencils in the correct colours for the listening task (red, blue, yellow, green, orange and grey). Say *Take out your pencils, please. Show me your (red) pencil,* etc. Students hold up the correct colours.
- Give students time to look at the picture, and ask, e.g. *Where's the go-kart?* Students point. They can also do this in pairs.
- Play the beginning of the recording and show students the example (the grey bike).

For script see TB p120.

- Tell students to listen and mark each object with the correct colour (without colouring the whole thing). Play the rest of the recording, pausing for students to choose the colours and mark.
- Play the recording for students to check.
- Elicit answers, e.g. *What colour is the (plane)?* Students finish colouring in class or for homework.

Key: train: yellow, plane: blue, car: orange, computer game: green, go-kart: red

2 WB p28 Look and write.

Aim: to practise reading and writing

Key: colour is purple, toy is her/a bike

Ending the lesson

Aim: to play a game

- Mime a phrase with a toy and an adjective, e.g. *An old plane.*
- Students ask yes/no questions, e.g. *Is it a plane? Is it big?*
- The student who guesses correctly comes to the front to mime a different phrase, e.g. *A big ball.*

Extension activity

Aim: to practise writing, reading and speaking

- In pairs, students draw two to four pictures of toys.
- They colour the pictures and write one sentence about each picture: some true, some false, e.g. *It's a new red go-kart.*
- Pairs swap pictures and sentences with another pair. They tick or cross the sentences. They swap back to check.

Learning outcomes:
- to listen for specific information
- to ask, answer and write about favourite things

New language: *things, What's your favourite number/colour/ toy? My favourite number's/ colour's … My favourite toy's my (bike).*

Recycled language: toys, adjectives, colours

Creative thinking: Creates texts that express personal interests, emotions, or identity

Materials: coloured pens or pencils

Warm-up

Aim: to review colours and adjectives
- Choose a known item and say, e.g. *I can see something in this room. It's big and red.*
- Students take turns to guess, e.g. *Your desk.*
- Repeat with other known items.

1 33 SB p29 Listen and draw lines.

Aim: to give students practice in listening for specific information
- Tell students to look carefully at the colours, pictures and numbers and say what they see. Ask *How many toys/colours/numbers can you see? What colour is the (kite)?*
- Read the children's names aloud. Students repeat until they are familiar with the sounds.
- Tell students they are going to listen to someone talking to Ruby and then Nathan. Explain that the woman is going to ask about their favourite things. Ask different students *What's your favourite colour/number/toy?*
- Read the instructions aloud. Make sure students know that they have to draw lines.
- Play the recording through once without stopping for students to listen only.

For script see TB p120.

- Play it again, pausing for students to draw lines.
- Students compare their answers in pairs.
- Play the recording again. Check with the class. Ask students which colour, number and toy they didn't use (yellow, eight, doll).

Key: Ruby: favourite colour orange, favourite number 10, favourite toy kite; Nathan: favourite colour green, favourite number 3, favourite toy bike

2 SB p29 Ask and answer.

Aim: to give students practice in asking and answering questions
- Demonstrate the activity and practise pronunciation of the questions with the whole class.
- Give students thinking time to prepare their answers.
- Students take turns to ask and answer in pairs. Encourage them to work with someone they don't know very well.
- Check and give further practice in open pairs.

3 SB p29 Draw and write about your favourite things.

Aim: to give students practice in writing from a model
- Read the text to the class and explain the task.
- Remind students to use adjectives.
- Students draw a picture of their favourite toy, number and colour.
- Check students' writing, and then ask them to copy out a final version next to their picture.

1 WB p29 Read, number and colour.

Aim: to practise reading for detail

Key: 2 d blue, 3 a green, 4 g black, 5 c red, 6 h purple, 7 b black, 8 e pink

Ending the lesson

Aim: to practise speaking
- Volunteer students take turns to show their pictures from SB Activity 3 and to read out what they have written.
- While listening, students can spot the number of toys mentioned.

Extension activity

Aim: to practise listening for detail
- Do a simple picture dictation with the class. Say, e.g. *Please draw a big blue ruler, a green book, a small red toy train and a beautiful yellow monster.* Students listen only.
- Read the instruction a second time in short phrases, allowing time for them to draw and mark the correct colour for each item. They finish colouring in class or for homework.

Stronger students: Students can repeat the activity in pairs.

1 (33) Listen and draw lines.

2 Ask and answer.

What's your favourite colour?

What's your favourite number?

What's your favourite … ?

My favourite …

3 Draw and write about your favourite things.

My favourite things

My favourite colour is blue.

My favourite number is nine.

My favourite toy is my doll.

Think and learn

2D shapes

What toys do you know?

1 34 Listen and point.

2 Look at Activity 1. Read and match.

1 The triangle is …
2 The circle is …
3 The kite is …
4 The square is …
5 The rectangle …

a red.
b yellow.
c orange.
d brown.
e green.

3 Look and draw the next shapes. Then describe the shapes.

A small blue circle, a big …

1
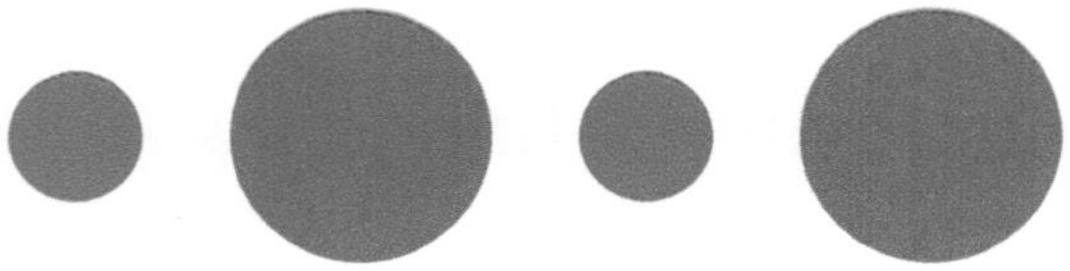

2
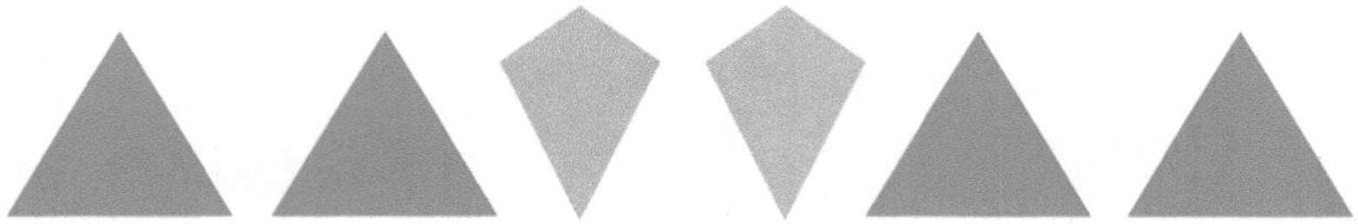

3
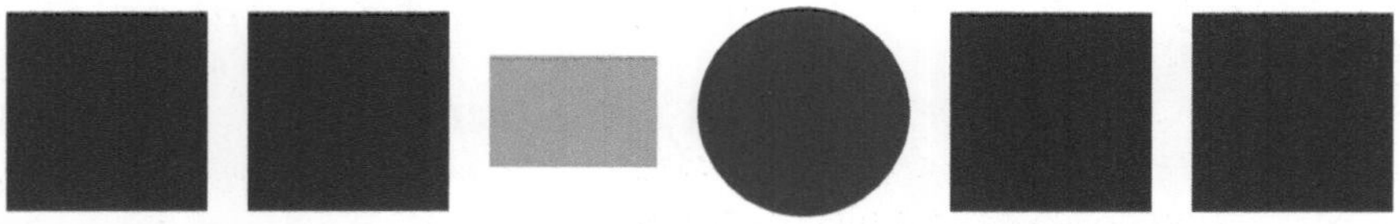

Learning outcomes:
- to integrate other areas of the curriculum through English: Maths
- to practise reading for information and instruction

BIG QUESTION to explore the Big Question *What do toys look like?*

New language: *shape, triangle, circle, kite, square, rectangle, brown, next*

Recycled language: colours, toys

Critical thinking: Draws conclusions from given information

Warm-up

Aim: to raise awareness of shapes, and present names of shapes
- Draw a circle and a square on the board and teach *shape*.
- Ask students what other shapes they know. Some students come and draw them.
- Draw a triangle, a kite shape and a rectangle.
- Teach the names of the shapes and write them below the pictures.

SB p30 What toys do you know?

Aim: to raise students' awareness of shapes in toys
- With Student's Books closed, ask *What toys do you see?* Play the video. Students answer (they may use L1 for some words, e.g. *robot, bricks*).

For videoscript see TB p120.

- Write the toys in the video on the board: *bricks, bike, go-kart, kite, plane, car, computer.*
- Students watch again to see which shapes are in each toy.
- Play the video again and pause to elicit answers.

Key: bricks – squares, bike – triangles, go-kart – circles, kite – kite, plane/car/computer – rectangle

1 34 SB p30 Listen and point.

Aim: to practise identifying shapes
- Play the recording. Students listen and point to the shapes.

For script see SB p30.

- Play the recording again. Students repeat the words.

2 SB p30 Look at Activity 1. Read and match.

Aim: to practise reading and identifying shapes and colours
- Teach *brown* using items in the classroom.
- Read item 1 aloud and elicit the answer.
- Students complete the matching task individually, looking at the shapes in Activity 1.
- Check answers with the class.

Key: 1 e, 2 c, 3 b, 4 d, 5 a

3 SB p30 Look and draw the next shapes. Then describe the shapes.

Aim: to encourage students to identify repeating patterns
- Read the instruction aloud. Check understanding of *next*, e.g. by counting and asking *1, 2, 3, 4 … What's next?*
- Talk about the first repeating pattern as an example, eliciting a phrase for each picture, e.g. *A small blue circle, a big red circle.*
- Students work on the rest of the shape sequences in pairs, drawing and colouring the missing shapes.

Extra support: Elicit answers before students draw and colour.
- Monitor and encourage students to talk about the shapes in English.
- Check with the class and elicit the answers, using the speech bubble as a model.

Key: 1 A small blue circle, a big red circle. 2 Two yellow kites, two green triangles. 3 An orange rectangle, a purple circle, two brown squares.

1 WB p30 Look and write.

Aim: to practise spelling the shape words

Key: 2 square, 3 circle, 4 triangle, 5 kite

2 WB p30 Look and match.

Aim: to practise identifying shapes and reading

Key: 2 b, 3 e, 4 a, 5 c

Ending the lesson

- Write the following prompt on the board: *Today I've learnt about …*
- Elicit ideas from students, e.g. *shapes and repeating patterns.*
- Write it on the board. Students copy it into their notebooks.

Extension activity

Aim: to reinforce awareness of shapes
- In pairs, students look around the room and write down all the shapes they can see in two minutes. They can use L1 for the item name and English for the shape, if necessary.
- Give one or two examples to help them, e.g. the board, the door (rectangle).
- Students compare ideas.

Learning outcomes:
- to extend the focus on Maths through English
- to complete a project

BIG QUESTION Your students will be able to talk about the Big Question *What do toys look like?* using shape words.

New language: *Which (shapes are in the toys)?*

Recycled language: colours, toys, *shape, triangle, square, circle, kite, rectangle*

Critical thinking (WB): Sorts and classifies objects and activities according to key features (e.g. types of animal or transport)
Chooses options to create something new

Cognitive control functions: Cognitive flexibility

Materials: real toys with obvious shapes in them (optional), paper, coloured pens or pencils, digital or print portfolios

Warm-up

Aim: to review shape words to describe toys
- Draw shapes on the board and revise the words.
- Write the Big Question *What do toys look like?* on the board. Show real toys or flashcards. Students say as much as they can in English about what they look like. Prompt, e.g. *What colour is it? What shapes can you see?* or model by describing a toy.

4 SB p31 Ask and answer.

Aim: to practise identifying and talking about shapes in toys
- Read question 1 and look at the example speech bubbles. Elicit the name of each toy.
- Students talk about each toy in pairs. Choose pairs to share their ideas with the class.
- Read question 2. Ask a volunteer to stand up and point to a shape in the classroom (e.g. *Look! A square.*)
- Say *Stand up and find shapes!* Students walk around and stop when they have found an item with a shape. Set a time limit of two minutes. Then ask different students to make a phrase about their item. Alternatively, students stay in their seats, look around the classroom and raise their hands when they have thought of a phrase.

Key: b The plane. Two triangles, ten squares and two circles. c The bike. Three circles, four triangles and a rectangle. d The kite. A kite or four triangles, and 14 triangles.

5 Project SB p31 Design a toy and write.

Aim: to enable students to apply what they have learnt about shapes
- Students work in pairs. Give each pair a piece of paper and ask them to choose a toy to design. Encourage them to look back through the unit for ideas.
- Pairs look at the example. Ask them to think about what shapes their chosen toy might have. Encourage students to use their imagination and be creative.
- Students draw and colour their toys. They label each of the different shapes that they can see in the toy. Encourage students to talk about their designs as they work.
- The final designs can be displayed around the classroom. Alternatively, take photos of their work and save it in students' digital portfolios.

3 WB p31 Which shapes are in the toys? Look and tick ✓ or cross ✗.

Aim: to practise recognising shapes

Key: 2 a ✗ b ✓ c ✓, 3 a ✓ b ✓ c ✓

4 WB p31 Read and look at Activity 3. Write the names of the toys.

Aim: to practise writing

Key: 2 train, 3 kite

5 WB p31 Choose, write and draw.

Aim: to practise identifying shapes and writing

Lesson review

- Write the following prompt on the board: *Today I've …*
- Elicit what students did today, e.g. *talked about shapes in toys, and designed a toy.*
- Write it on the board. Students copy it into their notebooks.

Extension activity

Aim: to review shapes
- Write the words for the shapes in jumbled letter order on the board.
- Students unjumble the words and write them in the correct order. Then they draw the matching shapes in their notebooks.

4 Ask and answer.

1 Which shapes are in the toys?

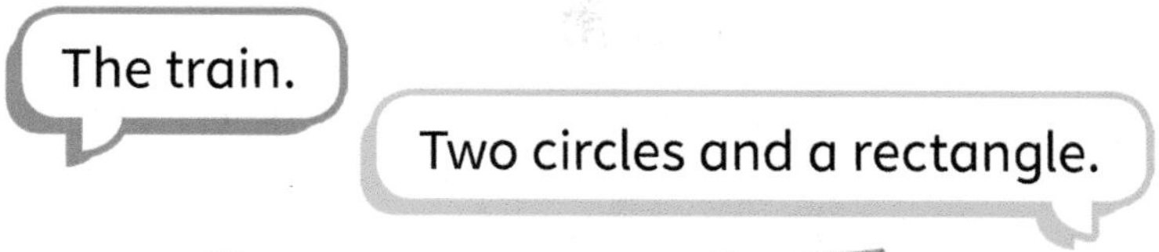
The train.
Two circles and a rectangle.

a
b
c
d

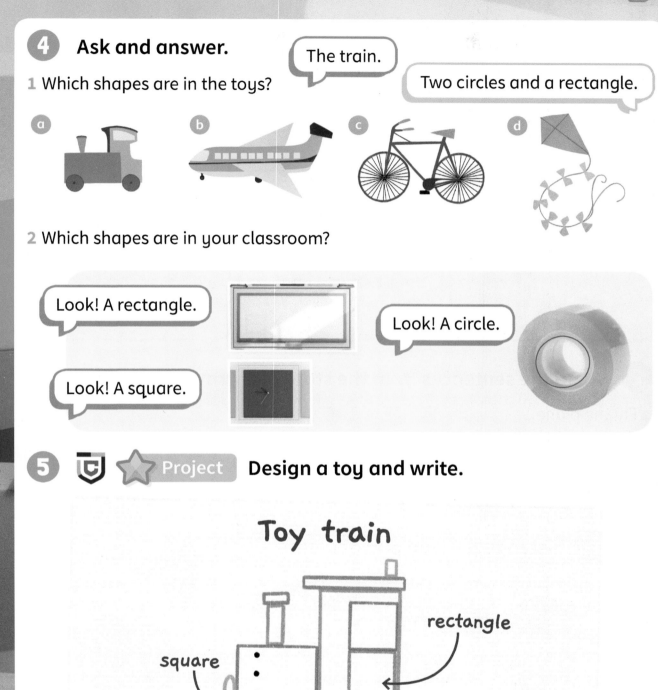

2 Which shapes are in your classroom?

Look! A rectangle.
Look! A circle.
Look! A square.

5 Project Design a toy and write.

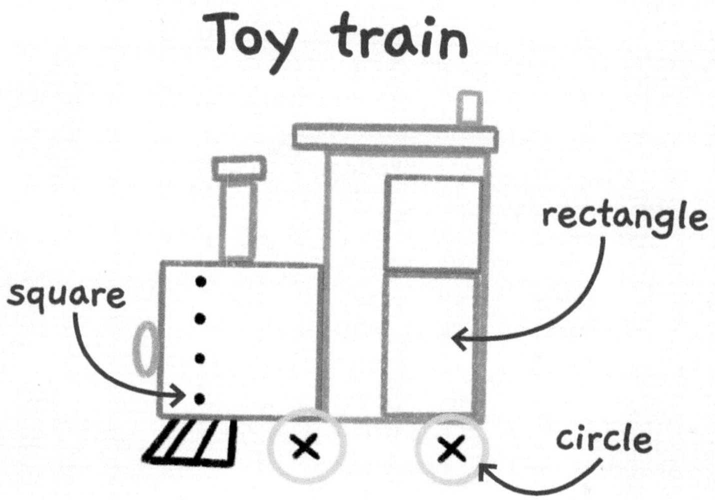
Toy train
rectangle
square
circle

Do that!

1 (35) **Listen and act out with your teacher. Then listen again and number the pictures.**

2 **Read the sentences from the story and draw lines.**

a Fly the plane.	b Ouch.
c Take a piece of paper.	d It's a plane!
e Fold the piece of paper.	f Where's the plane?

3 **Listen to a friend and act out.**

Take a piece of paper.
Cut the paper.
It's a kite!

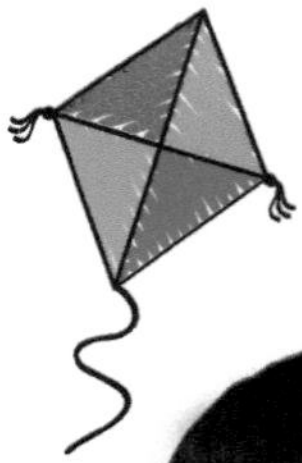

Learning outcomes:

- to practise the language through listening and responding physically
- to practise giving instructions

New language: *piece of paper, fold, take, Fly (the plane), Where's the plane? Ouch! Cut the paper.*

Recycled language: toys, shapes, imperatives

Creative thinking: Participates in investigative, exploratory, open-ended tasks

Creative thinking (WB): Uses different media to make and describe his/her own designs

Materials: paper for each student, scissors; For the WB making activity: paper, coloured pens, staplers, hole punches, string

Warm-up

Aim: to review instructions

- Give students some simple instructions, e.g. *Point to a square. Hold up a rectangle.*
- Students take turns to give other instructions to the class.

1 35 SB p32 Listen and act out with your teacher. Then listen again and number the pictures.

Aim: to practise listening and following instructions

- Tell students to look at the pictures and say what they can see. Elicit, e.g. *boy, paper, plane.* Explain that the pictures are not in the correct order, but they make a short story about the boy and his plane.
- Say *Listen and act out.* Play the recording. Mime each action and encourage students to copy you.

For script see TB p120.

- Play the recording again and repeat.
- Say *Now listen and number.* Make sure students know that they have to write numbers in the small boxes next to the pictures. Ask them to guess which is the first picture before they listen.
- Play the recording again for students to check their answers. Then elicit answers.

Key: 2, 6, 5, 3, 1, 4

2 SB p32 Read the sentences from the story and draw lines.

Aim: to give students practice in reading

- Look at the example and make sure students know they have to link the dots in the correct order.
- Check they recognise the written forms of the words *piece* and *Ouch.*
- Students read and draw lines between the dots individually. Check answers by eliciting the story in the correct order.
- Give out paper and show students how to make a paper plane. Give instructions in English. Demonstrate at the front of the class.

Key: c, e, d, a, f, b

3 SB p32 Listen to a friend and act out.

Aim: to give students practice in creating and giving instructions

- Give students time to think about how to make something simple from paper. Ask them to think which instructions to use in English. Write key words *Take, Fold, Cut* on the board.
- Students work in pairs. They each give instructions to make something. The student who is listening either mimes or actually makes the item. Encourage students to use as much English in their instructions as they can.
- Choose volunteers to show what they made.

1 WB p32 Make a paper kite.

Aim: to enable students to follow a set of instructions to make a kite

- Students work in pairs. Make sure students have all the items they need by reading the list and saying, e.g. *Show me a stapler.*
- Read the instructions, helping students make their kite, step by step.

Ending the lesson

Aim: to practise language from the lesson

- Ask students to give you instructions to make a kite. Write key words from the instructions in WB Activity 1 on the board as prompts, e.g. *colour, fold, bend, staple.*

Extension activity

Aim: to enable students to try out paper planes or kites

- Go into the school playground or hall and let students try out their planes (or kites) in pairs or small groups. Encourage them to say *Fly your kite/plane!* and *Where's the/my/your …?*

Learning outcomes:
- to review language from Units 1 and 2
- to collaborate and reflect on learning

BIG QUESTION to think about how the unit has helped them talk about the Big Question *What do toys look like?*

Recycled language: vocabulary and grammar from Units 1 and 2

Creative thinking: Substitutes words and phrases to create new texts

Creative thinking (WB): Creates texts that express personal interests, emotions, or identity

Cognitive control functions: Working memory

Cognitive control functions (WB): Cognitive flexibility

Materials: flashcards 25–34 (toys) or real toys, coloured pens or pencils

Warm-up

Aim: to review toys
- Hide a toy flashcard or toy. Give clues, e.g. *This is my favourite toy. It's small and blue. I can see a circle on it.* Students guess. You could allow only three guesses and keep score on the board.

1 SB p33 How many words can you remember? Draw pictures.

Aim: to review vocabulary
- Write the headings *Toys* and *Classroom objects* on the board. Elicit the items in Activity 1.
- Students copy the category headings in their notebooks and draw more items in each group. Students share their pictures in small groups.

2 SB p33 Write and say the words.

Aim: to review pronunciation and spelling of vocabulary
- Students write labels below the pictures they drew for Activity 1. Check spelling.
- In pairs, students take turns to point to one of their pictures and say the word.

3 36 SB p33 Listen and number.

Aim: to practise listening and revise unit language
- Remind students that the speech bubbles are in the wrong order.
- Play the recording for students to listen only.

For script see TB p121.

- Play it again, pausing so they can write numbers. Check answers. You may wish to explain that the word *roar* means the noise a monster makes (and that's why the monster is called Rory).
- Play the recording again for students to listen and repeat. They can practise the dialogue in pairs, swapping roles.

Key: 4, 2, 3, 1

4 SB p33 Write a new dialogue. Act it out.

Aim: to review grammar, and practise writing and speaking
- Show students how to make a new dialogue by completing the gaps, e.g. *What's this? It's a doll. What's her name? It's Carmen.*
- In pairs, students write a new dialogue. Help with spelling.
- Students practise their dialogue in pairs.

1 WB p33 Write and circle.

Aim: to enable students to assess their own learning

Key: 2 His, 3 He's

2 WB p33 Write the words. Then draw.

BIG QUESTION Aim: to enable students to revisit the Big Question and consolidate learning
- Check as a class and ask students to think of another way to describe toys (colour).

Key: 2 rectangle, 3 circle, 4 triangle, 5 kite

3 WB p33 Read. Then draw and write.

Aim: to enable students to personalise the topic

Picture dictionary

Aim: to review vocabulary for toys
- Students complete the Picture dictionary page for toys (WB p120).

Key: bike, car, computer game, doll, go-kart, kite, monster, plane, train

Ending the lesson

Aim: to enable students to express their preferences
- Ask students what their favourite activity is from the unit and have a class vote.
- Repeat the most popular activity with the class.

Extension activity

Aim: to enable students to share what they have learnt
- Students work in groups. They take turns to read aloud what they have written for WB Activity 3 and say something about their pictures.

Group check units 1 and 2

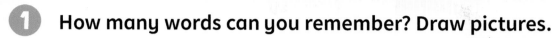

1 How many words can you remember? Draw pictures.

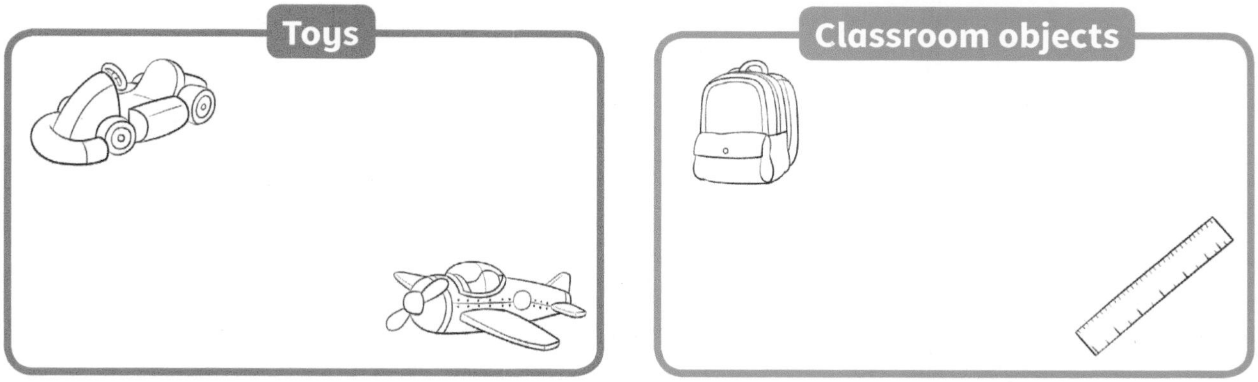

2 Write and say the words.

3 36 Listen and number.

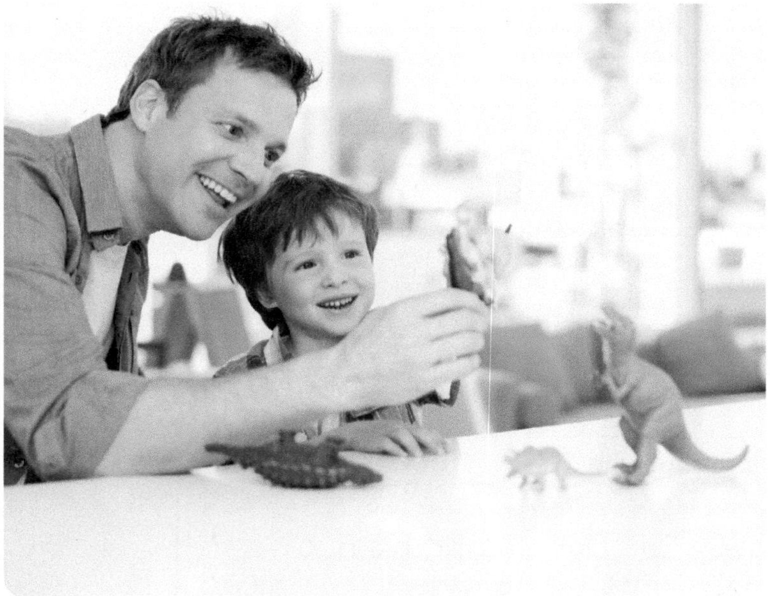

His name's Rory. ☐

It's a monster. ☐

What's his name? ☐

What's this? ☐

4 Write a new dialogue. Act it out.

What's this?

It's ______________.

______________ name?

______________.

3 Pet show

1 37 Listen and look. Then listen and say the words.

BIG QUESTION What do animals need?

2 38 **Listen and chant.**

Pet show, pet show,
Look at all the pets.

Whisper and his spider,
Daisy and her dog,
Lenny and his lizard,
Sandra and her frog.

Donnie and his duck,
Katie and her cat,
Thunder and his elephant,
Misty and her rat.

Pet show, pet show,
Look at all the pets ...

Learning outcomes:
- to name and talk about animals
- to say a chant

BIG QUESTION to start to think about the Big Question *What do animals need?*

New language: *donkey, elephant, spider, cat, rat, frog, duck, lizard, dog, pet show, need (What do animals need?), all, bring your pets, Welcome, What's the problem? I don't know.*

Recycled language: *cat, look at (all the pets), and, his, her, animals, speak (to), favourite*

Cognitive control functions: Working memory

Flashcards: 35–43 (animals)

Warm-up

Aim: to activate vocabulary
- Elicit the names of the Super Friends.
- Focus on Whisper's super power (he can speak to animals).
- Write *Animals* on the board in a circle. Elicit the animal Whisper speaks to in the story (*a cat*) and start a word map by writing it near the heading *Animals*.
- Elicit other animals students know in English and write them on the word map.

Presentation

Aim: to present animals
- Hold up each flashcard in turn. Say the word for the class to repeat. Do this three times.
- Hold up each flashcard for students to say the word without your help.
- Stick the flashcards around the room.

1 37 SB p34 Listen and look. Then listen and say the words.

Aim: to practise animals
- Students look at the picture in their Student's Books. Elicit who they can see (*Misty, Thunder, Whisper, Flash and the teacher*).
- Ask where they think the characters are and point to the unit title. Teach *pet* and ask if the students have any pets. Explain that a *pet show* is an event when people bring their pets to show others.
- Play the recording. Students point to the animals as they hear them.

For script see TB p121.

- Play the recording again. Students repeat the words.
- Students practise pointing and naming in pairs.

BIG QUESTION What do animals need?

Aim: to encourage students to find out about what animals need
- Read the Big Question. Ask students to think about what animals need (all types of animals, not just pets).
- Students work in pairs. Elicit ideas (e.g. *food, a place to live*) and discuss them briefly.
  Note: Some of the discussion will need to be in your students' first language (L1).

2 38 SB p34 Listen and chant.

Aim: to give students further practice saying the animals
- Play the recording. Students listen and follow the chant in their Student's Books.

For chant script see SB p34.

- Play the recording again, pausing after each verse for students to repeat. Do the chant as a class and then in groups.
- Make nine groups. Hand out a flashcard to each group. Students do the chant again. Groups with the relevant flashcard stand up when they say the animal.
- Elicit which of the animals in the picture isn't a pet (*the toy elephant*) and which one everyone in the picture is frightened of (*the spider*).

1 WB p34 Look and write.

Aim: to give students practice in writing the new words

Key: 2 frog, 3 dog, 4 elephant, 5 lizard, 6 duck, 7 rat, 8 cat, 9 donkey

2 WB p34 Write and draw.

Aim: to enable students to personalise the language

Ending the lesson

Aim: to review key language from the lesson
- Hold a flashcard so students cannot see it.
- Students try to guess, e.g. *Is it a frog?*
- The student who guesses correctly chooses the next flashcard for the class to guess.

Extension activity

Aim: to personalise the chant
- Do the chant again, substituting student names for character names, e.g. *Paolo* for *Daisy*.
- When students hear their names, they mime holding the animal.

Learning outcomes:
- to understand and say where things are, using prepositions
- to play a game

New language: *in, on, under, chair, hat, It's / The (frog's) (in/on/under) my (bag). It's not (in/on/under) my (chair). Where is it? It's (really) there. It isn't there.*

Recycled language: numbers *one* to *ten*, toys, classroom objects, animals

Materials: flashcards 35–43 (animals), Unit 3 stickers, scissors, animal soft toy and/or hat (optional)

Warm-up

Aim: to review animal vocabulary
- Review the animal words with the flashcards.
- Make four teams. Teams stand one behind the other, facing the board.
- Whisper a different animal to the first student in each team. This student whispers the animal to the person behind them and so on, to the end of the line. The student at the end runs to the board and writes the animal. This student then stands at the front of the line.
- Repeat three or four times with different animals.
- The team(s) who write the most animal names correctly is/are the winners.

Presentation

Aim: to present *in, on, under*
- Put a classroom object or soft toy on, in and then under a bag or box. Say the relevant sentence each time, e.g. *It's on the bag.* Students repeat the sentence. Repeat with different items.

1 39 SB p35 Listen and stick.

Aim: to practise *in, on, under*
- Give students time to look at the pictures and the stickers. Elicit *frog* and *desk*. Say, e.g. *Show me the yellow frog*. Students point to the correct sticker.
- Play the recording. Students listen, cut out the correct stickers and place them in position. Check answers before they attach the stickers.

For script see TB p121.

Key: 1 Green frog – on the desk,
2 Yellow frog – in the desk,
3 Red frog – under the desk

2 40 SB p35 Watch, listen and say.

Aim: to focus students on grammatical form
- Play the *Penny the penguin* video. Students watch and listen, then watch and read. Check understanding of the grammar and the word *hat*.
- Play the audio. Students follow in their Student's Book and join in.

For script see SB p35.

- Students practise the sentences with actions for the different places (*in my bag, under my chair*, etc.)

3 SB p35 Play the description game.

Aim: to give students further practice with the prepositions
- Make a statement about a picture, e.g. *The spider is under the book.* Students find the correct picture and say, e.g. *Number five.* Repeat several times.
- Students practise in open pairs and then in closed pairs.

1 WB p35 Look and tick ✓.

Aim: to give students extended practice with prepositions

Key: 2 No, 3 No, 4 Yes, 5 No

2 WB p35 Look and write.

Aim: to practise writing prepositions

Key: 1 in, 2 under, 3 on

Ending the lesson

Aim: to review language from the lesson
- Ask a student to close their eyes. Hide an animal flashcard or soft toy in, on or under a known object, e.g. a book.
- The student walks around, looking for the item. The rest of the class say *Yes* when the student gets near, or *No* if they are moving away. Say, e.g. *Is it in his bag? It's not under my chair* as the student searches. When they find it, elicit, e.g. *It's on the book.*

Extension activity

Aim: to practise writing sentences with prepositions
- Students each write three sentences about the pictures in SB Activity 3.

1 39 Listen and stick.

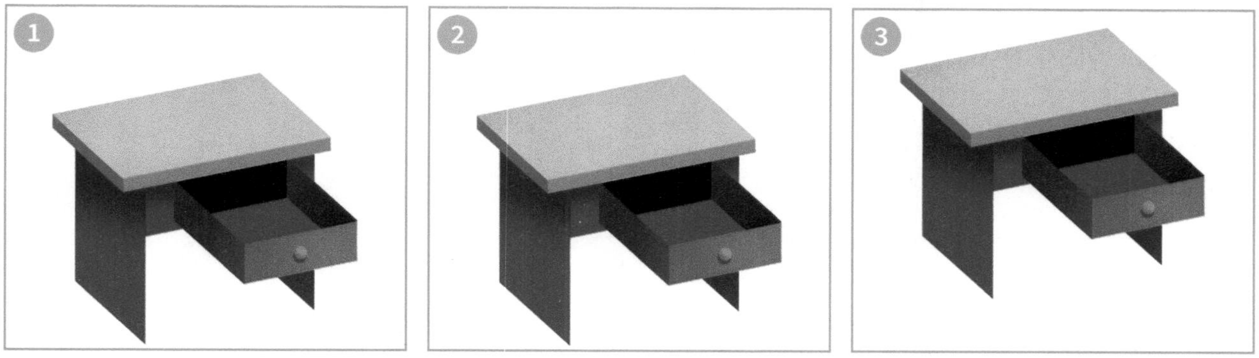

2 40 Watch, listen and say.

Language focus

The frog's **in** my bag.
It's **under** my chair.
The frog's **on** my hat.
It's really there.

My frog? Where is it?
It's not **in** my bag.
It's not **under** my chair.
It's not **on** my hat.
It isn't there.

3 Play the description game.

The cat …

Number …

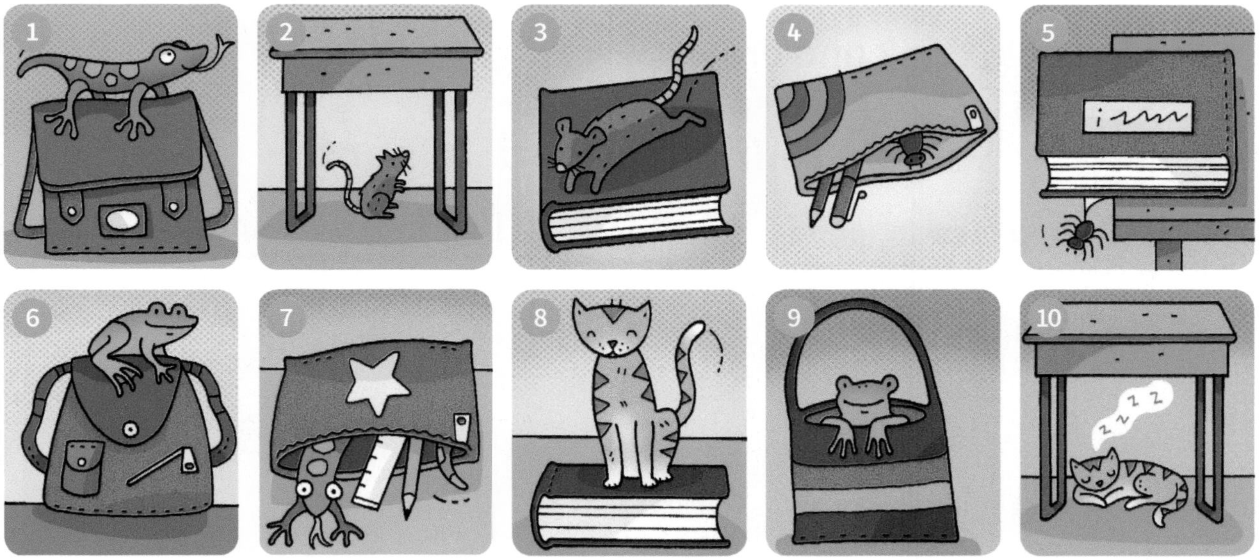

1 41 Listen and sing. Then tick ☑ the animals in the song.

The frog's on a bag
And that's not good.
Put the frog in the pond,
Yes, the pond in the wood.

There's a pond, there's a pond
There's a pond in the wood.
There's a pond in the wood,
And that's good!

The duck's under the car
And that's not good.
Put the duck on the pond,
Yes, the pond in the wood.

There's a pond, there's a pond

The fish's in the net
And that's not good.
Put the fish in the pond,
Yes, the pond in the wood.

There's a pond, there's a pond ...

2 Look, think and draw.

Which animals need a pond?

Need a pond	Don't need a pond

Learning outcomes:
- to sing a song
- to practise prepositions

New language: *pond, wood, fish, net, that's (not) good, Put the (frog) in/on/under the (pond). There's a (pond in the wood).*

Recycled language: animals, prepositions (*in, on, under*)

BIG QUESTION Your students will think again about the Big Question *What do animals need?*

Critical thinking: Sorts and classifies objects and activities according to key features (e.g. types of animal or transport)

Cognitive control functions: Cognitive flexibility

Cognitive control functions (WB): Working memory

Materials: flashcards 35–43 (animals), coloured pens or pencils, soft toy animal (optional)

Warm-up

Aim: to review prepositions
- Ask a student to close their eyes. Hide an animal flashcard or soft toy in, on or under a known object.
- The student walks around, looking. The rest of the class say *Yes* when the student gets near, or *No* if they are moving away. Say, e.g. *Is it in this bag? It's not on my chair* as the student searches. When they find the object, elicit, e.g. *It's under the desk*.
- Repeat with different students.

1 41 ▶ 42 SB p36 **Listen and sing. Then tick ✓ the animals in the song.**

Aim: to sing a song with the class and practise listening for specific details
- Elicit the animals in the picture that students know. Teach *fish* and *net*.
- Ask *What's under the car?* (*A duck*) *What's on a bag?* (*A frog*)
- Play the audio (41). Students follow the song in their Student's Books.

For song lyrics see SB p36.

- Play the audio again for students to tick the animals. Check answers.
- Play the song video, pausing after each verse for students to repeat.
- Use the karaoke version of the audio (42) or video to practise the song. Students can do actions for *frog, duck, fish, wood* and *pond*.

Key: Students tick the frog, duck and fish.

2 SB p36 **Look, think and draw.**

Aim: to encourage students to think about which animals need to live near water
- Remind students of the Big Question *What do animals need?* and explain that many animals need to live in a particular place. Read the question at the top of the table: *Which animals need a pond?*
- Make sure students realise that they need to draw pictures of the animals they know, according to which animals need to live near a pond.
- Students work in pairs. Monitor and help.
- Copy the table on the board, elicit each animal name and ask *Does it need a pond?*

Key: Need a pond: frog, fish; Don't need a pond: cat, dog, elephant, donkey, spider, lizard, rat

1 11 WB p36 **Can you remember? Listen and write.**

Aim: to give further practice with prepositions

For song lyrics see SB p36.

Key: 2 frog, 3 in, 4 under, 5 duck, 6 in

2 WB p36 **Read, draw and colour.**

Aim: to give further practice with prepositions

Key: Students complete the picture according to the instructions.

Ending the lesson

Aim: to review key language from the lesson
- Students sing the song from SB Activity 1 again, with the actions.

Extension activity

Aim: to practise listening and instructions with prepositions
- Give out the animal flashcards. Give the students with flashcards instructions, e.g. *Put the dog in your bag.* Students place the flashcards wherever you say.
- Ask the rest of the class where each flashcard is, e.g. *Where's the dog?* (*In her bag*) and collect them in.

Learning outcomes:
- to use *I like / don't like* to express preferences

New language: *I like / don't like (frogs). What about you? I like (frogs), too. Croak!*

Recycled language: prepositions, animals, *big*

Materials: flashcards 35–43 (animals), soft toy animal (optional)

Warm-up

Aim: to review prepositions
- Hide a soft toy animal or an animal flashcard before the lesson. When the students come in, say *There's an animal in the classroom. Where is it? Stand up and look!* Students walk around looking for the animal. Give clues, e.g. *It's not in my bag. It's not under the chair.*

Presentation

Aim: to present *like* and *don't like*
- Hold the flashcard of, e.g. the lizard, close to you and look happy. Say *I like lizards.*
- Put the flashcard of, e.g. the cat, on the other side of the room, look unhappy and say *I don't like cats.*
- Repeat for more animals.

1 (43) SB p37 Listen and circle what the spider says.

Aim: to practise *like* and *don't like*
- Elicit the animal in the main picture. Tell students the spider is speaking about the animals in pictures 1 to 4. Elicit *dog, cat, lizard, spider.*
- Check students understand the happy face means *like* and the sad face means *don't like*. Say *Show me 'like'* (students all smile), *Show me 'don't like'* (they look unhappy).
- Ask students to guess which animals the spider likes before listening. Make sure they know they have to circle a face for each animal.
- Play the recording, pausing for students to circle.

For script see TB p121.

- Play the recording again. Elicit a sentence for each, e.g. *I like dogs.*

Key: 1 ☺, 2 ☹, 3 ☹, 4 ☺

2 ▶ (44) SB p37 Watch, listen and say.

Aim: to focus students on grammatical form
- Play the *Penny the penguin* video. Students watch and listen, then watch and read.
- Ask how to say *too* in L1 and make sure students realise that *Croak!* is the sound frogs make in English. Point out the shortened form *don't* replaces *do not.*
- Play the audio. Students follow in their Student's Book and join in.

For script see SB p37.

- Students practise the sentences in pairs.

3 SB p37 Ask and answer.

Aim: to practise asking and answering questions and expressing preferences
- Demonstrate the activity, e.g. Teacher: *I like frogs. What about you?* Student: *I like frogs, too.*
- Students practise in open pairs, and then in closed pairs.

1 WB p37 Read and write the numbers.

Aim: to practise reading sentences with *like* and *don't like*

Key: b 3, c 6, d 5, e 1, f 2

2 WB p37 Write the words.

Aim: to practise writing *I like* and *I don't like*

Key: 1 I like, 2 I don't like

Ending the lesson

Aim: to review new language from the lesson
- Practise gestures with the class to show *like* and *don't like.*
- Say a sentence about an animal, e.g. *I like dogs*. Ask *What about you?* Students mime their preference.

Stronger students: Students respond, e.g. *I like dogs, too* or *I don't like dogs.*

Extension activity

Aim: to play a game
- Students work in groups of four. They each draw a 4 x 4 table. They write the names of four animals as the headings of the rows, and their own name and the names of the other three students in their group as the column headings.
- They complete the first column with happy/sad faces to show which animals they like and dislike.
- They ask the people in their group (as in SB Activity 3) and record the information in their table.

1 🎧 43 Listen and circle what the spider says.

2 ▶ 🎧 44 Watch, listen and say.

Language focus

I **like** frogs.	Croak, croak!
What about you?	I **don't like big** frogs!
I **like** frogs, too.	Croak. Croak!

3 Ask and answer.

The spider

1 45 Where's the spider in picture 3?

Whisper: Come back. He's beautiful. Look!
Flash: Oh, no. I don't like spiders.

Whisper: Touch him, Misty.
Misty: Wow!

Whisper: Look, he's under the table.

Flash: He's clever.
Thunder: He's amazing.

Misty: I like spiders.
Flash: They're great.

Spider: They like spiders! I've got an idea.
Whisper: What?

Learning outcomes:
- to listen to, read, watch and act out a picture story
- to review language from the unit

New language: *touch (him), table, clever, amazing, great, I've got an idea, brothers and sisters, tree, They like (spiders).*

Recycled language: character names, *under, in, spider, beautiful*

Value: being brave

Critical thinking (WB): Identifies characters, setting, plots and theme in a story
Sorts and classifies objects and activities according to key features (e.g. types of animal or transport)

Warm-up

Aim: to review the characters and the story
- Elicit the names of the four Super Friends and ask students to mime their special powers.
- Elicit what Whisper can do (*speak to animals*).
- Write *I like animals* and *I don't like animals* on the board. Elicit which Whisper says (*I like animals*).

The spider

1 45 SB pp38–39 Where's the spider in picture 3?

Aim: to present a picture story
- Elicit which animal is in the story. Ask students to look at the beginning of the story and guess which of the Super Friends really likes spiders (*Whisper*) and which Super Friend doesn't like spiders (*Flash*).
- Teach *touch, table* and *tree* using the pictures.
- Ask *Where's the spider in picture 3?*
- Play the audio. Students listen for the answer to the question.

For script see SB pp38–39.

- Elicit the answer. Point out that in the story the spider is called *he* because it can speak, but usually we use *it* to refer to animals.
- Play the whole *Super Friends* video. Then play the video again, pausing to check comprehension. Explain the meaning of *clever, amazing* and *great* and make sure students realise that Flash changes her mind about spiders. Ask what the spider is doing in picture 6. Mime thinking and then having an idea to explain *I've got an idea.* Ask who the spiders are at the end of the story, and check comprehension of *brothers and sisters.*
- Talk with the class about the value (being brave). Ask who is brave in the story (*Flash, because she overcomes her fear of the spider*).

Key: He's under the table.

1 12 WB p38 Who says it? Listen and tick ✓.

Aim: to review phrases from the story

For script see TB p121.

Key: 1 Whisper (2nd picture), 2 Spider (1st picture), 3 Flash (2nd picture)

2 WB p38 Look and match. Draw lines.

Aim: to review the storyline

Key: 1 b, 2 c, 3 a

3 WB p38 Order the pictures in the story. Write numbers.

Aim: to check comprehension

Key: 2 a, 3 d, 4 b

Ending the lesson

Aim: to practise the story
- Put students in groups of five. They each take a role of one of the characters.
- Play the recording. Students repeat in role.
- Students practise the role play in their groups.
- Volunteer groups role play for the class.

Extension activity

Aim: to discuss the value of being brave
- Elicit from students why it's important to be brave, and elicit examples of when they have been brave.
Note: This discussion will probably need to take place in L1.

Learning outcomes:
- to interpret deeper meaning from a story
- to practise saying the short vowel sound /ɪ/, as in *him*
- to review language from the story and the unit

New language: *silly, pan*

Recycled language: language from the story, animals, classroom objects, colours

Phonics focus: Your students will be able to identify and say the letter sound /ɪ/ and contrast it with the letter sounds /æ/ and /e/.

Value: being brave

Critical thinking (WB): Demonstrates understanding of links between new ideas

Flashcards: 35–43 (animals)

Warm-up

Aim: to review the story
- Write *Whisper* and *Flash* on the board and draw a spider. Teach students a mime for *Whisper* (e.g. whisper with your hand to your mouth), *Flash* (e.g. run on the spot) and *spider* (e.g. link your hands at the thumbs and wiggle the remaining fingers).
- Say phrases from the story, spoken by Whisper, Flash or the spider, e.g. *I like spiders. I don't like spiders. They like spiders.*
- Students call out *Whisper, Flash* or *Spider* and do the appropriate mime.
- Give students time to re-read the story as you play the recording.

2 SB p39 Read and circle *yes* or *no*.

Aim: to practise reading and to check comprehension of the story
- Revise *clever.*
- Students read the four sentences silently and circle *yes* or *no*. They compare answers in pairs.
- Check with the class.

Key: 1 no, 2 yes, 3 yes, 4 no

3 SB p39 Find who says ...

Aim: to present the letter sound /ɪ/
- Write *him* and *Misty* on the board, using a red pen for the *i*.
- Students repeat *Touch him, Misty* after you.
- Students find the sentence in the story (picture 2).

Key: Whisper

4 46 SB p39 Listen and say.

Aim: to practise the sound /ɪ/, a short vowel sound
- Play the recording. Students look at the picture, read and repeat. Teach *silly*.

For script see TB p121.

- Repeat the sentence as a class without the recording. Say it loudly, slowly, quickly, whisper it, etc.
- Students take turns to repeat in pairs.

1 WB p39 Which boy is brave? Tick ☑ the correct picture.

Aim: to focus students on the value of being brave

Key: Picture 2

2 13 WB p39 Read, draw and colour. Listen and say.

Aim: to practise reading and saying words with the letter sounds /ɪ/, /e/ and /æ/

For script see WB p39.

Key: Students draw and colour according to the instructions on the page.

Ending the lesson

Aim: to review the story and focus on the value of being brave
- Elicit the value in the story and ask students who is brave at the beginning and why (*Whisper, because he's holding the spider*).
- Ask students how Whisper helps his friends be brave in the story. Elicit examples of people who help the students feel braver.
  Note: This discussion will probably need to take place in L1.

Extension activity

Aim: to play a game
- Stick a picture of a happy face on one wall of the classroom. Point to it and say *I like*. Stick a picture of a sad face on the opposite wall and say *I don't like*. Say each phrase several times. Students point to the correct picture.
- Say *Stand up and listen. Go to 'I like' or 'I don't like'*. Say, e.g. *Lizards.* Students move to the appropriate wall. Elicit sentences, e.g. *I like lizards. / I don't like lizards.*
- Repeat for different animals.

Spider: My brothers and sisters are in the tree!

Whisper: Oh, no!
Misty, Flash and Thunder: Aagh!

2 Read and circle *yes* or *no*.

1 In picture one, Flash and Whisper like the spider. yes / no
2 In picture three, the spider is under the table. yes / no
3 In picture four, the spider is clever. yes / no
4 In picture eight, Misty, Thunder and Flash like the spiders. yes / no

Phonics

3 Find who says …

Touch him, Misty.

4 46 Listen and say.

This is Tim and his silly sister Kim.

Skills

1 47 **Listen and stick.**

2 **Look and say.**

The cat's …

Learning outcomes:
- to listen for specific information
- to read for specific information
- to describe where things are

New language: *Get (the cat), grass*

Recycled language: animals, prepositions, *pond, tree*

Critical thinking (WB): Critically compares ideas, objects, eras etc. to find differences or similarities

Cognitive control functions (WB): Cognitive flexibility

Materials: flashcards 35–43 (animals), Unit 3 stickers, scissors (optional)

Warm-up

Aim: to review animals
- Place the flashcards on the board and elicit the animal words. Write each word under the relevant flashcard.
- Students draw a 2 x 2 grid in their notebooks and write an animal word (or draw a picture) in each square.
- Call out the animals at random. Students cross out the words or pictures in their grid as they listen.
- The first student(s) to cross out all four is/are the winner(s).

1 47 SB p40 Listen and stick.

Aim: to practise listening and following instructions
- Give students time to look at the picture. Elicit items they know (*tree, bag, pond, kite, book*). Teach *grass*.
- Explain that students need to listen and put the animal stickers in the correct place in the picture. Elicit the animals (*cat, dog, lizard, rat, duck*). Students guess where they might be (e.g. *The dog is under the tree.*)
- Students find their stickers and cut them out together with the backing paper.
- Play the recording. Students listen and place the stickers on the picture (without sticking).

For script see TB p121.

- Students check in pairs.
- Play the recording again. Check answers by asking, e.g. *Where's the cat?*
- Students stick the stickers on the picture.

Key: The cat's in the tree. The duck's under the kite. The lizard's in the bag. The rat's under the ball. The dog's on the grass.

2 SB p40 Look and say.

Aim: to practise using prepositions to describe a picture
- Say a sentence about the completed picture in Activity 1, e.g. *The cat's in the tree* or *There's a cat in the tree*. Elicit more examples.
- In pairs, students talk about where things are in the picture.

1 WB p40 Read and write the numbers.

Aim: to practise reading

Key: b 1, c 3, d 2

2 WB p40 Look and find three differences. Circle and write.

Aim: to practise writing

Key: Picture 1: three frogs, two dogs; Picture 2: four frogs, one dog

Ending the lesson

Aim: to practise describing a picture
- Draw a simple scene on the board with a tree, a pond, some grass and one or two more known items, e.g. a car and a chair.
- Say *Let's put animals in the picture. Where's the rat?* Choose a student to decide and tell you, e.g. *On the car.* Draw the animal wherever the student suggests. Continue, asking questions and accepting suggestions, e.g. *There's a cat under the tree.*
- When the picture is complete, call a student to stand with his/her back to the board and try to remember what's in the picture and where. When he/she makes a mistake, call another student to try.

Extension activity

Aim: to practise information transfer and organisational strategies
- Draw two circles on the board. Write *I like* in one and *I don't like* in the other. Create two word maps of animal words to show which animals you like and which you don't like.
- Students do the same in their notebooks. They can extend the information to include other animals.

Learning outcomes:
- to read for specific information
- to listen for specific information
- to use *There are* to say what is in a picture
- to write about likes and dislikes

Recycled language: animals, numbers *one* to *ten*, prepositions

Creative thinking: Participates in investigative, exploratory, open-ended tasks

Cognitive control functions (WB): Cognitive flexibility

Materials: coloured pens or pencils, flashcards 35–43 (animals), sticky tape (optional)

Warm-up

Aim: to review animals and *I like / don't like*

- Clear space in the classroom. Make a line in the middle with sticky tape or string on the floor.
- Gesture to one side of the tape and say *I like*. Gesture to the other and say *I don't like*.
- Students stand one behind the other. Call the first student to stand near the line. Say an animal, e.g. *Rats!* The student jumps to one side of the line to show 'like' or 'don't like' and says, e.g. *I like rats!* He/She then goes to the back. Repeat, saying different animals.

1 SB p41 Read and circle the correct picture.

Aim: to practise reading

- Revise *pet show* using the pictures (ask *Where are the animals?*)
- Students read and circle the correct picture individually, and then compare answers.

Stronger students: Ask students to describe the pictures they didn't circle.

Key: Picture 3

2 SB p41 Look at Activity 1. Make sentences.

Aim: to give students practice in speaking **Exam skills**

- In pairs, students look at the pictures and take turns to make sentences with *There are*.

3 SB p41 Make a poster.

Aim: to practise writing and language from the unit

- Elicit the animals on the poster. Students match each one with a sentence.
- Students make their own poster, using the model.
- They compare posters in small groups.

1 14 WB p41 Listen and draw lines. **Exam skills**

Aim: to practise listening for specific information

- Elicit the animals in the picture and other features (*pond, tree*).
- Tell students to listen carefully and draw a line from each animal to the correct place.
- Play the recording through. Then play it again, pausing for students to draw lines.

For script see TB p121.

- Students check with their friends.
- Play the recording again and check answers.

Key: duck – on the pond, dog – under the table, cat – in the tree, spider – on the chair

2 WB p41 Look at the picture in Activity 1 and write.

Aim: to practise paying close attention to pictures and writing key information

Key: 2 on the pond, 3 under the table, 4 in the tree, 5 on the chair

Ending the lesson

Aim: to practise listening for detail

- Say, e.g. *At the pet show there are four elephants.* Choose a student to add an animal. He/She says, e.g. *At the pet show there are four elephants and six lizards.*
- Continue the chain, choosing students to add the next number and animal. They can't repeat animals or numbers.

Extension activity

Aim: to practise productive speaking

- Hand out animal flashcards and say *Come to the pet show!* Students who have flashcards come to the front, show their 'pets' to the class and talk about them, e.g. *This is my pet. I like lizards.*

Stronger students: Students can think of a name, e.g. *His name is Leo.*

- Award an imaginary prize to the 'best pet'.

1 Read and circle the correct picture.

Pet show

Come to the pet show. See two dogs, two lizards, four cats, two big spiders and two donkeys!

1

2

3

2 Look at Activity 1. Make sentences.

> There are eight dogs.

3 Make a poster.

Animals

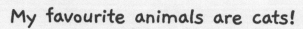

I like spiders and lizards.

My favourite animals are cats!

I don't like rats.

Think and learn

Nature

What do animals drink?

1 48 Listen and point.

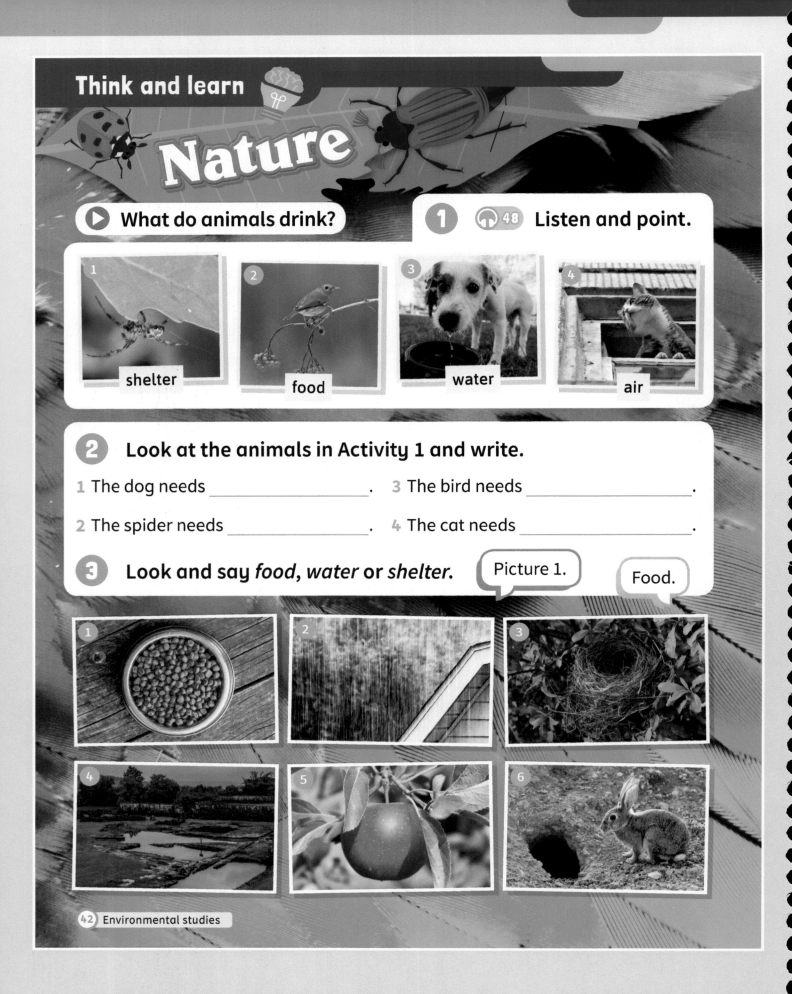

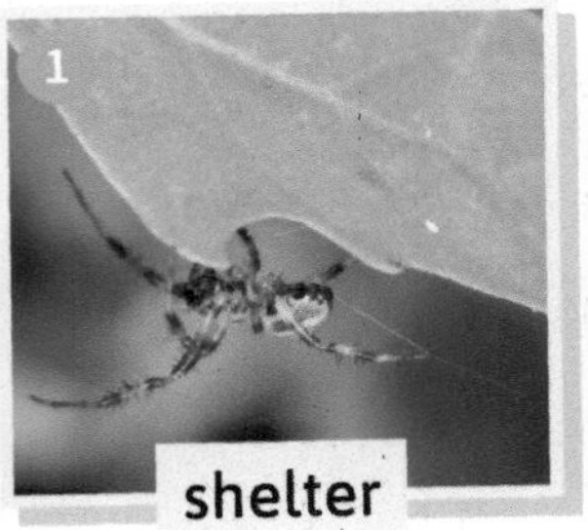

2 Look at the animals in Activity 1 and write.

1 The dog needs ________________.
2 The spider needs ________________.
3 The bird needs ________________.
4 The cat needs ________________.

3 Look and say *food*, *water* or *shelter*.

Picture 1.

Food.

Learning outcomes:
- to integrate other areas of the curriculum through English: Environmental studies
- to identify and name basic needs of animals

BIG QUESTION to explore the Big Question *What do animals need?*

New language: *shelter, food, water, air, live, eat, drink, bird*

Recycled language: animals, *need*

Critical thinking (WB): Demonstrates understanding of links between new ideas

Warm-up

Aim: to introduce the idea of needs of animals
- Write the Big Question *What do animals need?* on the board.
- Draw a picture of a dog or cat and ask *What does it need?* Elicit ideas. Students can answer in L1.
- Write some ideas on the board and ask students to try to work out what four things all animals (both wild animals and pets) need, from their ideas. Do not confirm answers at this stage.

SB p42 What do animals drink?

Aim: to raise students' awareness of basic animal needs
- With Student's Books closed, play the video.

For videoscript see TB p121.

- Ask students what animals they remember (*cat, dog, donkey, lizard, spider, elephant*). They can use L1 to tell you about the other things (*water, bird*). Teach *bird* and *drink* using gesture, and write the words on the board.
- Ask students to watch again and answer *What do animals drink?* Play the video again and elicit the answers (students can answer in L1 – teach *water*).

Key: Animals drink water.

1 48 SB p42 Listen and point.

Aim: to present words to talk about the needs of animals
- Play the recording. Students listen and point to the photos.

For script see SB p42.

- Make sure they realise that *shelter* means a place to live and *food* means things to eat.
- Play the recording again. Students repeat.

2 SB p42 Look at the animals in Activity 1 and write.

Aim: to practise words to talk about the needs of animals
- Check students know what to do.
- They complete the sentences by looking at the pictures in Activity 1 and copying the words.
- In pairs, students compare answers. Check as a class.

Key: 1 water, 2 shelter, 3 food, 4 air

3 SB p42 Look and say *food*, *water* or *shelter*.

Aim: to identify each need of animals
- Read the activity instruction aloud and check understanding.
- Practise the activity with the class responding in chorus, then in open pairs, then closed pairs.

Key: Picture 2. Water. Picture 3. Shelter. Picture 4. Water. Picture 5. Food. Picture 6. Shelter.

1 WB p42 Look and write.

Aim: to practise identifying animals' needs and writing new language

Key: 2 water, 3 air, 4 food

2 WB p42 What does it need? Tick ☑ the objects.

Aim: to enable students to apply what they have learnt about the needs of animals

Key: Students tick pictures 3 and 5.

Lesson review

Aim: to review what students have learnt in the lesson
- Write the following prompt on the board: *Today I've learnt about …*
- Elicit from students what they learnt today, e.g. *things animals need*.
- Write it on the board for students to copy.

Extension activity

Aim: to extend discussion from the lesson
- Ask students who have pets to say how they provide their basic needs of shelter, food and water.
- Discuss briefly what problems wild animals have getting some of their basic needs (their habitat could be disappearing, there might be a drought, their food might be taken away).

Note: This discussion will probably need to take place in L1.

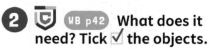

Learning outcomes:
- to extend the focus on Environmental studies through English
- to complete a project

New language: *I think, That's right, web, It lives/eats/drinks …*

Recycled language: *shelter, food, water, air, need, good,* animals

Critical thinking: Demonstrates understanding of links between new ideas

Creative thinking: Uses different media to make and describe his/her own designs

Critical thinking (WB): Sorts and classifies objects and activities according to key features (e.g. types of animal or transport)

Cognitive control functions: Cognitive flexibility

Materials: a paper plate per pair of students, plenty of wool, paper, pens, sticky tape, scissors, digital or print portfolios

Warm-up

Aim: to review the concept of animals' needs
- Elicit things all animals need from the previous lesson and write them on the board (*shelter, food, water, air*).
- Above them (in random order) write *drink, eat, live, breathe*. Ask students to match each need with a word above. Draw lines (*drink – water, eat – food, live – shelter, breathe – air*). Say *Animals drink water. Animals eat food. Animals live in shelter. Animals breathe air.*
- Repeat the sentences with the last word missing – students finish the sentences in chorus.

4 SB p43 Look and say.

Aim: to enable students to match resources to animals and express an opinion
- Read the activity instruction and the speech bubbles. Teach *I think* … using mime. Draw a tick on the board and teach/explain *That's right.*
- Students match the food, water and shelter to the animals at the top.
- Elicit ideas from the students and write them on the board. Encourage them to use *I think …*

Key: a food for a donkey, b food for a rat, d water for a donkey, e shelter for a donkey, f shelter for a rat, g shelter for a dog

5 Project SB p43 Make a spider's web.

Aim: to enable students to creatively engage with the concept of shelter
- Students work in pairs. Give each pair a paper plate and some wool. Teach *web*. Tell the class they are going to make a web.
- Students cut about 15 small grooves around the rims of their paper plates.
- Students tape the end of their wool to the back of the paper plate and then wind the wool over and across the plate, fitting it into each of the grooves to make a web.
- When there is wool over each groove, students cut the wool and tape that end on the back of the plate.
- Students draw and colour a spider on a piece of paper.
- The spiders and webs can be placed around the classroom. Alternatively, take photos of them to save to students' digital portfolios.

Stronger students: Students talk about their project, using the speech bubble as a model.

3 WB p43 What is it? Write the numbers.

Aim: to give practice in classifying needs of animals

Key: food: 2, 4, 6; water: 5, 8; shelter: 3, 7, 9

4 WB p43 Draw and write about an animal.

Aim: to enable students to consolidate new language

Lesson review

Aim: to review what students have learnt in the lesson
- Write the following prompt on the board: *Today I've …*
- Elicit from students what they learnt today, e.g. *made shelter for a spider – a web.*
- Write it on the board. Students copy it into their notebooks.

Extension activity

Aim: to extend students' understanding of the needs of animals
- Write the prompt from SB Activity 5 on the board: *This animal lives in a … for shelter. It eats … It drinks …*
- Show pictures of different animals. Elicit ideas to complete the sentences. **Note:** This discussion will probably need to take place in L1.

4 Look and say.

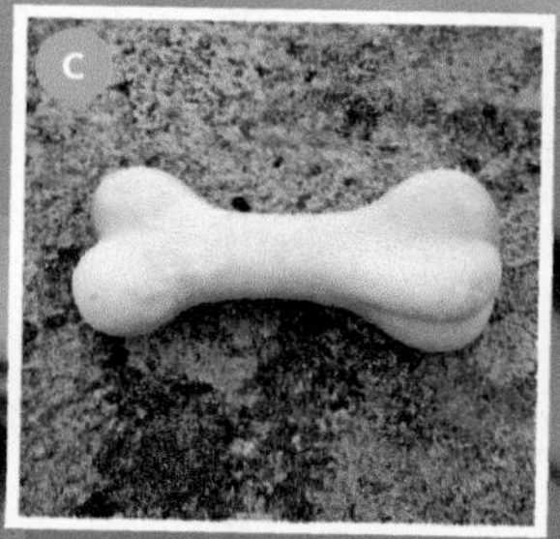

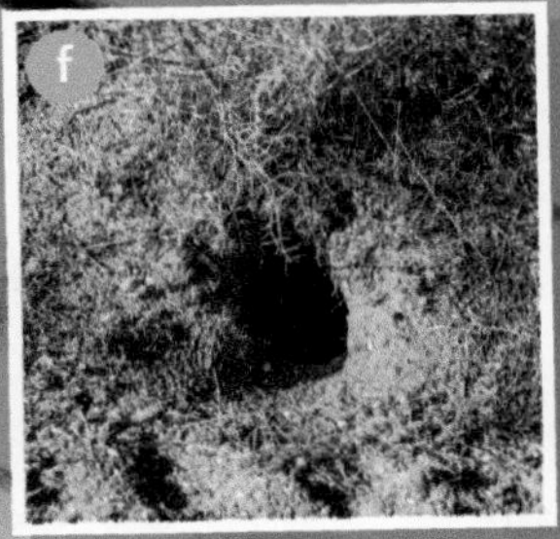

I think c is a good food for a dog.

That's right.

5 Project Make a spider's web.

My spider lives in a … for shelter. It eats … . It drinks … .

Create that!

1 49 **Listen and imagine. Then draw your picture.**

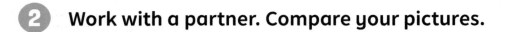

2 **Work with a partner. Compare your pictures.**

The animal in my picture is …

In your picture there's …

Learning outcomes:
- to listen, imagine and draw to demonstrate meaning
- to describe an animal

New language: *paper plate, scissors, coloured pens, hole punch, elastic, string*

Recycled language: animals, imperatives, *What colour is it? big, small, Where is (the animal)? Is it (big or small)? picture, pencil*

Creative thinking: Chooses options to create something new

Creative thinking (WB): Uses different media to make and describe his/her own designs

Cognitive control functions: Inhibitory control

Materials: coloured pens or pencils, paper plate for each student, scissors, hole punch, elastic or string (for students to attach to their masks), music CD (for Extension activity)

Warm-up

Aim: to review imperatives and animals
- Give students some simple instructions for them to carry out or mime, e.g. *Show me a red pencil. Put your book on your desk. Be an elephant!*
- Students take turns to give instructions to the class.

1 49 SB p44 Listen and imagine. Then draw your picture.

Aim: to give students practice in listening and following instructions
- Explain the activity. Make sure students have coloured pens or pencils and that they know the meaning of *imagine* and *draw*.
- Play the recording for students to follow the instructions.

For script see TB p121.

- Play the recording again before students draw, if necessary, and explain the new questions.
- Circulate as they draw their pictures, asking, e.g. *What's your animal? Is it big or small? What food does it need? Draw the food. Where does it live – what shelter does it need? Draw the shelter.*
- Praise students for using their imagination and for their originality.

2 SB p44 Work with a partner. Compare your pictures.

Aim: to practise speaking
- Students work in pairs. They show each other their pictures. Encourage them to say as much as they can.

1 WB p44 Make an animal mask.

Aim: to enable students to follow a set of instructions to make a mask
- Read the list of items students need and show each thing in turn. Students check they have what they need on their desk.
- Work through the instructions before students begin, showing them how to make a mask at the front of the class.
- Students make their masks. Help them with cutting, making holes, measuring and attaching the elastic, etc.

Ending the lesson

Aim: to enable students to use their masks
- Students sit in groups, with other students who have used the same animal for their mask.
- Give instructions for them to listen and follow, naming the animal group first, e.g. *All the donkeys, stand up and turn around. All the frogs, show me your pencil case.*

Extension activity

Aim: to enable students to use their masks
- Find a large space, e.g. the school hall or playground. Students put on their masks.
- Play a music CD. Say, e.g. *Let's see the cats.*
- The students who are wearing cat masks come to the middle of the room and move in the same way as their animal.
- Repeat for the other animals that the students have chosen for their masks.

Learning outcomes:
- to review language from the unit by doing a quiz
- to reflect on learning

BIG QUESTION to think about how the unit has helped them talk about the Big Question *What do animals need?*

Recycled language: vocabulary and grammar from the unit, imperatives, *This is a …*

Creative thinking (WB): Creates texts that express personal interests, emotions, or identity

Cognitive control functions (WB): Cognitive flexibility

Materials: flashcards 35–43 (animals), soft toy for each pair of students (optional)

Warm-up

Aim: to review animals and prepositions
- Revise animals with the flashcards. Use one animal flashcard or a soft toy to demonstrate *Simon says.*
- Call a student to the front and explain the rules (he/she follows your instructions only if you say *Simon says* first).
- Hand the student a flashcard or soft toy and give instructions, e.g. *Simon says 'Put the elephant under a chair.' Simon says 'Put the elephant in Carla's bag.'* and so on. Then say an instruction without *Simon says*, e.g. *Put the elephant in my hand.* If the student does it, he/she is out.
- Students play the same game in pairs (with one flashcard or soft toy per pair). They see who can follow instructions for the longest time, without making a mistake.

1 SB p45 Read and circle.

Aim: to enable students to review language from the unit by doing a quiz
- Remind students to answer by circling one option for each sentence, using the picture clues. Do the first item as an example, if necessary.
- Students do the quiz in pairs. The first time, they do it without looking back through the unit.
- Pairs check their work with other pairs.
- Students then look back to check questions they did not know.
- Check answers with the class.

Key: 1 b, 2 a, 3 c, 4 b, 5 b, 6 a, 7 c, 8 c

1 WB p45 Write and circle.

Aim: to enable students to assess their own learning

Key: 2 in, 3 under

2 WB p45 Read and tick ✓ or cross ✗.

BIG QUESTION **Aim:** to enable students to revisit the Big Question and consolidate learning
- Check as a class and ask students to give examples of food, shelter and water sources for particular animals (e.g. a donkey). Students use L1 to give examples.

Key: 1 ✗ 2 ✗ 3 ✓ 4 ✓ 5 ✓

3 WB p45 Read. Then draw and write.

Aim: to enable students to personalise the topic

Picture dictionary

Aim: to review vocabulary for animals
- Students look at the Picture dictionary page for animals (WB p121).
- In pairs, they take turns to point to one of the pictures and say the word.
- Then students write the words under the pictures.

Key: dog, duck, elephant, frog, lizard, rat, spider, donkey

Ending the lesson

Aim: to enable students to express their preferences
- Ask students what their favourite activity is from the unit (e.g. the song, chant or one of the games) and have a class vote.
- Repeat the most popular activity with the class.

Extension activity

Aim: to enable students to share what they have learnt
- Put students into groups of four.
- Each student opens their Workbook at p45.
- Students take turns to read aloud what they have written for Activity 3 and to say something about their pictures.
- Encourage students to compare what they have written and drawn.

1 Read and circle.

1 **This is a …**

a lizard. b donkey. c cat.

2 **This is a …**

a rat. b frog. c spider.

3 **The lizard is … the desk.**

a on b in c under

4 **The duck is … the pond.**

a on b in c under

5 **I … spiders.**

a like b don't like

6 **I … cats.**

a like b don't like

7 **In the story, … pet is a spider.**

a Thunder's b Misty's c Whisper's

8 **This is … for the duck.**

a food. b water. c shelter.

4 Lunchtime

1 (50) **Listen and look. Then listen and say the words.**

BIG QUESTION Where does food come from?

2 (51) **Listen and chant.**

Lunchtime! Lunchtime!
What's for lunch?

I don't like chicken,
And I don't like cheese.
I don't like pizza,
And I don't like peas.

Lunchtime! Lunchtime!
What's for lunch?

Oh, I like apples,
And I like steak.
Oh, I like carrots,
And I like cake!
Yummy!

Learning outcomes:
- to name and talk about food
- to say a chant

BIG QUESTION to start to think about the Big Question *Where does food come from?*

New language: *apple, banana, cake, pizza, sausage, cheese sandwich, fish, chicken, peas, steak, carrots, lunchtime, What's for lunch?*

Recycled language: plurals, *I like (apples). I don't like (chicken).*

Critical thinking (WB): Solves simple puzzles (e.g. word puzzles)

Cognitive control functions: Working memory

Flashcards: 44–54 (food)

Warm-up

Aim: to revise talking about likes and dislikes

- Draw a picture of a cake on the board / show the flashcard. Smile, look hungry and say *I like cake*. (Name), *what about you?* Ask other students. Encourage them to say *I like cake* or *I don't like cake*.
- Ask *What about pizza?* Students make new sentences.

Presentation

Aim: to present foods

- Teach the food words using the flashcards, as usual.
- Write *Food* in the middle of the board and stick the flashcards around it to make a word map.

1 50 SB p46 Listen and look. Then listen and say the words.

Aim: to practise foods

- Students look at the picture in their Student's Books. Elicit the characters and where they are (in the school canteen).
- Play the recording. Students point to the foods. Ask students what they think Misty is saying.

For script see TB p121.

- Play the recording again. Students repeat.
- Students point and name the food in pairs, saying *I like* or *I don't like* each item.

BIG QUESTION Where does food come from?

Aim: to encourage students to find out about where food comes from

- Read the Big Question. Ask *Which food is from plants? Which food is from animals?* Write *From plants* and *From animals* on the board as column headings.
- Elicit ideas (From plants: *banana, apple, peas, carrots*; From animals: *sausage, chicken, steak, fish, cheese*).
  Note: Some of the discussion will need to be in your students' first language (L1).

2 51 SB p46 Listen and chant.

Aim: to give students further practice saying the foods

- Pre-teach *lunchtime*, *What's for lunch?* and *Yummy!*
- Play the recording. Students listen and follow the chant in their Student's Books.

For chant script see SB p46.

- Play the recording again, pausing after each verse for students to repeat. Do the chant as a class and then in groups. Check that students are using singular and plurals correctly.
- Teach actions for *lunch* (e.g. pretending to use a knife and fork), *I like* (e.g. thumbs up), *I don't like* (e.g. thumbs down) and *Yummy!* (e.g. licking lips and rubbing your stomach). Students do the chant with the actions.

1 WB p46 Look and number.

Aim: to give students reading practice

Key: 2 b, 3 f, 4 a, 5 g, 6 e, 7 h, 8 c

2 WB p46 Circle the food words.

Aim: to give practice in spelling and word recognition

Key: carrot, fish, bananas, pizza, apple, peas

Ending the lesson

Aim: to review key language from the lesson

- Hold a flashcard so students can't see it. Say *Yummy! I like this food. What is it?*
- Students guess, e.g. *Is it cake?*

Extension activity

Aim: to personalise the chant

- In groups of four, students personalise the chant by changing the foods. Groups practise their chant, and then perform for the class.

Learning outcomes:
- to say what they've got and haven't got

New language: *I've got (a/an), I haven't got, Me too, Look what I can do, go away, parrot*

Recycled language: food, *silly*, *lunch(box)*

Materials: flashcards 44–54 (food), Unit 4 stickers, a lunchbox with known food inside (optional)

Warm-up

Aim: to review food vocabulary
- Stick the flashcards around the room.
- Make sentences about the food items, e.g. *I like cheese sandwiches*. Students point to the correct flashcard.
- If possible, show students a closed lunchbox (with real food inside). Say *This is my lunchbox! What's in my lunchbox?* Students guess foods. Show them items they guess. Then show all the food and say *Look at my lunch! Yummy!*

Presentation

Aim: to present *have got* and *haven't got*
- Choose a flashcard and hide it from the students. Say *I've got a food*. Say, e.g. *I haven't got pizza. I haven't got a banana. I haven't got carrots. I haven't got a cheese sandwich.*
- Students guess what you have got. Say, e.g. *Yes! I've got steak!*

1 52 SB p47 Listen and draw lines.

Aim: to practise listening and *have got / haven't got*
- Ask students *What colour is your lunchbox? What's in your lunchbox?*
- Point to the first lunchbox in Activity 1 and elicit the food (*banana, pizza*). Repeat for others.
- Play the recording for students to listen only.

For script see TB p121.

- Play the recording again, pausing for students to draw lines.
- Check as a class.

Key: 1 c, 2 d, 3 a, 4 b

2 53 SB p47 Watch, listen and say.

Aim: to focus students on grammatical form
- Use the picture to review *carrot*. Teach *parrot*.
- Play the *Penny the penguin* video. Students watch and listen, then watch and read.
- Explain that the apostrophe replaces the letters *ha* (*I have got* becomes *I've got*). Check understanding of *go away*, *silly* and *Look what I can do*.
- Play the audio. Students follow in their Student's Book and join in.

For script see SB p47.

- Students practise the sentences in pairs. Then they swap roles.

3 SB p47 Choose your lunch and stick. Find a friend with the same lunch.

Aim: to give students further practice with *I've got / I haven't got*
- Point to the picture and say *This is your lunchbox. Put four foods in the box.* Students choose four food stickers and stick them in the lunchbox. Draw a lunchbox with four food items on the board.
- Point to your picture and say, e.g. *I've got a sandwich*. One student looks at his/her lunchbox with stickers and says *I haven't got a sandwich* or *Me too!* Practise pronunciation of *Me too!*
- Students talk about their lunchboxes in pairs. Swap pairs two or three times. They try to find another student with the same lunch.
- Alternatively, students can walk around the classroom, stopping to talk to other students, until they find someone with the same lunch as their own.

1 WB p47 Look and circle.

Aim: to give students practice reading *have got* and *haven't got*

Key: 2 haven't got, 3 've got, 4 haven't got, 5 've got, 6 've got

2 WB p47 Read and match.

Aim: to give students extended reading practice

Key: 2 a, 3 c, 4 b

3 WB p47 Look and write.

Aim: to practise writing the new language

Key: 1 got, 2 've, 3 haven't

Ending the lesson

Aim: to review new language
- Put three food flashcards on the board and elicit, e.g. *I've got cake, a cheese sandwich and an apple.*
- Change the flashcards and elicit new sentences.

Extension activity

Aim: to personalise the new language
- Students choose a lunch and draw it.
- They write sentences, e.g. *I've got steak and bananas. I haven't got pizza.*

1 52 Listen and draw lines.

1
2
3
4

a
b
c
d

2 53 Watch, listen and say.

Language focus

I’**ve got** a carrot.
I’**ve got** a carrot.
Look what I can do.

Oh, go away,
You silly parrot.
Now I **haven’t got** a carrot!

3 Choose your lunch and stick. Find a friend with the same lunch.

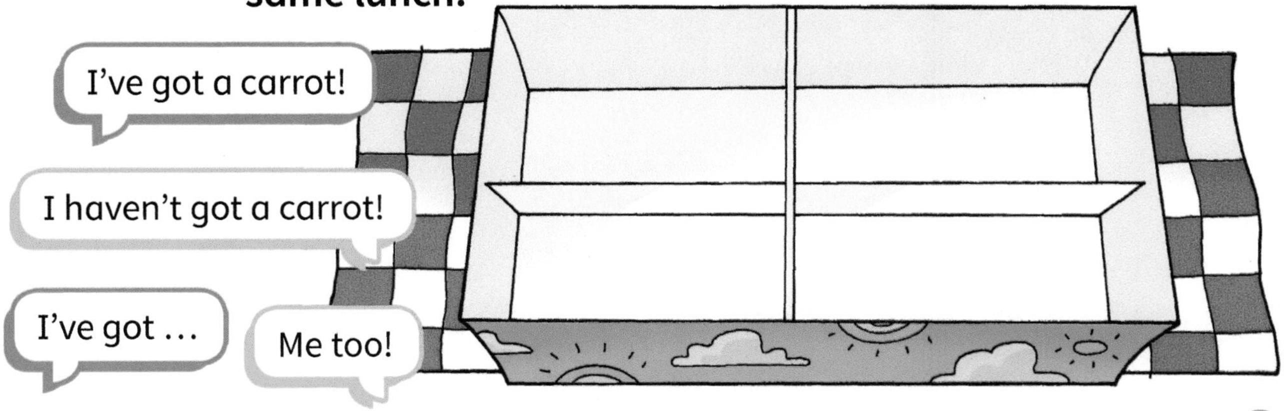
I’ve got a carrot!
I haven’t got a carrot!
I’ve got …
Me too!

1 54 Listen and sing. Then tick ✓ the food in the song.

I've got a magic tree
With lots of things to eat.
I've got a magic tree.
Let's go and get a treat.

Pick an ice cream from the tree.
Pick an orange from the tree.
Pick an apple from the tree.
It's there for you and me.

I've got a magic tree
With lots of things to take.
I've got a magic tree.
Let's go and get a cake.

Pick an ice cream from the tree ...

2 Look, think and write.

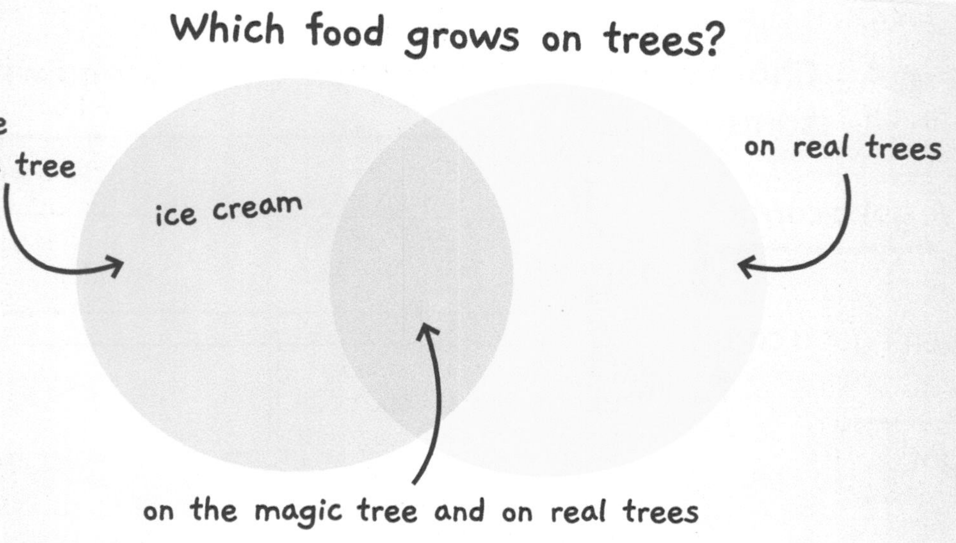

Learning outcomes:
- to sing a song
- to practise *I've got / I haven't got* and food

New language: *magic tree, real tree, things to eat/take, Let's go, get a treat/cake, pick, ice cream, orange, there*

Recycled language: food, *I've got / I haven't got*

BIG QUESTION Your students will think some more about the Big Question *Where does food come from?*

Critical thinking: Compares different types of information (factual and fictional)

Creative thinking (WB): Participates in investigative, exploratory, open-ended tasks

Cognitive control functions: Cognitive flexibility

Cognitive control functions (WB): Working memory

Flashcards: 44–54 (food)

Warm-up

Aim: to review food and *have/ haven't got*

- Hand the food flashcards out. Each student shows his/ her flashcard and makes a sentence, e.g. *I've got an apple*, and then hides the card.
- A volunteer without a flashcard tries to remember the order, e.g. *an apple, pizza, sausages*. If he/she is right, the student with the flashcard turns it around and says, e.g. *Yes. I've got an apple.* If not, he/she hides the flashcard and says *No. I haven't got (pizza).*

1 54 ▶ 55 SB p48 Listen and sing. Then tick ✓ the food in the song.

Aim: to sing a song with the class and practise listening

- Students look at the picture. Say *It's a magic tree! There are lots of things to eat.* Ask *What's on the tree?* (*Cake, apple, carrots, pizza, banana*) Teach *ice cream* and *orange*.
- Pre-teach *pick* by miming picking something from a tree.
- Play the audio (54). Students follow the song in their Student's Books.

For song lyrics see SB p48.

- Explain *treat*.
- Play the audio again for students to tick the food they hear.
- Play the song video, pausing after each verse for students to repeat.
- When students have learnt the song, use the karaoke version of the audio (55) or video to practise. Students can mime picking things from a tree as they sing.

Key: Students tick the ice cream, orange, apple and cake.

2 SB p48 Look, think and write.

BIG QUESTION **Aim:** to help students think about where food comes from

- Copy the diagram on the board without headings.
- Point and say *This is a magic tree. It isn't a real tree.* Write the headings for the Venn diagram on the board.
- Ask *Which food grows on real trees?* (*Apples, oranges, bananas*) Write these in the right-hand circle, together with other suggestions from students. Ask *What about the magic tree?* (*Ice cream, cake, pizza, carrots*) Write these in the left-hand circle. Elicit the items which grow on both (*apples, oranges, bananas*) and move these into the overlapping section.
- Students copy the diagram in their notebooks.

1 15 WB p48 Can you remember? Listen and write.

Aim: to give further practice with food words

For song lyrics see SB p48.

Key: 2 tree, 3 ice cream, 4 orange, 5 apple, 6 tree, 7 tree, 8 cake

2 WB p48 Which foods grow on trees? Draw.

Aim: to review food and think about the Big Question

Ending the lesson

Aim: to review key language from the lesson

- Students sing the song from SB Activity 1 with actions.

Extension activity

Aim: to give students further practice using Venn diagrams

- Make a Venn diagram with your name next to one circle, a student's name next to the other circle, and *Both* for the overlap. Say *I like cheese. Do you like cheese?* to the student. Write *cheese* in the appropriate section. Repeat with other foods.
- Students ask and answer and make Venn diagrams in pairs.

Learning outcomes:
- to ask and answer questions using *have got*

New language: *Have we got any (chicken)? Yes, we have, No, we haven't, I'm hungry, (orange) juice*

Recycled language: food

Flashcards: 44–54 (food)

Warm-up

Aim: to review food and drink
- Draw two shopping baskets on the board. Label them *Food* and *Drink*.
- In pairs, with books closed, students write words in the two categories.
- Elicit ideas and add them to the board.

Presentation

Aim: to present *Have you got …? Yes, we have. / No, we haven't.*
- Put five food flashcards face up on a desk at the front. Call two students to the desk.
- Say, e.g. *Have you got any chicken?* Students look for the chicken flashcard and hold it up if it's on the desk. Prompt *Yes, we have. / No, we haven't.*
- Repeat the question with other food words. Then repeat the activity with different students.

1 SB p49 Follow the lines. Read and tick ☑.

Aim: to practise *Have we got any …? Yes, we have. / No, we haven't.*
- Elicit the food in the pictures and teach *orange juice.*
- Students trace the lines to see which items are in the basket. They tick the correct answers.

Key: 1 Yes, we have. 2 Yes, we have. 3 No, we haven't. 4 Yes, we have.

2 ▶ 56 SB p49 Watch, listen and say.

Aim: to focus students on grammatical form
- Teach *I'm hungry* using mime. Students practise the phrase and do the mime.
- Play the *Penny the penguin* video. Students watch and listen, then watch and read. Check understanding of the grammar.
- Play the audio. Students follow in their Student's Book. They join in and do mimes for *I'm hungry* and *No, we haven't*, *Yes, we have* and *fish.*

For script see SB p49.

- Students practise the sentences in pairs.

Stronger students: Students can say the chant with different kinds of food instead of *fish.*

3 SB p49 Ask and answer.

Aim: to give students practice asking and answering questions using *have got*
- Demonstrate the activity with a volunteer. Point to the shopping trolley and say *This is our food and drink. What have we got? Have we got any sausages?* The student answers *Yes, we have.* Ask *Have we got any fish?* The student answers *No, we haven't.*
- Students ask and answer about the shopping in the same way in pairs. Monitor and check they are taking turns and using the question form correctly.
- Volunteer pairs perform one exchange for the class.

1 WB p49 Who says what? Look and circle.

Aim: to give students practice in reading the new language

Key: 1 Paul, 2 Penny, 3 Penny

2 WB p49 Look at the picture and answer the questions.

Aim: to give students practice in writing the short answers

Key: 3 No, we haven't. 4 Yes, we have.

3 WB p49 Look and write questions.

Aim: to give students practice in reading and writing the new language

Key: 2 Have we got any bananas? 3 Have we got any carrots?

Ending the lesson

Aim: to review new language from the lesson
- Ask questions about things you haven't got in the classroom, e.g. *Have we got any animals in our classroom?* Students respond.
- Students take turns to ask the class similar questions, using their own ideas.

Extension activity

Aim: to review vocabulary
- In pairs, students make word snakes of at least six words, using WB p46 Activity 2 as a model.

1 Follow the lines. Read and tick ☑.

1 Have we got any cheese?
- ☐ Yes, we have.
- ☐ No, we haven't.

2 Have we got any orange juice?
- ☐ Yes, we have.
- ☐ No, we haven't.

3 Have we got any sausages?
- ☐ Yes, we have.
- ☐ No, we haven't.

4 Have we got any fish?
- ☐ Yes, we have.
- ☐ No, we haven't.

2 56 Watch, listen and say.

Language focus

Penny, I'm hungry.
Have we **got any** fish?
No, we **haven't**.
We haven't got any fish.

Penny, I'm hungry.
Have we **got any** fish?
Yes, we **have**!
Yes, we've got a fish!

3 Ask and answer.

Have we got any pizza?

Yes, we have.

The pizza

1 Which food can you see in picture 8?

Thunder: Where's Misty?

Misty: Mmm … pizza. My favourite!

Whisper: Look at Misty!
Flash: Hey! That isn't fair.

Misty: Pizza, please.
Woman: Sorry. We haven't got pizza.

Misty: OK. Sausages and peas, please.

Woman: Here you are.
Misty: Thank you.

Learning outcomes:
- to listen to, read, watch and act out a picture story
- to review language from the unit

New language: *Where's (Misty)? What have you got? hot*

Recycled language: character names, *please, have got, haven't got, nice, fantastic, favourite, look at, that isn't fair, new, here you are*

Value: waiting your turn

Critical thinking (WB): Sorts and classifies objects and activities according to key features (e.g. types of animal or transport)

Warm-up

Aim: to review the characters and the story
- Elicit the names of the four Super Friends.
- Ask students to mime their special powers.
- Elicit what the characters learnt in the last episode (*to be brave and overcome their fear of spiders*).

The pizza

1 57 SB pp50–51 Which food can you see in picture 8?

Aim: to present a picture story
- Elicit who students can see in the first picture of the story (*Whisper, Flash and Thunder*) and where they are (*in the school canteen*). Elicit what they are doing (students can answer in L1 that they are queuing for lunch).
- Remind students that the names of the speakers in the story are on the left, and teach *Woman*, using the pictures.
- Ask *Which food can you see in picture 8?* Play the audio. Students listen and read to find out what the food is in picture 8.

For script see SB pp50–51.

- Elicit the answer. Explain the meaning of *nice* and *hot*.
- Play the whole *Super Friends* video. Then, play the video again, pausing to ask questions: *Who's missing?* (*Misty*), *What's Misty's favourite?* (*Pizza*), *What does Misty want?* (*Pizza*), *What's the problem?* (*There isn't any pizza*), *What's Misty got?* (*Sausages and peas*), *What have the other Super Friends got?* (*Pizza*)
- Talk with the class about the value (waiting your turn) and ask who doesn't wait their turn (Misty).

Key: Pizza, sausages, peas, apples and bananas.

1 16 WB p50 Who says it? Listen and tick ✓.

Aim: to review the story

For script see TB p121.

Key: 1 Thunder (2nd picture), 2 Flash (2nd picture), 3 Woman (1st picture)

2 WB p50 Look and match. Draw lines.

Aim: to match phrases from the story with pictures

Key: 1 (Thunder) We've got pizza. – picture of pizza, 2 (Misty) Pizza, please. – picture of sausages and peas

3 WB p50 Look and write.

Aim: to practise writing and to review the story

Key: 1 Here you are. 2 What have you got?

Ending the lesson

Aim: to practise the story
- Put students in groups of five (one student is the woman).
- Students each take a role of one of the characters.
- Play the recording. Students repeat in role.
- Students practise the role play in groups. They can use paper plates and serving spoons as props.
- Volunteer groups role play for the class.

Extension activity

Aim: to discuss the value of waiting your turn
- Focus on the part of the story where Misty jumped the queue and got her lunch before her friends.
- Elicit why the value of waiting your turn is important, and elicit examples from the students of when they have had to wait their turn or when other people haven't waited their turn.
  Note: This discussion will probably need to take place in L1.

Learning outcomes:
- to interpret deeper meaning from a story
- to practise saying the short vowel sound /ɒ/ as in *hot*
- to review language from the story and the unit

New language: *Who says …? sorry, stop, shop, hot dog*

Recycled language: language from the story, food, colours, classroom objects, toys

Phonics focus: Your students will be able to identify and say the short vowel sound /ɒ/ in the sound sentence.

Value: waiting your turn

Critical thinking (WB): Demonstrates understanding of links between new ideas

Flashcards: 44–54 (food)

Warm-up

Aim: to review the story
- Write *Misty* on the board and draw a plate of sausages and peas and a plate of pizza (or put the flashcards on the board).
- Ask *What has Misty got in the story? Sausages and peas or pizza?* Elicit why she hasn't got pizza, to review the value (waiting your turn).

2 SB p51 Read and tick ✓ or cross ☒.

Aim: to check comprehension of the story
- Check students know what to do, and their understanding of *Who says …?* Students read the five sentences silently.
- They tick or cross in the table and compare answers in pairs.
- Check with the class.

Key:

Who says …?	Misty	Whisper	Flash	Thunder
I've got pizza.	☒	✓	✓	✓
I've got an apple.	☒	✓	☒	✓
I've got sausages.	✓	☒	☒	☒
I've got peas.	✓	✓	☒	☒
I've got a banana.	✓	☒	✓	☒

3 SB p51 Find who says …

Aim: to present the short vowel sound /ɒ/
- Write *sorry* and *got* on the board, using a red pen for the *o*.
- Students repeat *Sorry. We haven't got pizza* after you.
- Students find the sentence in the story (frame 4).

Key: The woman

4 58 SB p51 Listen and say.

Aim: to practise the sound /ɒ/, a short vowel sound
- Teach *shop* and *hot dog* using the picture. Play the recording. Students look at the picture, read and repeat.

For script see TB p122.

- Repeat the sentence as a class without the recording. Say it loudly, slowly, quickly, whisper it, etc.
- Students take turns to repeat in pairs.

1 WB p51 Read and match. Tick ✓ the correct picture.

Aim: to focus students on the value of waiting your turn

Key: Picture 1

2 17 WB p51 Listen and colour. Point and say.

Aim: to practise recognising the sounds /æ/, /e/, /ɒ/ and /ɪ/

For script see TB p122.

Key: The objects should be coloured as follows:
black – 5 bag
red – 4 desk, 6 pen
orange – 2 doll, 7 box
pink – 3 fish, 8 six

Ending the lesson

Aim: to review and write decodable words with the sound /ɒ/ and distinguish it from the sounds /æ/, /e/ and /ɪ/
- Students close their Student's Books.
- Dictate the sound sentence while students write. They compare their sentences with a partner before checking spelling in the Student's Book.
- Write these sentences on the board: *A pink six and a red ten. An orange dog with a black hat.* Students draw and colour pictures to match the sentences.

Extension activity

Aim: to create a pizza
- Tell students to draw their ideal pizza in their notebooks. They add the toppings they like. Go around the class, supplying words as necessary.
- Students label their toppings.
- More confident students present their pizzas to the class, e.g. *I've got a pizza with sausage, mushroom and tomato.*

7

Thunder: Look!
Woman: A new pizza. Nice and hot.
Flash: Fantastic!

8

Misty: What have you got?
Whisper, Thunder and Flash: We've got pizza. Nice and hot!

2 Read and tick ✓ or cross ✗.

Who says ... ?				
I've got pizza.				
I've got an apple.				
I've got sausages.				
I've got peas.				
I've got a banana.				

Phonics

3 Find who says ...

Sorry, we haven't got pizza.

4 58 Listen and say.

Polly stops at the shop for a hot dog.

Skills

1 59 **Listen and say the numbers.**

eleven | twelve | thirteen | fourteen | fifteen

sixteen | seventeen | eighteen | nineteen | twenty

2 60 **Listen and write.**

In the fridge

__________ carrots

13 __________

1 __________

__________ sausages

3 **What's in your fridge? Think and write.**

In my fridge

14 pizzas

Learning outcomes:
- to listen for specific information
- to say and write numbers 11–20

New language: numbers 11–20, *fridge, What's in the/your fridge?*

Recycled language: food, numbers *one* to *ten*, *Just a minute, Have we got any (sausages)? We've got … Yummy!*

Materials: flashcards 55–64, 44–54 (numbers 11–20, food), soft ball for each group of students (optional)

Warm-up

Aim: to review numbers *one* to *ten*

- Make groups of up to ten students. Each group stands in a circle. Make a ball out of paper for each group (or use a real soft ball).
- The first student says *One* and then throws the ball to another student who says *Two*. This student throws the ball and says *Three*, and so on.
- When groups get to *Ten*, they start to count backwards.

1 59 SB p52 Listen and say the numbers.

Aim: to present and practise numbers 11–20

- Students look at the pictures in the Student's Book.
- Play the recording twice. Students listen and repeat.

For script see SB p52.

- Use the flashcards to practise the numbers. Show the flashcards first in sequence while students say the numbers. Then show the cards at random and elicit the numbers.

2 60 SB p52 Listen and write.

Aim: to practise listening for specific information

- Use the picture to teach *fridge*. Ask students what they think the boy in the picture is asking (*What's in the fridge?* or *What have we got in the fridge?*) Elicit some questions he could ask with *Have we got any …?* (e.g. *Have we got any cheese? Have we got any orange juice?*)
- Tell students that the boy is called Tom and they are going to listen to Tom and his dad talking about what's in the fridge.
- Play the recording for students to listen only.

For script see TB p122.

- Play the recording again for students to listen and complete the list of food.
- They compare answers in pairs before the class check. If necessary, play the recording again.

Stronger students: Ask *What do they need for the party?* (*Steak and sausages*)

Key: 16, apples, steak, 4

3 SB p52 What's in your fridge? Think and write.

Aim: to enable students to personalise the language and practise listening and writing

- Students work individually to complete a list of items in their own fridge. They write six items. Monitor to check spelling and ask *What's in your fridge?* or *Have you got any (sausages)?*
- Students work in pairs. Student A tries to guess what is on Student B's list by asking, e.g. *Have you got any (orange juice)?* Student B replies *Yes, I have* or *No, I haven't*. Then they swap roles. The activity can be competitive – students lose a 'life' each time their partner says *No, I haven't.*

1 WB p52 Look at the numbers. Look at the letters. Write the words. Exam skills

Aim: to practise spelling numbers 11–20

Key: 2 seventeen, 3 fifteen, 4 twelve, 5 twenty, 6 eighteen

2 WB p52 Look and write.

Aim: to practise writing numbers 11–20

Key: 2 eleven carrots, 3 twenty apples, 4 seventeen peas

Ending the lesson

Aim: to give students practice in sequencing numbers

- Call 20 students to the front of the class.
- Say a number between 1 and 20 to each student at random.
- Students quickly arrange themselves in a line in numerical order.

Extension activity

Aim: to practise alphabet skills

- In pairs, students put the new number words into alphabetical order.

Learning outcomes:
- to read for specific information
- to write and talk about a shopping list

New language: *shopping list, We need …*

Recycled language: food, numbers 11–20, *I've got …, I haven't got …, lunch*

Creative thinking: Participates in investigative, exploratory, open-ended tasks

Critical thinking (WB): Compares different types of information

Flashcards: 55–64 (numbers 11–20)

Warm-up

Aim: to review numbers 11–20
- Students close their Student's Books. Stick the number flashcards on the board (showing the figure).
- Call volunteers in turn to write a number as a word under the flashcard.
- The rest of the class help with the spelling. Turn the cards over for students to check.

1 SB p53 Look, read and circle the five mistakes in the texts. Exam skills

Aim: to give students practice in reading for specific information
- Tell students to look carefully at the picture and think about what each person has got (and how many of each thing they've got). Ask questions about each person, e.g. *Has Emily got oranges? What has she got?* (*Bananas*)
- Explain that there are mistakes in the captions below the pictures (five mistakes in total). Read the instructions.
- Students do the activity silently and on their own. They then compare their answers in pairs and re-read to check when their answers differ.
- Check with the class.

Key: Students circle the following words:

Noah: I've got twelve sausages and **two** cheese sandwiches. I haven't got any steaks. I've got a chicken.

Peter: I've got **thirteen** apples. I **haven't** got a cake. I haven't got a pizza.

Emily: I've got **three** bananas and twelve carrots. I haven't got four fish. I **haven't** got a chicken.

2 SB p53 Make a shopping list for a school lunch.

Aim: to personalise the language and give students speaking practice
- Pre-teach *shopping list* by writing your own shopping on a piece of paper. As you write items on the list look thoughtful and say *I need …* Ask students if their parents/carers make lists before they go shopping and if they sometimes help with deciding what to buy.
- Students work in small groups. They agree on a shopping list for a school lunch. Monitor and prompt students to use as much language as possible. Ask *What have you got on your list? Have you got any drinks?* Ask students to explain why they have chosen particular items.
- Groups share their lists with the class. You can have a class vote about which lunch students would like to eat.

1 18 WB p53 Listen and tick ✓.

Aim: to practise listening for detail

For script see TB p122.

Key: 1 b, 2 c

2 WB p53 Read and match. Write numbers.

Aim: to give students practice in close reading

Key: 2 a, 3 b, 4 c

Ending the lesson

Aim: to practise writing a description from notes
- Students write a description of what's on their shopping list in SB Activity 2. Write the beginning on the board for students to copy, e.g. *On our shopping list we've got …*

Extension activity

Aim: to practise listening for detail
- Play a chain game. Say, e.g. *On my list I've got 12 bananas.* Student A says *On my list I've got 12 bananas and 16 cakes.*
- Continue the chain around the class, choosing students at random to add new items. They cannot repeat food or numbers.
- Start another chain when you have eight foods on the list.

1 Look, read and circle the five mistakes in the texts.

Noah: I've got twelve sausages and two cheese sandwiches. I haven't got any steaks. I've got a chicken.

Peter: I've got thirteen apples. I haven't got a cake. I haven't got a pizza.

Emily: I've got three bananas and twelve carrots. I haven't got four fish. I haven't got a chicken.

2 Make a shopping list for a school lunch.

Think and learn

Food

What types of food do you know?

1 Listen and point. (61)

1 fruit

2 vegetables

3 plant

4 tree

5 soil

2 Read, look and match.

a

1 fruit on a plant

2 fruit on a tree

3 vegetables in the soil

4 vegetables on a plant

b

c

d

3 Look, think and write *yes* or *no*.

Is it from a plant?

- Yes → Is it from a tree?
  - 1 ______ → apple
  - 2 ______ → carrot
- No → Is it from an animal?
  - 3 ______ → water
  - 4 ______ → sausage

Learning outcomes:
- to integrate other areas of the curriculum through English: Science
- to practise classifying and categorising

BIG QUESTION to explore the Big Question *Where does food come from?*

New language: *fruit, vegetables, plant, soil, come(s) from, grow (on a tree / under the ground), Is it from a (plant)?*

Recycled language: food, *tree, in, on, under, pick, shop*

Critical thinking: Draws conclusions from given information

Critical thinking (WB): Sorts and classifies objects and activities according to key features (e.g. types of animal or transport)

Materials: flashcards 44–54 (food), a real carrot (optional)

Warm-up

Aim: to introduce the idea of food stories
- Write the Big Question *Where does food come from?* on the board. Show the carrots flashcard or a real carrot, and ask *Where do carrots come from? From a tree?* Elicit that a carrot comes from a plant and grows under the ground. Draw a diagram of a carrot growing and teach *ground*.
- Mime and ask students *Do we dig carrots up?* Talk about how carrots are grown by farmers, who harvest them. They are transported to a shop and then we buy them.

SB p54 What types of food do you know?

Aim: to raise students' awareness of where food comes from
- With Student's Books closed, play the video. Ask students what they remember.

For videoscript see TB p122.

- Ask students to watch again and answer *What types of food do you know?* Play the video again and elicit answers (students say the food words they know in English).

1 61 SB p54 Listen and point.

Aim: to present words to describe where food comes from
- Play the recording. Students listen and point to the photos.

For script see SB p54.

- Play the recording again. Students repeat.

2 SB p54 Read, look and match.

Aim: to encourage students to think about where different foods come from
- Students read and match individually. Then they check their answers in pairs.

Key: 1 c, 2 a, 3 d, 4 b

3 SB p54 Look, think and write *yes* or *no*.

Aim: to practise reading and categorising foods
- Copy the diagram on the board, with the writing lines.
- Show students how it works, by following one of the answers to the first question. Elicit the missing words and write them on the board. Students copy the diagram in their books.
- Ask for more examples of foods for the four categories at the bottom of the diagram.

Key: 1 yes, 2 no, 3 no, 4 yes

1 WB p54 Look and write.

Aim: to give students practice in writing the new words

Key: 2 plant, 3 fruit, 4 tree, 5 vegetables

2 WB p54 Where does the food grow? Look and match. Then write *fruit* or *vegetable* under the pictures.

Aim: to give students practice in reading and applying knowledge

Key: 2 in the soil, 3 on a tree, 4 on a tree, 5 in the soil, 6 on a plant

2 vegetable, 3 fruit, 4 fruit, 5 vegetable, 6 fruit

Lesson review

Aim: to review what students have learnt in the lesson
- Elicit what students learnt today and write it on the board, e.g. *Today I've learnt about different types of food.* Students copy in their notebooks.

Extension activity

Aim: to personalise the lesson topic
- Ask students which fruit and vegetables they have in their country and which they eat at different times of year.

Learning outcomes:
- to extend the focus on Science through English
- to complete a project

New language: *potato, salad, now, breakfast*

Recycled language: *food, soil, lunch, in, big, shop*

Creative thinking: Based on a model, develops new games, dishes, clothes, etc.

Critical thinking (WB): Demonstrates understanding of links between new ideas

Creative thinking (WB): Participates in investigative, exploratory, open-ended tasks

Cognitive control functions: Cognitive flexibility

Materials: flashcards 44–54 (food), paper and coloured pens or pencils, a real carrot or potato, a banana and an apple (optional), some apples and pears and a knife (optional), digital or print portfolios

Warm-up

Aim: to review classifying food
- Write headings on the board: *Fruit, Vegetables, Other.* Hand out the food flashcards randomly. Call students to put their flashcard under the correct heading.
- Show a real carrot or potato, a banana and an apple. Hold up each one in turn and ask *Where is it from? Where does it grow?* Students say *In the soil / On a plant / On a tree.*

4 SB p55 Look, read and write the numbers.

Aim: to enable students to apply their own knowledge and experience
- Use the pictures to teach *potato* and *salad* and review *big* and *shop*.
- Students read and match. They compare answers in pairs.
- Say one of the sentences. Students say the number of the picture. Ask *Do you like potatoes?*

Key: a 3, b 1, c 4, d 2

5 Project SB p55 Write a story about a fruit.

Aim: to enable students to apply what they have learnt about food production
- In pairs, students read and look at the example food story. Check comprehension of *breakfast*. Ask different students *What do you eat for breakfast?*
- Pairs choose a fruit to write about. Brainstorm fruits and write them on the board.
- In pairs, students make notes for their story. They think about four different parts: the beginning, how the fruit grows, where it goes next, and where/when it is eaten.
- Give each pair a piece of A4 paper. They divide it into four sections.
- Pairs draw a picture and write each section of their story.
- Pairs present their stories to the class. Student A reads the story and Student B acts it out.
- The presentations could be recorded (audio or video) and saved to students' digital portfolios.

3 WB p55 Order the pictures. Write numbers.

Aim: to enable students to apply real-world knowledge

Key: 2 a, 3 d, 4 b

4 WB p55 Look at Activity 3. Write the words to complete the sentences.

Aim: to enable students to practise writing the new language

Key: b dinner, c in the soil, d in a shop

5 WB p55 Find out about the food in your house. Draw and write.

Aim: to enable students to personalise the new language

Lesson review

Aim: to review what students have learnt in the lesson
- Write on the board: *Today I've …*
- Elicit what students did today, e.g. *made a food story*.
- Write it on the board. Students copy it into their notebooks.

Extension activity

Aim: to reinforce and extend students' understanding of fruit and how it grows
- Cut a fruit with seeds (e.g. an apple or a pear) in half and show students the different parts of the fruit.
- Draw the section of fruit on the board and label, e.g. *flesh, skin, seeds*.
- Students work in groups of four. Hand out a halved fruit to each group. They draw and label it.

4 Look, read and write the numbers.

1 The potato is in the soil.

2 Now it's a big potato.

3 The potato is in a shop.

4 It's lunchtime! The potato is in a salad. Yum!

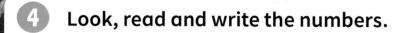

The story of a potato

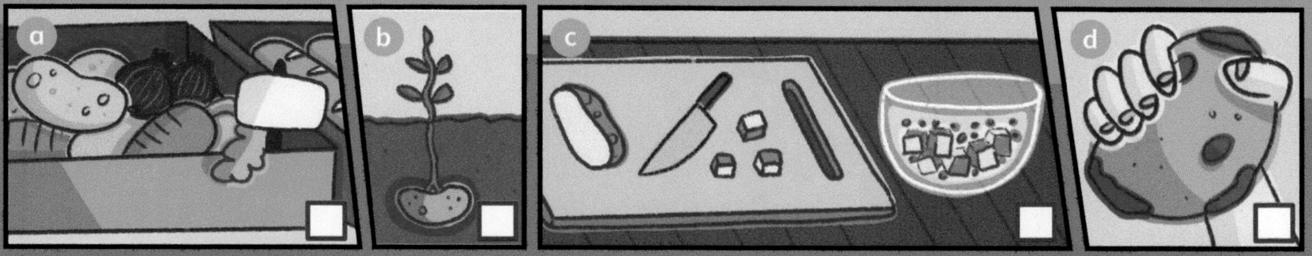

5 Project Write a story about a fruit.

The story of a banana

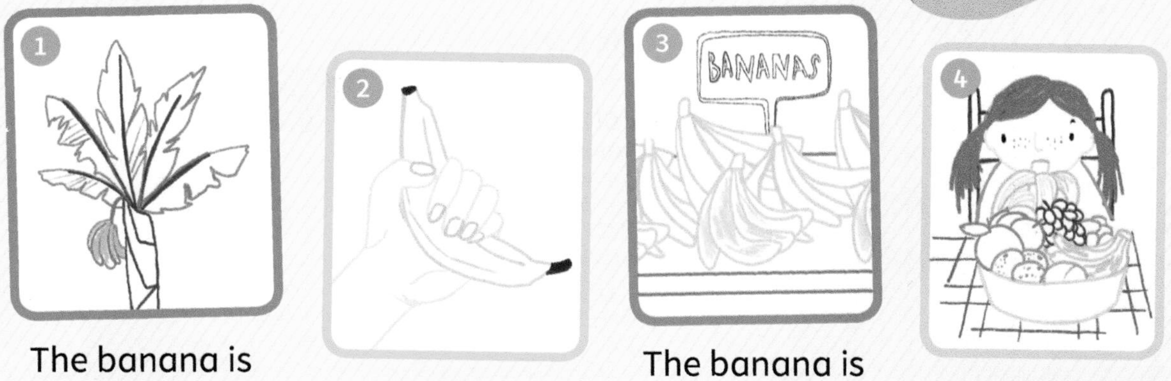

1 The banana is on the tree.

2 Now it's a big banana.

3 The banana is in a shop.

4 It's breakfast. I eat the banana. Yum!

Do that!

1 62 **Listen and act out with your teacher. Then listen again and number the pictures.**

2 **Read the sentences from the story and draw lines.**

a Buy a banana. • → • b You slip on the banana peel. Ouch!

c Eat the banana. • • d Go out of the shop.

e Throw the peel down! • • f You are hungry.

3 **Listen to a friend and act out.**

Buy fifteen chickens.

Eat the chickens.

You've got a stomach-ache. Ouch!

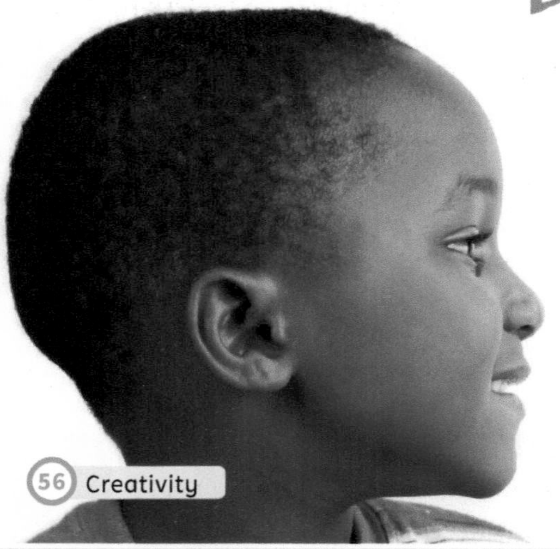

Learning outcomes:
- to stimulate imagination and review new language through listening
- to practise following a set of instructions

New language: *buy, eat, peel, throw (down), slip, go out of, stomach-ache (You've got a stomach-ache), place mat*

Recycled language: food, imperatives, *hungry, shop, Ouch!*

Creative thinking: Participates in investigative, exploratory, open-ended tasks

Creative thinking (WB): Uses different media to make and describe his/her own designs

Materials: flashcards 44–54 (food), a real banana (optional), real fruit and vegetables (some produced locally, some from abroad), world map (optional); For the WB making activity: card, magazines, scissors, glue, coloured pens

Warm-up

Aim: to review vocabulary
- Say *It's lunchtime! What's for lunch today? What do you like?*
- Elicit favourite foods.

1 62 SB p56 Listen and act out with your teacher. Then listen again and number the pictures.

Aim: to give students practice in listening and following instructions
- With Student's Books closed, show a real banana or draw one on the board. Ask *Where do bananas grow? (On a plant) Where do we buy bananas?* (*In a shop*) Teach *peel*. Say *I'm hungry* and mime eating a banana (or eat a real banana!) Teach *throw (down)* by miming throwing away the peel. Mime slipping on the skin and teach *slip*.
- Play the recording and show students the actions. Repeat the recording until students are able to listen and follow.

For script see TB p122.

- Students look at the pictures in Activity 1. Say *Now listen and number.* Ask them to guess which is the first picture before they listen.

Stronger students: Students try to write all the numbers in pencil before listening.
- Play the recording again. Students number the pictures.

Key: 4, 6, 1, 3, 5, 2

2 SB p56 Read the sentences from the story and draw lines.

Aim: to give students practice in reading
- Remind students that the sentences are the story they have just listened to.
- Students read and draw lines between the dots individually. Check answers by eliciting the story in the correct order.

Key: a, d, f, c, e, b

3 SB p56 Listen to a friend and act out.

Aim: to enable students to personalise the language
- Read the example speech bubbles and explain the new language.
- Students work on their own to write a simple set of instructions (the number of turns depends on their ability). They work out an action for each instruction. Monitor and help.
- In pairs, students take turns to give their instructions and teach the actions. Choose pairs to show the class their role plays.

1 WB p56 Make a place mat.

Aim: to enable students to follow a set of instructions to make a place mat
- Students work in pairs. Make sure students have all the items they need by saying, e.g. *Show me the glue.*
- Read the instructions, helping students make their place mat, step by step.

Ending the lesson

Aim: to review language from the lesson
- Give instructions from SB Activity 2 in the wrong order. Students do the appropriate actions.

Extension activity

Aim: to think about the Big Question *Where does food come from?*
- Show a selection of fruit and vegetables. Ask students to guess which one has travelled the furthest to the shop.
- Using a world map, help students work out which fruit or vegetable has travelled the furthest. Talk briefly about the problems of transporting food for long distances by plane, compared with the advantages of buying food transported by ship or seasonal local food.

Learning outcomes:
- to review language from Units 3 and 4
- to collaborate and reflect on learning

BIG QUESTION to think about how the unit has helped them talk about the Big Question *Where does food come from?*

New language: *Oh dear!*

Recycled language: vocabulary and grammar from Units 3 and 4

Creative thinking: Substitutes words and phrases to create new texts

Creative thinking (WB): Creates texts that express personal interests, emotions, or identity

Cognitive control functions: Working memory

Cognitive control functions (WB): Cognitive flexibility

Materials: flashcards 35–43, 44–54 (animals, food), coloured pens or pencils

Warm-up

Aim: to review food
- Write six to eight food words from the unit in jumbled letter order on the board.
- Students work in pairs and write each word correctly.

1 SB p57 How many words can you remember? Draw pictures.

Aim: to review vocabulary
- Write the headings *Pets* and *Food* on the board. Elicit the names of the animals and items in Activity 1.
- Students copy the category headings in their notebooks and draw more items in each group. Students share their pictures.

2 SB p57 Write and say the words.

Aim: to review pronunciation and spelling of vocabulary
- Students write labels below the pictures they drew for Activity 1. Check spelling.
- In pairs, students take turns to point to one of their pictures and say the word.

3 63 SB p57 Listen and number.

Aim: to practise listening and to revise unit language
- Remind students that the speech bubbles are in the wrong order.
- Play the recording for students to listen only.

For script see TB p122.

- Play it again, pausing so they can write numbers. Check answers. Explain when we use the expression *Oh dear!*

Key: 4, 5, 2, 3, 1

- Play the recording again for students to listen and repeat. They can practise the dialogue in pairs, swapping roles.

4 SB p57 Write a new dialogue. Act it out.

Aim: to review grammar and practise writing
- Show students how to make a new dialogue by completing the gaps, e.g. *Have we got any oranges? No, we haven't. Oh dear! I'm very hungry. There's a banana in my bag. I like bananas. Thanks.*
- In pairs, students write a new dialogue. Help with spelling.
- Students practise their dialogue in pairs.

1 WB p57 Write and circle.

Aim: to enable students to assess their own learning

Key: have

2 WB p57 Look, read and circle.

BIG QUESTION Aim: to enable students to revisit the Big Question and consolidate learning
- Check as a class and ask students to give more examples of foods.

Key: 1 in the soil, 2 on a tree, 3 on a plant

3 WB p57 Read. Then draw and write.

Aim: to enable students to personalise the topic

Picture dictionary

Aim: to review vocabulary for food
- Students complete the Picture dictionary pages for food and numbers (WB pp122–123).

Key: cake, carrots, cheese sandwich, chicken, peas, pizza, sausages, steak, fish, bananas; twelve, thirteen, fourteen, fifteen, sixteen, seventeen, eighteen, nineteen, twenty

Ending the lesson

Aim: to enable students to express their preferences
- Ask students what their favourite activity is and have a class vote.
- Repeat the most popular activity.

Extension activity

Aim: to enable students to share what they have learnt
- Students work in groups. They take turns to read aloud what they have written for WB Activity 3 and say something about their pictures.

1 **How many words can you remember? Draw pictures.**

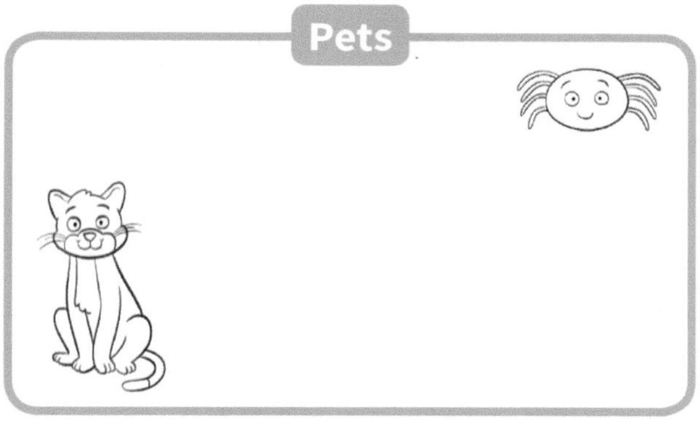

2 **Write and say the words.**

3 63 **Listen and number.**

There's an apple in my bag. ☐

I don't like apples. ☐

No, we haven't. ☐

Oh dear! I'm very hungry. ☐

Have we got any bananas? ☐

4 **Write a new dialogue. Act it out.**

Have we got ________________________________?

No, ________________________________.

Oh dear! I'm very hungry.

There's ________________ in my ________________.

I ________________________________.

5 Free time

1 64 Listen and look. Then listen and say the words.

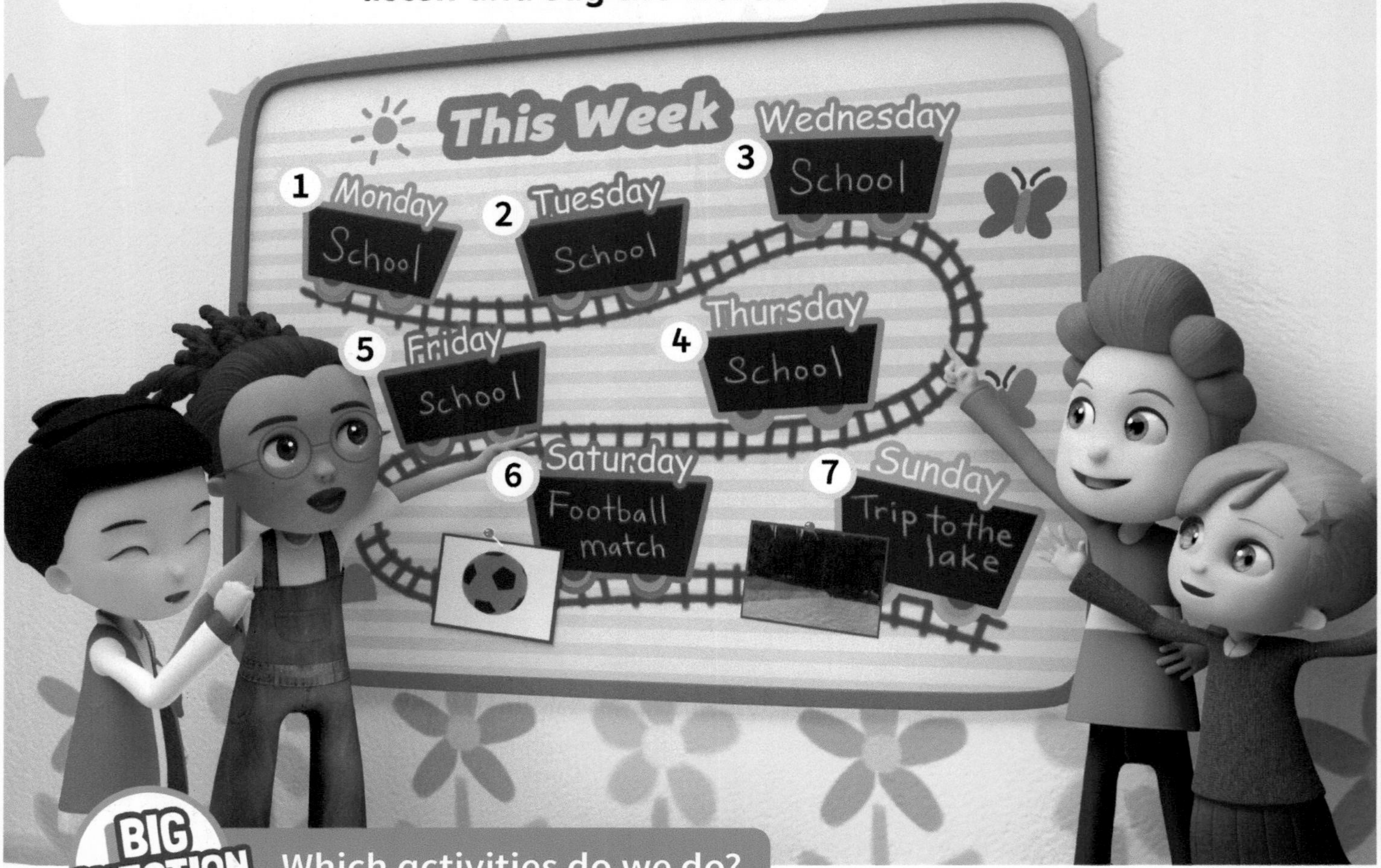

BIG QUESTION Which activities do we do?

2 65 Listen and chant.

Monday and Tuesday
Are fantastic days!
Wednesday and Thursday
Are fantastic days!

Friday and Saturday
Are fantastic days!
But Sunday's best.
We just play and rest!

Learning outcomes:
- to name and talk about days of the week
- to say a chant

BIG QUESTION to start to think about the Big Question *Which activities do we do?*

New language: *Monday, Tuesday, Wednesday, Thursday, Friday, Saturday, Sunday, football match, trip, lake, fantastic, day, best, just, play, rest*

Cognitive control functions: Working memory

Cognitive control functions (WB): Cognitive flexibility

Flashcards: 65–71 (days of the week)

Warm-up

Aim: to activate vocabulary
- Ask students which days of the week they know in English. Point out that all the days end with *day* and explain what it means. Elicit what day it is today, e.g. *It's Monday.*

Presentation

Aim: to present the days of the week
- Hold up each flashcard in turn. Say the word for the class to repeat. Do this three or four times.
- Hold up each flashcard for students to say the word without your help.
- Write *Days of the week* on the board. Call students to the front to help you stick the flashcards in order (Monday to Sunday).

1 64 SB p58 Listen and look. Then listen and say the words.

Aim: to practise days of the week
- Students look at the picture in their Student's Books. Elicit the names of the Super Friends. Check that students realise they are looking at a plan for the week on a noticeboard. Use the small pictures to teach *trip to the lake* and *football match.*
- Ask questions about the plan, e.g. *What have they got on (Monday)? (They've got school / a football match / a trip to the lake.)*
- Play the recording. Students point to the days when they hear them.

For script see TB p122.

- Play the recording again. Students repeat the words.
- Students practise pointing and naming the days in pairs.

Stronger students: Students ask and answer *What have they got on (Monday)?*

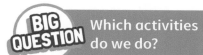

BIG QUESTION Which activities do we do?

Aim: to encourage students to find out about which activities we do
- Read the Big Question. Ask students to think about activities they do in their free time.
- In pairs, students think about other activities they do. Accept any reasonable suggestions and ask, e.g. *When have you got (gymnastics)?*

Note: Some of the discussion will need to be in your students' first language (L1).

2 65 SB p58 Listen and chant.

Aim: to give students further practice saying the days of the week
- Play the recording. Students listen and follow the chant in their Student's Books. Check comprehension of *fantastic.*

For chant script see SB p58.

- Play the recording again, pausing after each verse for students to repeat. Do the chant as a class and then in groups.
- Make seven groups. Hand out a flashcard to each group.
- Students do the chant again. They stand up when they say their day and add actions for *fantastic*, *play* and *rest*.

1 WB p58 Write the days of the week.

Aim: to give students practice in writing the days of the week

Key: 2 Sunday, 3 Wednesday, 4 Saturday, 5 Tuesday, 6 Thursday, 7 Monday

2 WB p58 Draw your favourite day and write.

Aim: to enable students to personalise the language

Ending the lesson

Aim: to review key language from the lesson
- Hold a flashcard so that students cannot see it. Students guess, e.g. *Is it Monday?*

Extension activity

Aim: to find out favourite days and favourite activities
- Put the flashcards around the room. Students stand under their favourite day, according to WB Activity 2.
- Draw a bar chart on the board to show how many students chose each day.

Learning outcomes:
- to talk about free time activities
- to practise present simple first person singular for habitual activities

New language: present simple: *go fishing, go swimming, play football, play the piano, ride my bike/pony/horse, on (Mondays), sea, being (with you), true, false, go flying*

Recycled language: days of the week, *I like …*

Materials: flashcards 65–71 (days of the week), Unit 5 stickers

Warm-up

Aim: to review days of the week
- Clap twice and say *Tuesday*. Students clap twice and say the next day (*Wednesday*). Students continue clapping and chanting until they get back to *Monday*.
- A student restarts the chant by clapping twice and saying a different day.

Presentation

Aim: to extend vocabulary for activities, and use the present simple
- Write the days of the week on the board.
- Under each day write an activity, e.g. *Monday – ride my pony, Tuesday – play football, Wednesday – go fishing, Thursday – play the piano, Friday – play football, Saturday – go swimming, Sunday – ride my bike.* Teach each new activity using mime.
- Point and say, e.g. *I ride my pony on Mondays*. Students repeat.
- Say a day, e.g. *On Wednesdays*, and students say, e.g. *I go fishing.*

1 66 SB p59 Listen and stick.

Aim: to practise the present simple
- Elicit the activities on the stickers. Read the names below the pictures, so students know what they sound like.
- Students find their stickers.
- Play the recording. Students listen and choose the stickers.

For script see TB p122.

- Students check in pairs.
- Play the recording again. Check answers with the class.
- Students stick the stickers in the correct place.

Stronger students: Play the recording again, pausing after each speaker to ask *What day?*

Key: Sandra – ride my bike, Pat – play the piano, Maria – play football, Oliver – ride my pony, Bill – go swimming

2 67 SB p59 Watch, listen and say.

Aim: to focus students on grammatical form
- Play the *Penny the penguin* video. Students watch and listen, then watch and read. Check understanding of the grammar and new phrases *in the sea, come and play with me* and *being with you*.
- Play the audio. Students follow in their Student's Book. They join in and mime each activity.

For script see SB p59.

- Students practise the sentences in pairs.

3 SB p59 Play the true or false game.

Aim: to give students further practice talking about habits
- Read the example speech bubbles and teach *go flying, true* and *false*.
- Make true or false statements, e.g. *I play the piano on Sundays*. Students say *true* or *false*. Say *Yes, it is* or *No, it isn't*.
- Students play the same game in pairs. Swap pairs and play the game again.

1 WB p59 Look, read and match. Write numbers.

Aim: to give students practice reading present simple sentences

Key: b 4, c 1, d 3

2 WB p59 Write the words in the correct order.

Aim: to enable students to evidence their understanding of word order of sentences

Key: 2 I play the piano on Fridays. 3 I go swimming on Saturdays. 4 I play football on Tuesdays. 5 I ride my bike on Wednesdays.

3 WB p59 Write the words.

Aim: to give students practice in writing the new language

Key: 1 go, 2 play, 3 like

Ending the lesson

Aim: to review new language from the lesson
- Mime one of the actions for students to guess.
- Students take turns to mime and guess in pairs.

Extension activity

Aim: to give students a personal record of the new language
- Students write three true sentences about what they do during the week in their notebooks.

1 66 Listen and stick.

Sandra	Pat	Maria	Oliver	Bill

2 67 Watch, listen and say.

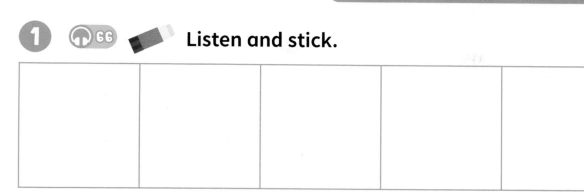

Language focus

I **go swimming** on Mondays,
Swimming in the sea.
I **play football** on Tuesdays.
Come and play with me!

I **go fishing** on Wednesdays,
On Thursdays and Fridays, too.
But on Saturdays and Sundays,
I like **being** with you!

3 Play the true or false game.

I go flying on Sundays.
That's false.
Yes, it is.

1 68 Listen and sing. Then write the days.

I'm bored. I'm bored.
I've got nothing to do!
I'm bored. I'm bored.
What can I do with you?

On Mondays, I play board games.
On Tuesdays, I play football.
On Wednesdays, I play tennis.
On Thursdays, I play them all!

I'm bored. I'm bored ...

On Fridays, I go swimming.
On Saturdays, I sing songs.
On Sundays, I ride my bike.
Why don't you come along?
Please come along.

2 Read, think and say.

How are you the same as the girl in the song? What do you do?

On Mondays, I play board games.

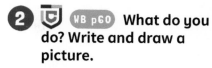

Learning outcomes:
- to sing a song
- to practise the present simple

New language: *I'm bored, nothing to do, What can I do (with you)? play board games, play tennis, sing songs, Why don't you come along?*

Recycled language: days of the week, *go fishing, go swimming, play football, play the piano, ride my bike/pony*

Creative thinking: Responds to songs, rhymes and poems in a variety of ways.

Creative thinking (WB): Creates texts that express personal interests, emotions, or identity

Cognitive control functions (WB): Working memory

Materials: A4 pieces of paper (optional)

Warm-up

Aim: to review free time activities
- Mime one of the activities from the previous lesson, e.g. *play the piano*. Students say the phrase. Write it on the board. Repeat for the rest of the activities.
- Students play a mime game in pairs, using the activities listed on the board and guessing the activities mimed.

1 68 69 SB p60 **Listen and sing. Then write the days.**

Aim: to sing a song with the class
- Students look at the pictures in the Student's Book. Ask how the boy sitting at the bottom of the picture is feeling and teach *bored*. Students mime and say *I'm bored.* Use the pictures to teach *play board games / tennis* and *sing songs*.
- Play the audio (68). Students follow the song in their Student's Books.

For song lyrics see SB p60.

- Play the audio again, pausing for students to write the days. Check answers.

Key: 1 Thursdays, 2 Wednesdays, 3 Sundays, 4 Tuesdays, 5 Saturdays, 6 Fridays, 7 Mondays

- Play the song video, pausing after each verse for students to repeat.
- When students have learnt the song, use the karaoke version of the audio (69) or video to practise the song with the whole class and then in groups.

2 SB p60 **Read, think and say.**

Aim: to encourage students to personalise the language
- Read the first speech bubble and explain the meaning of the question. Students listen, read and point to the day of the week.
- In pairs, students think and make sentences about things they have in common (it can be just the same activity, but on a different day).
- Elicit examples from students who do similar activities. Ask students who do different activities to make sentences about their habits.

1 19 WB p60 **Can you remember? Listen and draw lines.**

Aim: to give further practice with reading and listening

For song lyrics see SB p60.

Key: 2 c, 3 e, 4 f, 5 d, 6 a

2 WB p60 **What do you do? Write and draw a picture.**

Aim: to encourage creativity

Ending the lesson

Aim: to review key language from the lesson
- Students sing the song again, doing actions for *I'm bored* and for the different activities.

Extension activity

Aim: to review verb phrases
- Give each pair of students three A4 pieces of paper. Tell them to write *go* on one piece of paper, *play* on another and *ride* on the third.
- Say one of the nouns from the activities in the lesson, e.g. *swimming*. Students confer in their pairs to work out which verb to use and then hold up the correct piece of paper (e.g. *go*). Repeat with different nouns (*tennis, on my pony, fishing, on my bike, football*). When students get the idea, you can make the game competitive by eliminating pairs who make a mistake, until you have a winning pair.

Stronger students: Add in new verb phrases for students to guess: *go*, *ride* or *play*, e.g. *camping* (*go*), *shopping* (*go*), *a motorbike* (*ride*), *a scooter* (*ride*), *basketball* (*play*), *hockey* (*play*).

Learning outcomes:
- to use the present simple to talk about free time activities

New language: *watch TV, play computer games, Do you …? Yes, I do, No, I don't, at the weekend*

Recycled language: free time activities

Creative thinking (WB): Chooses options to create something new

Warm-up

Aim: to review days of the week
- Divide the class into seven groups, each named after a day of the week.
- Play the song from the previous lesson. Each group sings the line for their day. Everyone sings the chorus.

Presentation

Aim: to present *Do you …? Yes, I do. No, I don't.*
- Write days of the week on the board and teach *weekend*.
- Say, e.g. *I go swimming at the weekend*. Ask a student *Do you go swimming at the weekend?* Prompt *Yes, I do* or *No, I don't*.
- Students ask and answer in open pairs.

1 70 SB p61 Listen and tick ✓ or cross ✗.

Aim: to practise *Do you …? Yes, I do. / No, I don't.*
- Elicit the activities in the pictures and teach *watch TV*.

Extra support: Say a number between 1 and 6. Students make a sentence about the picture, e.g. *5 – I ride my bike*. In pairs, students practise in the same way.
- Play the recording. Students listen and tick or cross. They check in pairs.

For script see TB p122.

- Play the recording again for students to check their answers. Then check with the class.

Key: 1 ✓ 2 ✓ 3 ✓ 4 ✗ 5 ✗ 6 ✓

2 71 SB p61 Watch, listen and say.

Aim: to focus students on grammatical form
- Play the *Penny the penguin* video. Students watch and listen, then watch and read.
- Play the audio. Students follow in their Student's Book. They join in and do a mime for the activity in each question.

For script see SB p61.

- Students practise the sentences in pairs.

3 SB p61 Play the find someone game.

Aim: to give students practice of *Do you …? Yes, I do. / No, I don't.*
- Students write three sentences about things they do at the weekend, e.g. *I ride my bike at the weekend.*
- They walk around the class asking questions to find people who do the same activities. When they find someone who says *Yes, I do*, they write their name next to their sentence.

1 WB p61 Read and circle the correct words.

Aim: to give students practice in reading the new language

Key: 1 don't, 2 do

2 WB p61 Read and match. Then write answers.

Aim: to give further reading and writing practice with the new language

Key: 2 b, 3 d, 4 f, 5 a, 6 c, Students' own answers.

3 WB p61 Write and tick ✓.

Aim: to give further reading and writing practice with the new language

Key: 2 go, 3 watch, Students' own answers.

Ending the lesson

Aim: to review word order in question forms
- Write a question from the lesson on the board in jumbled word order for students to unjumble.

Extension activity

Aim: to do a survey about free time activities
- Draw a 5 x 5 grid on the board with the title *At the weekend* and four activities in the first column.
- Students copy the grid, adding the names of four friends to the top of columns 2 to 5.
- They ask and answer in groups and write ticks or crosses in the grid.

1 Listen and tick ✓ or cross ✗.

(Audio track 70)

1

☐

2

☐

3

☐

4

☐

5

☐

6

☐

2 Watch, listen and say.

(Video; audio track 71)

Language focus

Do you watch TV at the weekend?

No, I **don't**.

Do you play computer games?

Yes, I **do**.

Do you ride your horse at the weekend?

No, I **don't**.

Do you ride your bike with Paul?

Yes, I **do**.

3 Play the find someone game.

At the weekend …

I play tennis ____________ with my friend.

I sing ____________.

I go swimming ____________.

Do you sing at the weekend?

Yes, I do.

We're lost!

1 72 Which pictures is the rabbit in?

Misty: Where's the lake?
Flash: I don't know.
Thunder: We're lost!

Whisper: I've got an idea.
Flash: What?

Whisper: Wait and see.
Thunder: This isn't much fun.

Whisper: Rabbit, we're lost. Where's the lake?
Rabbit: Come with me.

Whisper: Thank you very much.
Thunder: Here you are, Rabbit.

Rabbit: Yippee!
Whisper: Watch out!

Learning outcomes:
- to listen to, read, watch and act out a picture story
- to review language from the unit

New language: *We're/I'm/He's lost, lake, I don't know, I've got an idea, wait and see, this isn't much fun, rabbit, thank you very much, here you are, Yippee! watch out, Are you OK?*

Recycled language: character names, *Where's ...?*

Value: asking for help when you need it

Critical thinking (WB): Sorts and classifies objects and activities according to key features (e.g. types of animal or transport)

Warm-up

Aim: to review the characters and the story

- Elicit the names of the four Super Friends and ask students to mime their special powers.
- Elicit what happened in the last episode (*Misty didn't wait her turn and didn't get pizza*).
- Ask who can speak to animals (*Whisper*). Teach *rabbit* and tell students there is a rabbit in today's story.

We're lost!

1 72 SB pp62–63 Which pictures is the rabbit in?

Aim: to present a picture story

- Elicit where the friends are (*in the countryside/forest*) and what they are doing (*walking/hiking*). Teach *lake* and *lost* using the pictures.
- Ask *Which pictures is the rabbit in?*
- Play the audio. Students listen and follow and look for the rabbit.

For script see SB pp62–63.

- Check answers by asking students to say the picture numbers.

Key: Pictures 4, 5, 6, 7 and 8

- Play the whole *Super Friends* video. Then play the video again, pausing to check comprehension. Say *The Super Friends are in the forest, but they aren't walking. Why?* (*They're lost*) Ask *What are they doing?* and check comprehension of *Wait and see* and *This isn't much fun.* Point to the hole in the picture and ask *Who lives there?* (*A rabbit*) Ask *What do they give the rabbit to say 'thank you'?* (*A carrot*) Make sure students realise that the rabbit hits its head because it's excited, and that's why Whisper asks *Are you OK?*
- Talk with the class about the value (asking for help when you need it). Ask who helps the Super Friends in the story (*the rabbit*) and who asks the rabbit for help (*Whisper*).

1 20 WB p62 Who says it? Listen and tick ✓.

Aim: to review the story

For script see TB p122.

Key: 1 Misty (2nd picture), 2 Whisper (2nd picture), 3 Rabbit (1st picture)

2 WB p62 Look and write the numbers.

Aim: to check understanding of key phrases in the story

Key: b 5, c 2, d 1, e 4

Ending the lesson

Aim: to practise the story

- Put students in groups of five. They each take a role of one of the characters (one student is the rabbit).
- Play the recording. Students repeat in role.
- Students practise the role play in groups. They can use something to represent the carrot, e.g. a pen or pencil.
- Volunteer groups role play for the class.

Extension activity

Aim: to stimulate students' creativity

- Students each choose one of the phrases in WB Activity 2. They make up a little, silent role play and include their short dialogue at the end.
- Help students with vocabulary. They can change words, e.g. *Here you are, Spider,* if they want.
- Students perform their short role plays for the class.

Learning outcomes:
- to interpret deeper meaning from a story
- to practise saying the short vowel sound /ʌ/ as in f**u**n
- to review language from the story and the unit

New language: *jump, mud*

Recycled language: language from the story

Phonics focus: Your students will be able to identify and say the sound /ʌ/ and contrast it with the sounds /æ/, /e/, /ɪ/ and /ɒ/.

Value: asking for help when you need it

Critical thinking (WB): Identifies characters, setting, plots and theme in a story

Warm-up

Aim: to review the story
- Write *Where's the ______? We're ______. I've got an ______. Wait and ______. Here you are, ______* on the board and elicit the complete sentences (the missing words are *lake, lost, idea, see, Rabbit*).

Extra support: Write the words on the board for students to choose from.
- Use these sentences to recap the story. Students help you to retell it.

2 SB p63 Look at the picture and tick ✓ the correct sentence.

Aim: to check comprehension of the story
- Students read the four sentences silently and choose the best one to match the picture.
- They compare their answer in pairs.
- Check with the class.

Key: 2 Come with me.

3 SB p63 Find who says ...

Aim: to present the letter sound /ʌ/
- Write *much* and *fun* on the board, using a red pen for the *u*. Separate out the three phonemes in the words and say each one separately (e.g. *f – u – n*) before saying the whole word.
- Students repeat *This isn't much fun* after you and find the sentence in the story (picture 3).

Key: Thunder

4 73 SB p63 Listen and say.

Aim: to practise the letter sound /ʌ/, a short vowel sound
- Students look at the cartoon picture. Elicit which birds they can see (*ducks*). Teach *mud* using the picture and check comprehension of *has fun*.
- Play the recording. Students look at the picture, read and repeat.

For script see TB p122.

- Repeat the sentence as a class without the recording. Say it loudly, slowly, quickly, whisper it, etc.
- Students take turns to repeat in pairs.

1 WB p63 Look and write.

Aim: to focus students on the value of asking for help when you need it

Key: 1 We're lost. 2 Come with me.

2 21 WB p63 Write the words. Listen and say the sentences.

Aim: to practise reading and saying words with the sounds /ʌ/, /æ/, /e/, /ɪ/ and /ɒ/

For script see WB p122 and Key.

Key: 2 pens, 3 milk, 4 dog, 5 rat, 6 rubber

Ending the lesson

Aim: to review and write decodable words with the sound /ʌ/ and distinguish it from /æ/, /e/, /ɪ/ and /ɒ/
- Students close their Student's Books.
- Dictate the sound sentence while students write. They compare their sentences with a partner before checking in the Student's Book.
- Write the names from WB Activity 2 on the board (*Mum, Ken, Jill, Polly, Sam, Gus*). Students try to remember what belonged to each person. They check their answers in the WB (*lunch, pens, milk, dog, rat, rubber*).

Extension activity

Aim: to discuss the value of asking for help when you need it
- Focus on the part of the story where Whisper asked for help.
- Elicit from students why it is important to admit we need help. Elicit examples of when the students have had to ask for help, why they needed it and what happened.

  Note: This discussion will probably need to take place in L1.

7

Whisper: Are you OK, Rabbit?

8

Rabbit: Now, I'm lost!
Whisper: Now, he's lost!

2 Look at the picture and tick ✓ the correct sentence.

1 Are you OK? ☐
2 Come with me. ☐
3 Here you are. ☐
4 I'm lost! ☐

Phonics

3 Find who says … This isn't much fun.

4 73 Listen and say.

On Sundays, Mum has fun with the ducks in the mud.

Skills

1 Listen and stick.

	Monday	Tuesday	Wednesday	Thursday	Friday	Saturday	Sunday
 Jim							
 Emily							

2 Ask and answer.

Do you ride your bike on Saturdays?

Do you play with your friends on Sundays?

	✓ Yes, I do.	✗ No, I don't.
Do you ride your bike on Saturdays?		
Do you play board games on Saturdays?		
Do you go swimming on Saturdays?		
Do you play with your toys on Sundays?		
Do you watch TV on Sundays?		
Do you play with your friends on Sundays?		

Learning outcomes:
- to listen for specific information
- to ask and answer about free time activities

Recycled language: days of the week, free time activities, *Do you (ride your bike) on (Saturdays)? Yes, I do, No, I don't.*

Materials: Unit 5 stickers, scissors, one soft ball per group of seven students (optional)

Warm-up

Aim: to review the days of the week
- Make groups of seven and arrange each group in a circle. Make a paper ball for each group (or use a soft ball).
- The student with the ball says a day of the week and then throws it to another student, who says the following day, and so on.

1 74 SB p64 Listen and stick.

Aim: to practise listening for specific information
- Students look at the stickers. Make sentences for them to point to the correct sticker (e.g. *I ride my horse.*)
- Make sure students understand how the table works (that they have to find the correct activities and stick them on the correct days). Ask them to guess which child does each activity.
- Students find their stickers and cut them out together with the backing paper.
- Play the recording. Students listen, choose the correct stickers and place them on the appropriate days (but don't stick them yet).

For script see TB p122.

- Students check in pairs.
- Play the recording again. Check answers with the class.
- Students stick the stickers in the table.

Stronger students: Ask about the completed table, e.g. *What days does Emily ride a horse? Does Jim play tennis on Tuesdays?*

Key: Jim plays tennis on Mondays, Wednesdays, Fridays and Saturdays. Emily rides a horse on Tuesdays, Thursdays, Saturdays and Sundays.

2 SB p64 Ask and answer.

Aim: to give students speaking practice
- Read through the table and check comprehension of the activities.
- Model the task, if necessary, by copying the table on the board and completing it with ticks and crosses, according to the answers of a volunteer.
- Students ask and answer the questions in pairs.

1 WB p64 Read and draw lines to make sentences.

Aim: to give students reading practice

Key: 2 g, 3 a, 4 f, 5 b, 6 c, 7 e

2 WB p64 Look at Activity 1. Write the days.

Aim: to give students practice matching words with pictures

Key: b Friday, c Saturday, d Thursday, e Monday, f Wednesday, g Sunday

Ending the lesson

Aim: to review free time activities
- Mime one of the free time activities. Students guess by asking questions, e.g. *Do you play board games?*
- The student who guesses the activity first does a mime for the rest of the class to guess.

Extension activity

Aim: to play a game to review language from the lesson
- Make four teams. Students stand one behind the other in a line in their team, facing the board.
- Whisper a sentence to the student at the back of each line.
- This student whispers the sentence to the person in front, and so on, and the student at the front of the line writes it on the board.
- Check the sentence and, if it's correct, award the team one point.
- This student then goes to the back of the line.
- Repeat with different sentences, e.g. *I play tennis on Mondays. I go swimming on Fridays. I play with my friends at the weekend.*

Learning outcomes:
- to read for specific information
- to write a poem from a model

New language: *poem, sleep, perfect*

Recycled language: present simple, days of the week, free time activities

Creative thinking: Writes own songs or poems to reflect personal interests, emotions, or identity

Critical thinking (WB): Draws conclusions from given information

Warm-up

Aim: to review free time activities with *play*
- Write *play* in a circle on the board.
- Elicit free time activities which use the verb *play*, e.g. *play the piano*.
- Create a word map around *play* with these activities.
- Students copy the word map into their notebooks.

1 SB p65 Read the poem and tick ✓ the pictures. Exam skills

Aim: to give students practice in reading for specific information
- Students look at the text. Elicit/Pre-teach *poem*. Read the title and check comprehension of *perfect*.
- Tell students to look carefully at the pictures and elicit the activities. Elicit/Teach *sleep* using picture c.
- Students read the poem silently to find out which activities are mentioned, and tick the pictures.
- They check their answers in pairs before the class check.

Stronger students: Ask *What does he do on (Mondays)?*
- Read the poem aloud. Students listen.
- Read the poem in sections. Students repeat.
- Read the whole poem with the students joining in, according to ability.

Key: Students tick pictures b, c, d, f, g and h.

2 SB p65 Write a poem about your perfect week.

Aim: to enable students to write their own poem from a model
- Next to the *play* word map on the board, brainstorm all the other free time activities from the unit.
- Elicit what students do on different days, using sentences in the same form as the poem, e.g. *On Fridays, I ride my bike.*
- Students write a poem, using the SB Activity 1 poem as a model.
- Go around the class to check and help as students are working. Point out that they need to use a comma after the days, because *On (day)* is at the start of the sentence.
- Students illustrate their poems (they can finish the pictures for homework).

1 22 WB p65 What do they do? Listen and tick ✓.

Aim: to practise listening for specific information

For script see TB p123.

Key: 2 On Wednesdays, Emma plays with her friends (3rd picture). 3 On Fridays, Charles watches TV (3rd picture). 4 On Saturdays, Hannah rides her horse (2nd picture).

2 WB p65 Look at Activity 1 and write the names.

Aim: to practise reading

Key: 2 Charles, 3 Emma, 4 Hannah

Ending the lesson

Aim: to practise spoken production
- In groups of five or six, students take turns to read their poems aloud.
- Students say *Snap!* when they have the same activity for the same day.

Extension activity

Aim: to practise speaking and writing skills about Sunday routines
- Students look at the free time activities in the pictures in WB Activity 1.
- Ask a student *What do you do on Sundays?* The student replies.
- Students continue to practise questions and answers in open pairs.
- Students then write three sentences in their notebooks about what they do on Sundays.
- Go around the class and help with vocabulary, if necessary.

1 Read the poem and tick ✓ the pictures.

My perfect week

a

☐

b

☐

c

☐

d

☐

On Mondays,
I play football.

On Tuesdays,
I ride my bike.

On Wednesdays,
I play tennis.

On Thursdays,
I go swimming.

On Fridays,
I play board games.

On Saturdays and Sundays,
I watch TV and sleep.

That's my perfect week.

e

☐

f

☐

g

☐

h

☐

2 Write a poem about your perfect week.

My perfect week
On Mondays, I play
with my friends.

Think and learn

Activities

What do we do?

1 (75) Listen and point.

1 go skiing

2 go surfing

3 go climbing

4 go running

5 go sledging

2 Look at the photos in Activity 1. Ask and answer.

What do they do in picture 1?

They go skiing.

3 Look, think and write.

go skiing | go surfing | go climbing | go running | go sledging | go swimming

1 ____________

2 ____________

3 ____________

4 (76) Listen and check.

Learning outcomes:

- to integrate other areas of the curriculum through English: Physical education
- to identify free time activities and categorise them

BIG QUESTION to explore the Big Question *Which activities do we do?*

New language: *go skiing, go surfing, go climbing, go running, go sledging, What do they do (in picture 1)? They go (skiing), in the snow, in the countryside, on the beach*

Recycled language: free time activities

Critical thinking: Sorts and classifies objects and activities according to key features (e.g. types of animal or transport)

Critical thinking (WB): Uses tables, charts, mind maps etc. to evaluate ideas or options

Warm-up

Aim: to review free time activities

- Write the Big Question *Which activities do we do?* on the board.
- Mime free time activities for students to guess (make sure you review *run, dance, ride a bike, sing*).
- Write each activity on the board.

SB p66 What do we do?

Aim: to raise students' awareness of free time activities

- With Student's Books closed, play the video.

For videoscript see TB p123.

- Students remember as many of the free time activities as they can.
- Students watch again and answer *What do we do?* Play the video again and elicit answers. Ask students which of the activities they have tried.

1 75 SB p66 Listen and point.

Aim: to present new free time activities

- Play the recording. Students listen and point to the photos.

For script see SB p66.

- Play the recording again. Students repeat.

2 SB p66 Look at the photos in Activity 1. Ask and answer.

Aim: to practise the new language and present simple third person plural

- Students point to the pictures in Activity 1 and ask and answer about each activity.

3 SB p66 Look, think and write.

- Students look at the table. Focus on the pictures and ask students which three categories they represent (students answer in L1). Teach *In the snow*, *In the countryside* and *On the beach*. Write the phrases on the board.
- Point to the first activity in the box and ask which column of the table it should go in (*1*). Students write it in the first column.
- In pairs, they complete the rest of the table. Monitor and help as necessary, but don't confirm answers.

4 76 SB p66 Listen and check.

- Play the recording for students to check answers.

For script see TB p123.

Key: 1 go skiing, go sledging 2 go climbing, go running, go swimming 3 go climbing, go running, go surfing, go swimming

1 WB p66 Look and write.

Aim: to practise writing the new language

Key: 2 go sledging, 3 go running, 4 go surfing, 5 go skiing, 6 go climbing

2 WB p66 Where can we do it? Look and write the numbers.

Aim: to reinforce learning from the lesson

Key: a 3, 4; b 2, 5, 6

Lesson review

Aim: to review what students have learnt in the lesson

- Elicit what students learnt today and write it on the board, e.g. *Today I've learnt about where we do different activities.* Students copy in their notebooks.

Extension activity

Aim: to discuss the healthy things students do in a day

- Write *healthy* in a circle on the board. In pairs, students think about what they do during the week that is healthy.
- Elicit ideas and create a word map. Talk about the importance of having a healthy lifestyle.

Learning outcomes:
- to extend the focus on Physical education through English
- to complete a project

New language: *We (play football). We don't (play football). I like / don't like +ing.*

Recycled language: free time activities, *go skiing, go surfing, go climbing, go running, go sledging, in the snow, in the countryside, on the beach*

Creative thinking: Creates texts that express personal interests, emotions, or identity

Cognitive control functions: Cognitive flexibility

Critical thinking (WB): Sorts and classifies objects and activities according to key features (e.g. types of animal or transport)

Solves simple puzzles (e.g. word puzzles)

Materials: A3 paper, coloured pens or pencils, magazines, scissors, glue, large signs with the phrases *in the snow, in the countryside* and *on the beach*, digital or print portfolios

Warm-up

Aim: to review new free time activities and places

- Make three signs with *in the snow, in the countryside* and *on the beach* in large letters. Check students remember the meaning.
- Stick the signs in three corners of the classroom.
- Students stand together in the middle of the room. Say an activity, e.g. *Go swimming.* Students move (or point) to the correct sign. Repeat with different activities. You can make the game competitive by eliminating students who go/point to the wrong sign.

5 SB p67 Look and say.

Aim: to practise new free time activities and third person plural

- Read the speech bubbles for Activity 5. Check comprehension of *we*.
- In pairs, students talk about which activities they could do in each place.
- Circulate and help as necessary. Elicit example sentences from different pairs.

6 Project SB p67 Make a poster.

Aim: to enable students to apply what they have learnt about activities

- Point to the model poster and elicit what the happy and sad faces mean (*I like / I don't like*).
- Tell students to imagine they made the poster and help them make sentences, e.g. *I like riding my horse. I don't like playing tennis.* Point out that after *like* we use verb + *-ing*.
- Give each student a piece of A3 paper. They draw a line down the middle, then a happy face top left and a sad face top right.
- Ask students to decide which activities to put on their poster.
- Students can draw pictures, find pictures online and print them, or cut and stick pictures from magazines.
- Students present their posters in small groups, saying what they like and don't like doing.
- Display the finished posters in the classroom. Alternatively, take photos of the posters and save them to students' digital portfolios.

3 WB p67 Read, look and match.

Aim: to enable students to practise reading, and review learning from the lesson

Key: 2 b, 3 a, 4 d, 5 c, 6 e

4 WB p67 What do they do? Look and write.

Aim: to practise writing new free time activities

Key: 2 go surfing, 3 go sledging, 4 go climbing

Lesson review

- Write on the board: *Today I've …*
- Elicit what students did today, e.g. *made a poster about my free time.*
- Write it on the board. Students copy it into their notebooks.

Extension activity

Aim: to give further practice in writing about their free time activities

- Students use the poster and WB Activity 4 to help them write sentences about their own free time activities, e.g. *I go climbing. I like running.*
- Go around the class to check their work before they write a final draft.

5 Look and say.

We play football in picture 3.

We don't play football in picture 4.

6 Project Make a poster.

I like football. I don't like surfing.

Create that!

1 77 Listen and imagine. Then draw your picture.

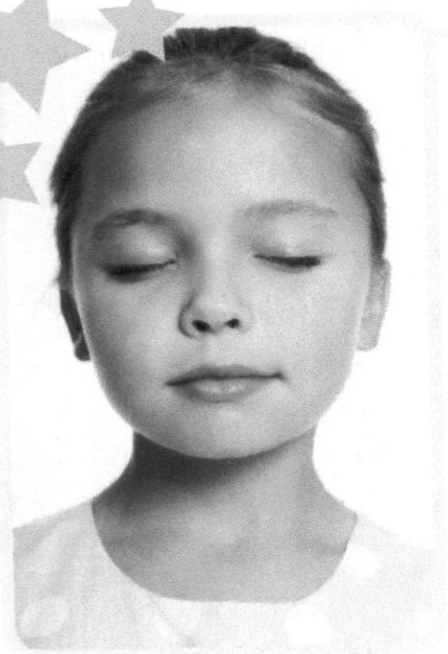

2 Work with a partner. Compare your pictures.

On my perfect Sunday, I ...

On your perfect Sunday, you ...

Learning outcomes:
- to listen, imagine and draw to demonstrate meaning
- to describe a perfect day

New language: *in bed, get out of (bed), On my perfect Sunday, guitar*

Recycled language: free time activities, days of the week, *Close your eyes, listen, imagine, perfect, Open your eyes, Draw the picture, sleep(ing), fun*

Creative thinking: Chooses options to create something new

Cognitive control functions: Inhibitory control

Creative thinking (WB): Uses different media to make and describe his/her own designs

Materials: coloured pens or pencils; For the WB making activity: tissue box, paint and brushes, elastic bands of different sizes; recording of guitar music (optional)

Warm-up

Aim: to review instructions
- Pretend you have lost your voice. Mime some of the instructions you usually give, e.g. *Pick up your books. Open your books. Take your pencil case. Find a red pencil.* Students give the instructions. Include *Close your eyes*, *Open your eyes* and *Listen.*

1 77 SB p68 Listen and imagine. Then draw your picture.

Aim: to give students practice in listening and following instructions
- Remind students how to do the activity. Pre-teach *bed* (by drawing a picture) and *get out of bed* using mime. Make sure students have coloured pens or pencils.
- Play the recording for students to follow instructions.

For script see TB p123.

- Play the recording again before students draw, if necessary.
- Circulate as they draw their pictures, asking *What do you do on your perfect Sunday? Do you go swimming? Who's this? Do you go with your friends?*
- Praise students for using their imagination and for their originality.

2 SB p68 Work with a partner. Compare your pictures.

Aim: to practise speaking
- Draw a picture of yourself doing two activities with your friends or family. Use colours if possible. Talk about the picture, starting with the prompt in the speech bubble (e.g. *On my perfect Sunday, I play tennis with my friends. I ride my horse with my sister.*)
- Students work in pairs. They show each other their pictures and describe. Encourage them to say as much as they can and to talk about their partner's picture, as in the example.

1 WB p68 Make a guitar.

Aim: to enable students to follow a set of instructions to make a guitar
- Read the list of items students need and show each thing in turn. Students check they have what they need on their desk.
- Work through the instructions before students begin, showing them how to make a guitar at the front of the class.
- Students make their guitars. Help as necessary.

Ending the lesson

Aim: to review language from the unit
- Tell students to listen and mime. Say, e.g. *It's Sunday. You're in bed, sleeping. It isn't much fun. You get out of bed. You run to the park. You say hello to your friends. You go climbing with your friends. You play tennis. You ride your horses. You run to the lake. You don't like surfing, but you like swimming. You go swimming. Then you run to the snow! You go skiing! Then you say goodbye to your friends and you go home. You go to bed.*

Extension activity

Aim: to enable students to try their guitars
- Tell students they are going to play their guitars along with some real music. Play some recorded guitar music. Encourage students to play along on their guitars, copying the rhythm of the music.

Learning outcomes:

Recycled language: vocabulary and grammar from the unit, *before, after*

Creative thinking (WB): Creates texts that express personal interests, emotions, or identity

Cognitive control functions (WB): Cognitive flexibility

Warm-up

Aim: to review days of the week

- Write the days of the week in jumbled letter order on the board.
- Students work in pairs to write each word correctly.
- When checking with the class, elicit what free time activities they do each day.

1 SB p69 Read and circle.

Aim: to enable students to review language from the unit by doing a quiz

- Remind students that they answer by circling one option for each sentence, using the picture clues, if appropriate. Revise *before* and *after* by asking *What's after Saturday? What's before Wednesday?*
- Do the first item in the quiz as an example, if necessary.
- Students do the quiz in pairs. The first time, they do it without looking back through the unit.
- Pairs check their work with other pairs.
- Students then look back to check questions they did not know.
- Check answers with the class.

Key: 1 c, 2 b, 3 c, 4 a, 5 b, 6 a, 7 b, 8 a

1 WB p69 Write and circle.

Aim: to enable students to assess their own learning

2 WB p69 Look and read. Tick ✓ or cross ☒.

BIG QUESTION

Aim: to enable students to revisit the Big Question and consolidate learning

- Check as a class and ask students to give examples of more activities we can do in each place.

Key: 1 ✓ 2 ☒ 3 ✓

3 WB p69 Read. Then draw and write.

Aim: to enable students to personalise the topic

Picture dictionary

Aim: to review days of the week and free time activities

- Students look at the Picture dictionary page for days of the week (WB p124).
- In pairs, they take turns to point to one of the pictures and say the activity.
- Then students write the days below the pictures in the correct order.

Stronger students: Make sentences, e.g. *On Mondays, I go swimming.*

Key: Tuesday, Wednesday, Thursday, Friday, Saturday, Sunday

Ending the lesson

Aim: to enable students to express their preferences

- Ask students what their favourite activity is from the unit (e.g. the song, chant or one of the games) and have a class vote.
- Repeat the most popular activity with the class.

Extension activity

Aim: to enable students to share what they have learnt

- In small groups, students take turns to read aloud what they have written for WB Activity 3 and to say something about their picture.
- Students compare what they have written and drawn.

1 Read and circle.

1 **The day after Monday is …**

a Sunday. b Wednesday. c Tuesday.

2 **The day before Friday is …**

a Monday. b Thursday. c Saturday.

3 **I … on Tuesdays.**

a go fishing b ride my horse c play tennis

4 **I … on Fridays.**

a watch TV b go swimming c play football

5 **Do you sing songs at the weekend?**

a Yes, I do. b No, I don't.

6 **Do you ride your bike at the weekend?**

a Yes, I do. b No, I don't.

7 **In the story, the Super Friends see a …**

a frog. b rabbit. c rat.

8 **On Mondays, I …**

a go skiing. b go climbing. c go running.

6 The old house

1 78 **Listen and look. Then listen and say the words.**

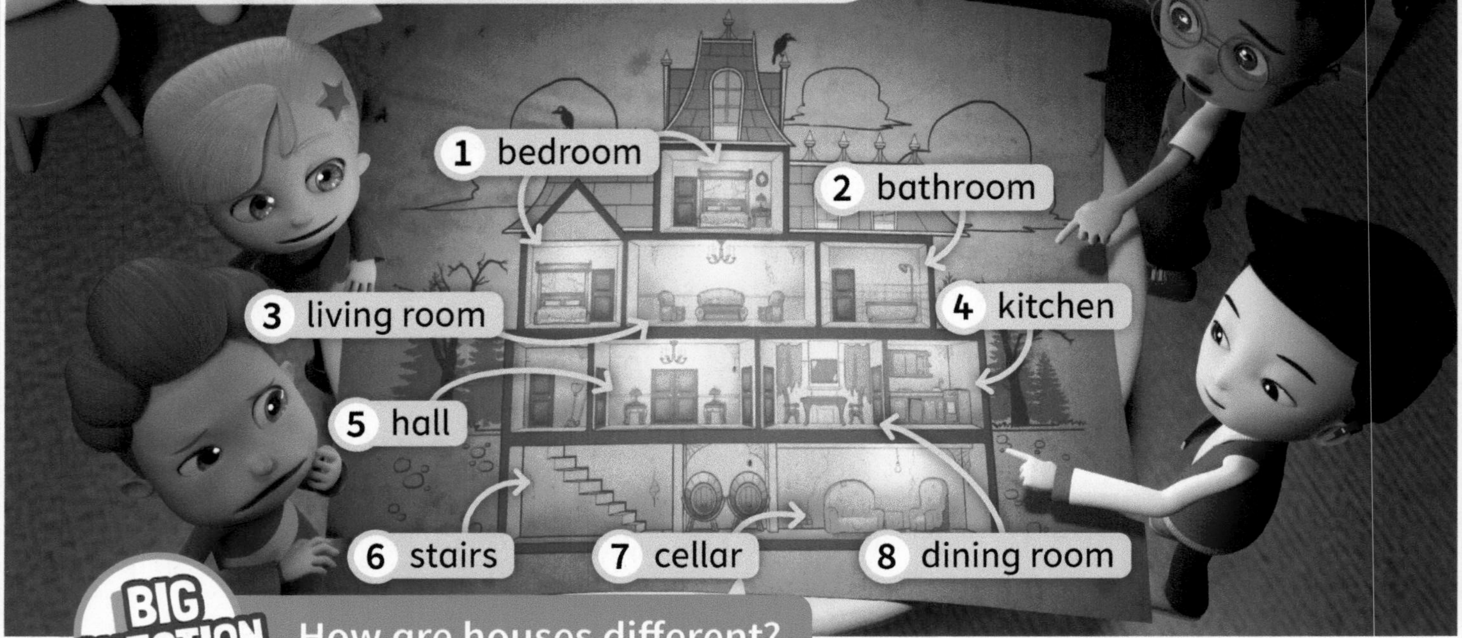

BIG QUESTION How are houses different?

2 79 **Listen and chant.**

Let's go to the scary house,
The scary house, the scary house.
Let's go to the scary house,
Let's go in!

What's in the bedroom?
What's in the bathroom?
What's in the cellar?
Let's go and see!

Let's go to the scary house,
The scary house, the scary house.
Let's go to the scary house,
Let's go in!

What's in the dining room?
What's in the living room?
What's in the kitchen?
Let's go and see!

Learning outcomes:
- to name and talk about parts of a home
- to say a chant

BIG QUESTION to start to think about the Big Question *How are houses different?*

New language: *house, bedroom, bathroom, living room, kitchen, hall, stairs, cellar, dining room, scary*

Recycled language: *old, Let's go …, different*

Cognitive control functions: Working memory

Cognitive control functions (WB): Cognitive flexibility

Flashcards: 72–80 (the home)

Warm-up

Aim: to activate vocabulary
- Draw a simple house on the board. Elicit or teach *house*.
- Elicit rooms that students know and write them next to your picture.
- Review *old, new, big, small, ugly, beautiful* by asking about your picture (*Is the house old or new? Is it big or small?* etc.)

Presentation

Aim: to present home vocabulary
- Hold up each flashcard in turn. Say the word for students to repeat in chorus.
- Do this three or four times.
- Hold up each flashcard for students to say the word in chorus.
- Stick the flashcards around your drawing of the house on the board to make a word map.

1 78 SB p70 **Listen and look. Then listen and say the words.**

Aim: to practise home vocabulary
- Students look at the picture in their Student's Books. Elicit who's in the picture and what they're looking at (*a picture of a house*). Ask *Is the house old or new?* Ask how Flash and Thunder feel (*scared*).
- Play the recording. Students point to the parts of the house.

Stronger students: Ask what the Super Friends are going to do (*go and see the house*).

For script see TB p123.

- Play the recording again. Students repeat the words.
- Students practise pointing and naming the parts of the house in pairs.

BIG QUESTION How are houses different?

Aim: to encourage students to find out about how houses are different
- Read the Big Question and explain *different*.
- In pairs, students think about as many different types of home as they can. Accept any reasonable suggestions, e.g. house boats, tree houses, tents.

  Note: Some of the discussion will need to be in your students' first language (L1).

2 79 SB p70 **Listen and chant.**

Aim: to give students further practice with home vocabulary
- Students look at the chant.
- Play the recording. Students listen and follow the chant in their Student's Books. Check comprehension of *scary house*.

For chant script see SB p70.

- Play the recording again, pausing after each verse for students to repeat. Do the chant as a class and then in groups.
- Students help you invent actions for *Let's go, scary* and for each of the rooms in the chant (e.g. sleeping for *bedroom*, showering for *bathroom*, looking under a trapdoor for *cellar*). Students do the chant again, including the actions.

1 WB p70 **Write the words.**

Aim: to give students practice in writing the home vocabulary

Key: 2 bedroom, 3 bathroom, 4 kitchen, 5 living room, 6 cellar, 7 dining room, 8 stairs

2 WB p70 **Choose a room. Write and draw.**

Aim: to enable students to personalise the language

Ending the lesson

Aim: to review key language from the lesson
- Hold a flashcard so that students cannot see it.
- Students try to guess, e.g. *Is it the cellar?*
- The first student who guesses correctly chooses a flashcard for the class to guess.

Extension activity

Aim: to enable students to talk about their houses or flats
- Pre-teach *flat*. Find out who lives in a house and who lives in a flat.
- Talk about your home, e.g. *In my flat I've got two bedrooms, a living room, a kitchen and a bathroom. I haven't got a hall.*
- Students exchange information about their homes in pairs.

Learning outcomes:
- to ask and answer about things in a home using *There's* and *There are*

New language: *There's, There are, log*

Recycled language: the home, animals, *monster*

Materials: flashcards 72–80 (the home), bag with items or pictures of known vocabulary (e.g. a toy car, three bananas, soft toy animals, two apples, four small balls)

Warm-up

Aim: to review vocabulary for the home
- Show the flashcards in different orders and elicit the home vocabulary.
- Stick the flashcards around the room.
- Say a room or place. Students point to the correct flashcard. Repeat.

1 80 SB p71 Listen and match the monsters with their bedrooms.

Aim: to present and practise *There's* and *There are*
- Give students time to look at the pictures of the bedrooms. Ask *What animals are in the rooms?* (*Frogs*) Say *Look and count the frogs.*
- Read the activity instruction and make sure students remember the meaning of *monster*. Say *Point to the (green) monster*. Students point to the correct monster.
- Play the recording. Students match the monsters with their bedrooms by writing numbers in the boxes.

For script see TB p123.
- Students compare answers in pairs.
- Play the recording again. Check with the class.
- Say each sentence for students to repeat.
- Write each sentence on the board: *There's one frog in my bedroom. There are four frogs in my bedroom. There are two frogs in my bedroom. There are five frogs in my bedroom*. Underline *There's* and *There are*.

Key: 1 c, 2 d, 3 a, 4 b

2 81 SB p71 Watch, listen and say.

Aim: to focus students on grammatical form
- Use the picture to review *fish*.
- Play the *Penny the penguin* video. Students watch and listen, then watch and read. Check understanding of the grammar.
- Play the audio. Students follow in their Student's Book and join in.

For script see SB p71.
- Students practise the sentences in pairs (holding up their fingers to show the numbers one to four).

3 SB p71 Play the description game.

Aim: to give students further practice with *There's* and *There are*
- Demonstrate the game (describe one of the rooms, and students guess the picture number). Then give practice in open pairs.
- Students take turns to say and guess in closed pairs.

1 WB p71 Look and circle.

Aim: to give students extended practice with *There's* and *There are*

Key: 2 There's, 3 There are, 4 There's, 5 There are, 6 There's

2 WB p71 Write the words.

Aim: to practise writing *There's* and *There are*

Key: 1 There's, 2 There are

Ending the lesson

Aim: to review new language from the lesson
- Put different items inside a bag or box (or use pictures) without students seeing. Take out the items and make sentences using *There's* and *There are*, e.g. *In my bag there's a car. There are two apples. There are three bananas. There's a doll. And there's a small ball.* Hold up the items and repeat your sentences as you put them back in your bag.
- Students try to remember what's in the bag. Choose individuals to make sentences with *There's* and *There are*. Take out items as students say correct sentences. Prompt if necessary, e.g. *There's some fruit. It's green. … And there's some yellow fruit, too.*

Extension activity

Aim: to give students a personal record of the new language
- Students write about three of the pictures from SB Activity 3 in their notebooks.
- Help with vocabulary as appropriate.

1 80 Listen and match the monsters with their bedrooms.

2 81 Watch, listen and say.

Language focus

There's a fish in the hall
And two fish in the living room.
There are three fish in the kitchen.
There are four fish in the dining room.

3 Play the description game.

In this picture, there's a …

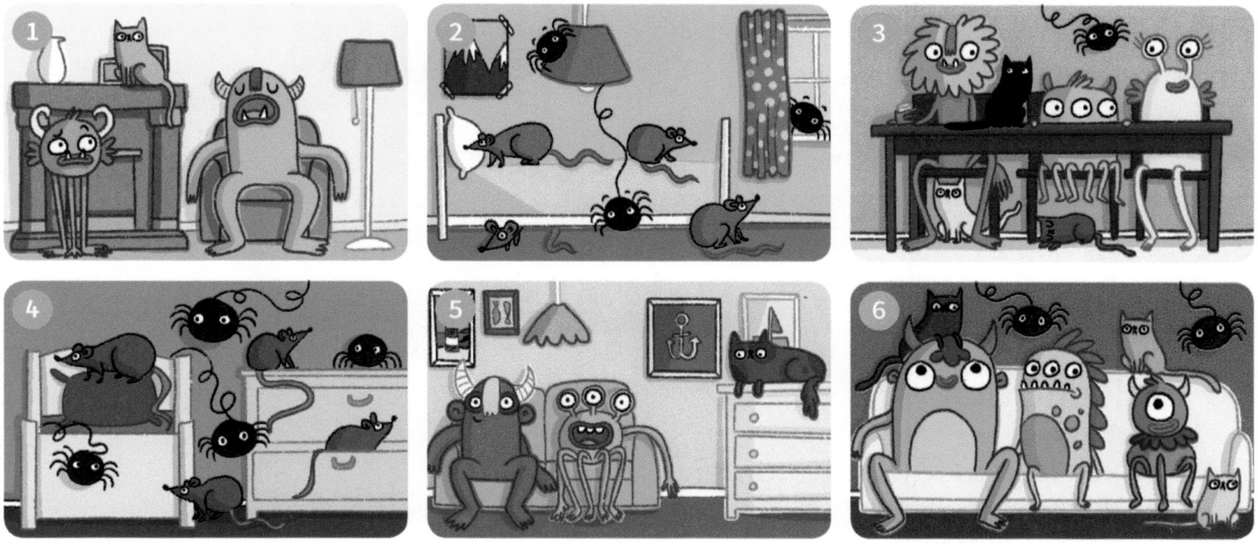

1 82 Listen and sing. Then look and draw lines.

We live in different homes
you and me
Me and you, you and me.
We live in different homes
you and me.
You live in a flat ●
And I live in a tree! ●

Some people live in houses,
Some people live in cars, ●
Some people live in flats,
Or in tents under the stars. ●

We live in different homes ...

Some homes are very old, ●
Some homes are new,
Some homes are very small, ●
Some have got beautiful views.

We live in different homes ...

2 Ask and answer.

Which is your favourite home?

My favourite home is ...

Learning outcomes:
- to sing a song
- to practise *There's* and *There are*

New language: *I/You/We live in (different homes), flat* (n), *some people/homes, stars*

Recycled language: the home, pets, food, *There is/are, very, old, new, beautiful, under, are, have got, Which is your favourite (home)? My favourite (home) is …*

Creative thinking (WB): Chooses options to create something new

Cognitive control functions (WB): Working memory

Flashcards: a selection of toys, animals and food

Warm-up

Aim: to review vocabulary and *There's / There are*

- Draw a large outline of a house on the board, with a bedroom (draw a simple bed), living room (draw a sofa), kitchen (draw the cooker and fridge), bathroom (draw a shower), dining room (draw a table and chairs) and stairs.
- Point to different areas and ask *What's this?* or *Is this the (bedroom)?*
- Hand out a selection of toy, animal and food flashcards.
- Call different students to put their flashcard in the correct place on the board, e.g. *There's a dog in the kitchen. There are carrots in the bedroom, on the bed.*
- Ask, e.g. *What's in the living room?* Students make sentences with *There's …* and *There are …*

1 82 ▶ 83 SB p72 Listen and sing. Then look and draw lines.

Aim: to sing a song with the class and practise reading

- Elicit what students can see in the pictures (*a house in a tree, a car, an old house, a small house*). Use the last two pictures to teach *tent, flat* (= *apartment*) and *view*. Review *beautiful*.
- Play the audio (82). Students follow the song in their Student's Books.

For song lyrics see SB p72.

- Read the second part of the instructions. Play the audio again for students to read and match each phrase which has a dot after it to one of the pictures (a–f).
- Students compare answers in pairs before the class check.
- Play the song video, pausing after each verse for students to repeat.
- When students have learnt the song, use the karaoke version of the audio (83) or video to practise the song with the whole class and then in groups.

Key: flat – f, tree – a, in cars – b, under the stars – e, very old – c, very small – d

2 SB p72 Ask and answer.

Aim: to personalise the song

- Practise the question and answer in the speech bubbles with the whole class.
- Students look at the pictures of the different homes in Activity 1. They ask and answer in pairs.
- Elicit opinions from different students and have a class vote on the favourite home.
- Ask students if they live in a house or a flat.

1 23 WB p72 Can you remember? Listen and write.

Aim: to practise listening for specific information

For song lyrics see SB p72.

Key: 2 tree, 3 cars, 4 tents

2 WB p72 Read and circle. Draw two homes.

Aim: to personalise the key language

Ending the lesson

Aim: to review key language from the lesson

- Write the rhyming words from the song in two columns on the board, but jumbled, e.g.

me	*stars*
cars	*views*
new	*tree*

- Students tell you which words rhyme.

Stronger students: Students tell you the two lines of the song which feature each rhyming pair.

Extension activity

Aim: to consolidate understanding of the vocabulary

- In their notebooks, students write *My favourite home in the song is …* and choose their favourite. They draw their own version of the home, with themselves inside it.

Learning outcomes:
- to use *Is there …? Are there …?* and *How many are there?* to talk about things in a town

New language: *Is there a …? Are there any …? Yes, there is, No, there isn't, Yes, there are, No, there aren't, How many … are there? There are (five), pears*

Recycled language: animals, food, toys, *park, school, house, tree*

Materials: Unit 6 stickers, scissors

Warm-up

Aim: to review *There's / There are*

- Play a chain game. Say *In my house there are two bedrooms.* A student says *In my house there are two bedrooms and there's a …* and adds another item, e.g. *cellar.* The next student repeats the list and adds another item, and so on.

1 84 SB p73 Listen, look and stick.

Aim: to practise the new language

- Students look at the picture. Review vocabulary, e.g. *Point to a green car. Point to the trees. Show me a boy in a house.*
- Students find their stickers and cut them out together with the backing paper. Then, ask students to read the questions.
- Play the recording. Students listen, look and place the stickers without sticking them.

For script see TB p123.

- Students compare answers in pairs. Play the recording again.
- Check with the class before students stick.

Key: 1 Yes, there is. 2 Yes, there are. 3 No, there aren't. 4 There are seven.

2 85 SB p73 Watch, listen and say.

Aim: to focus students on grammatical form

- Play the *Penny the penguin* video. Students watch and listen, then watch and read. Point out that we use *a* after *Is there* but *any* after *Are there.*
- Play the audio. Students follow in their Student's Book and join in. They practise it in pairs.

For script see SB p73.

- Ask questions about the picture in Activity 1 (without asking about items in Activity 3), e.g. *Are there any footballs? How many footballs are there?*

3 SB p73 Look at Activity 1 again. Ask and answer.

Aim: to give students practice asking and answering questions

- Check students know what all the small pictures show.
- Students take turns to ask and answer in pairs.

Key: 1 Is there a plane? Yes, there is. 2 Is there a rat? No, there isn't. 3 Are there any cars? Yes, there are. How many (cars) are there? There are four. 4 Are there any bikes? Yes, there are. How many (bikes) are there? There are three. 5 Is there a cake? Yes, there is. 6 Are there any kites? Yes, there are. How many (kites) are there? There are eight. 7 Are there any pears? No, there aren't. 8 Is there a go-kart? No, there isn't.

1 WB p73 Complete the questions.

Aim: to give students practice writing the new language

Key: 2 Is there, 3 Are, 4 Are there, 5 How many

2 WB p73 Look and write *Yes* or *No*. Then circle.

Aim: to give students further practice with the new language

Key: 2 No, aren't, 3 No, isn't, 4 Yes, are

Ending the lesson

Aim: to review word order in question forms

- Write three questions from the lesson on the board in jumbled word order for students to write.

Extension activity

Aim: to personalise the new language

- Elicit words for animals, toys and food and write them on the board
- Students draw a bag and secretly draw six things from the board inside it.
- In pairs, students take turns to ask and answer, using *Is there …? Are there …? How many …?*

Misty: There's no problem. You can come in.

Whisper: Misty, where are you?

Misty: Here I am.

Thunder: Help!

Flash and Whisper: Aagh!

2 Make sentences with a friend.

In picture one, there's a house.

In picture five, there are twelve spiders.

Phonics

3 Find who says … Help!

4 87 Listen and say.

In Harry's house there's a hairy spider.

1 88 Listen and write the numbers.

How many are there?

1 living rooms: ______
2 bathrooms: ______
3 kitchens: ______
4 bedrooms: ______
5 gardens: ______
6 dining rooms: ______

2 Write about your house.

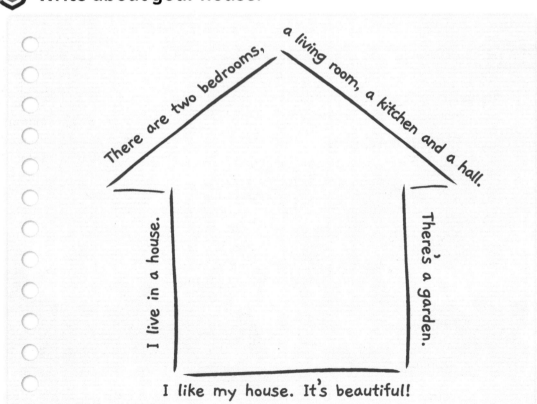

There are two bedrooms, a living room, a kitchen and a hall.

I live in a house.

There's a garden.

I like my house. It's beautiful!

Learning outcomes:
- to listen for specific information
- to write a description of a home from a model

New language: *garden*

Recycled language: the home, numbers 1–20, *flat, there's, there are, How many … are there? I live in a (house), I like, beautiful*

Creative thinking: Uses own ideas for doing creative activities like retelling stories

Critical thinking (WB): Draws conclusions from given information

Cognitive control functions (WB): Cognitive flexibility

Materials: soft ball for each group of seven/eight students (optional)

Warm-up

Aim: to review vocabulary sets
- Make circles of seven or eight students and give each group a soft ball (or a paper ball).
- The student holding the ball says a home word, e.g. *cellar,* and throws the ball to another student who says a different home word, and so on.
- Go around the groups and say a word from another set, e.g. an animal. Students practise that set in the same way.

1 88 SB p76 Listen and write the numbers. Exam skills

Aim: to practise listening for specific information
- Ask students what they think the man in the picture is talking about (*his home*). Use the picture to teach *garden*.
- Read *How many are there?* Ask students what they need to write on the lines (numbers of rooms). Tell them they can use figures or words.
- Play the recording. Students listen and write in pencil. They compare answers in pairs.

For script see TB p123.

- Play the recording again. Then check with the class.

Stronger students: Ask what the man is called (*Mr Big*) and why (*Because he's big and he's got a big house*).
- When students have the correct answers, use open pairs to ask and answer, e.g. *How many living rooms are there? There are six living rooms.*

Key: 1 six/6, 2 four/4, 3 two/2, 4 fifteen/15, 5 one/1, 6 three/3

2 SB p76 Write about your house.

Aim: to enable students to write a description of their own house
- Read the model and check comprehension.
- Students write a first draft of the sentences they want to use in their notebooks. Monitor and check.
- After you have seen and commented on their work, students draw an outline of a house or block of flats and write their sentences around it. They can add details to the picture or bring a photo of their home to the next lesson to stick inside the outline.

1 WB p76 Look and read. Write *yes* or *no*. Exam skills

Aim: to practise reading for specific information and following instructions

Key: 3 yes, 4 no, 5 yes, 6 no

2 WB p76 Look at Activity 1. Read and match.

Aim: to practise reading

Key: 2 a, 3 d, 4 b

Ending the lesson

Aim: to practise memory skills
- Students look at the picture in WB Activity 1 for 30 seconds and then close their Workbooks.
- Say true or false sentences about the picture. Students stand up (or stay standing) if they are true and sit down (or remain sitting) if they are false.

Extension activity

Aim: to enable students to share what they have learnt
- In small groups, students take turns to read aloud what they have written for SB Activity 2 and to say something else about their pictures.
- Students compare their pictures.

Learning outcomes:
- to read for specific information
- to ask and answer simple questions about pictures

Recycled language: the home, animals, toys, classroom objects, numbers, *How many (trains) are there? There are …*

Materials: coloured pens or pencils, four pieces of paper (optional)

Warm-up

Aim: to review the home
- Write *Homes* in a circle on the board. Students copy the heading in their notebooks.
- In pairs, with books closed, students brainstorm all the words connected with the home that they can think of in 30 seconds. They write them around the heading to make a word map.
- They swap word maps with another pair.
- Elicit all the words and write them on the board (or ask students to write them). Check spelling.
- Students correct their spelling and copy any items they didn't have onto the word map in their notebooks.

1 SB p77 Look, read and write *a*, *b*, *c*, *d*.

Aim: to practise reading for specific information
- Elicit which vocabulary sets are in the pictures.
- Read the activity instruction and check students know what to do.
- Students read silently, count and write the letters. Then they compare their answers in pairs.
- Check with the class using open pairs.

Stronger students: Ask students to make sentences about the other items in each picture, e.g. *Picture a – There are seven cats.*

Key: 1 c, 2 a, 3 c, 4 b, 5 d, 6 d

2 SB p77 Look at Activity 1 again. Ask and answer.

Aim: to give students practice in asking and answering questions
- Demonstrate the activity with a volunteer. Practise pronouncing the question with the whole class.
- In pairs, students take turns to ask and answer about the pictures.
- Go around the class to listen and check.

1 26 WB p77 Listen and colour. Exam skills

Aim: to practise listening for specific information

For script see TB p123.

Key: The objects in the picture should be coloured as follows: first cat – black, second cat – black and white, flowers – blue and yellow, leaves on the trees – orange, bike – green, football – blue and yellow

2 WB p77 Look at the picture in Activity 1 and complete the sentences.

Aim: to practise writing

Key: 2 are two, 3 is one, 4 are two

Ending the lesson

Aim: to practise spoken production
- Students look at SB Activity 1 for a minute. They try to remember which items are in each rectangle and how many there are.
- In pairs, students take turns to say as much as they can remember about each rectangle. Student A makes sentences (with book closed), while Student B looks at the book and checks. Then they swap roles.

Extension activity

Aim: to play a game
- Make four teams. Students in each team stand one behind the other, facing your desk. Put a piece of paper on your desk in front of each team (four pieces in total).
- Whisper a different home word to the student at the back of each line.
- This student whispers the word to the student in front of him/her and so on, to the front of the line. The student at the front writes the word for his/her team on the piece of paper on your desk.
- This student then goes to the back of the line.
- Repeat until everyone has written a word.
- Check papers for correct spelling and tell the class which team(s) is/are the winner(s).

1 Look, read and write *a*, *b*, *c*, *d*.

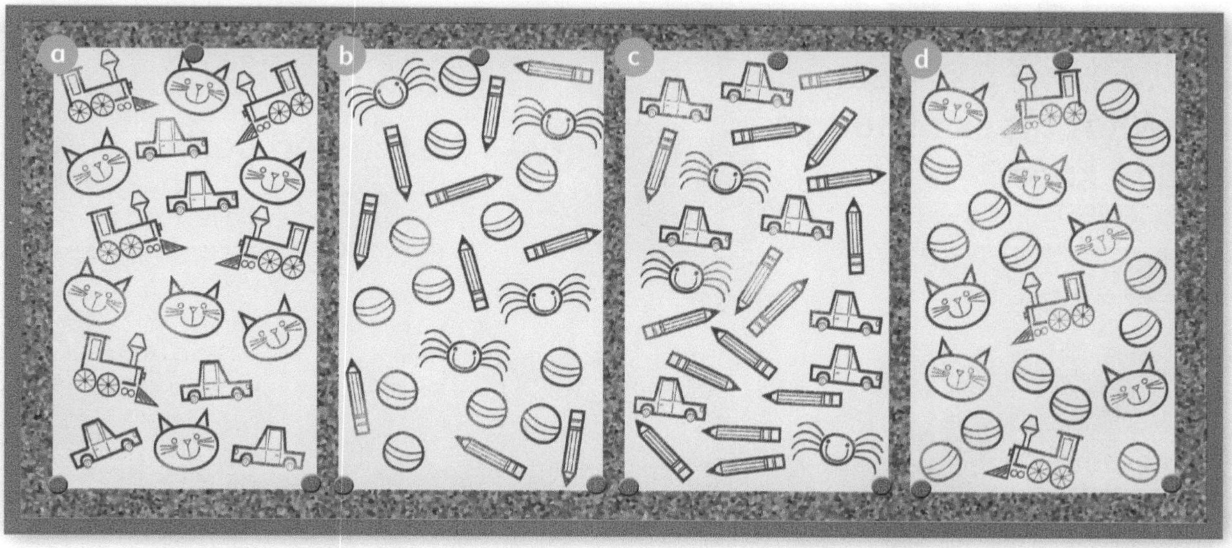

1 There are fifteen pencils. ☐

2 There are five trains. ☐

3 There are seven cars. ☐

4 There are four spiders. ☐

5 There are fourteen balls. ☐

6 There are six cats. ☐

2 Look at Activity 1 again. Ask and answer.

How many trains are there in picture d?
There are three.

Think and learn

Homes

What types of homes do you know?

1 89 **Listen and point.**

cave house

house boat

tree house

yurt

2 **Cover the photos in Activity 1. Ask and answer.**

What's picture 1?

It's a cave house.

3 **Look at Activity 1 again. Read and answer.**

Which home …

1 is on water? __________

2 is round? __________

3 has got stairs in it? __________

4 is small and in a tree? __________

Learning outcomes:
- to integrate other areas of the curriculum through English: Geography
- to identify and name different types of home

BIG QUESTION to explore the Big Question *How are houses different?*

New language: *type, house boat, cave house, tree house, yurt*

Recycled language: the home, *water, circle, small, tree*

Critical thinking: Demonstrates understanding of links between new ideas

Critical thinking (WB): Sorts and classifies objects and activities according to key features (e.g. types of animal or transport)

Materials: world map (optional)

Warm-up

Aim: to review the idea of how homes can be different
- Write the Big Question *How are houses different?* on the board.
- Say the beginning of sentences for students to complete: *Houses are big or … (small). Houses are new or … (old). Some people don't live in houses. They live in (flats, tents, trees).*
- Elicit more ideas about places to live.

SB p78 What types of homes do you know?

Aim: to extend students' awareness of unusual homes
- With Student's Books closed, play the video.

For videoscript see TB p123.

- Ask students what they remember. They can use L1 to tell you about the houses on wheels, the igloo, etc.
- Students watch again to answer *What types of homes do you know?* Play the video again and elicit answers. Ask students *Has anyone ever slept on a house boat or in a tent?*

1 89 SB p78 Listen and point.

Aim: to present words for unusual homes
- Play the recording. Students listen and point to the photos.

For script see SB p78.

- Play the recording again. Students repeat.

2 SB p78 Cover the photos in Activity 1. Ask and answer.

Aim: to practise the new vocabulary
- Students look at the photos in Activity 1 for 30 seconds.
- In pairs, they test each other on what is in each picture (Student A with book closed, Student B checking the page, then swapping roles).

3 SB p78 Look at Activity 1 again. Read and answer.

Aim: to link new language to previous knowledge, and practise reading
- Check comprehension of *Which home …?*
- Students read the rest of the questions in pairs and find the answers in Activity 1. Monitor and help, as necessary.
- Elicit answers and ask *Which home do you like?* Have a class vote on the most popular unusual home.

Key: 1 house boat, 2 yurt, 3 cave house, 4 tree house

1 WB p78 Look and write.

Aim: to practise reading and writing the new language

Key: 2 yurt, 3 cave house, 4 house boat

2 WB p78 Read and write the numbers.

Aim: to check students' understanding of types of homes

Key: 2 c, 3 a

Lesson review

- Elicit what students learnt today and write it on the board, e.g. *Today I've learnt about different types of homes*. Students copy in their notebooks.

Extension activity

Aim: to learn about locations of unusual homes
- Use a world map to show students where some of the unusual homes from the lesson are, e.g. Matera, Southern Italy (cave house), Amsterdam, the Netherlands (house boat), Papua New Guinea (tree house), Central Asia / Mongolia (yurt). Talk about the advantages and disadvantages of each type of home.

  Note: Some of the discussion will need to be in your students' first language (L1).

Learning outcomes:
- to extend the focus on Geography through English
- to complete a project

New language: *It's got, It hasn't got, What haven't they got?*

Recycled language: homes, *house boat, cave house, tree house, yurt, How many (rooms) are there? which, there are*

Creative thinking: Based on a model, develops new games, dishes, clothes, etc.

Cognitive control functions: Cognitive flexibility

Critical thinking (WB): Compares different types of information

Creative thinking (WB): Substitutes words and lines to a song or poem

Materials: coloured pens or pencils, paper, digital or print portfolios

Warm-up

Aim: to review unusual homes
- Ask students which homes they remember from the previous lesson and write them on the board (*house, flat, house boat, cave house, tree house, yurt*).
- Make a sentence about a home, e.g. *This home is on water.* Students say the home.
- Repeat with different sentences, e.g. *This home is round.* (*Yurt*) *This home can be in a tall tower.* (*Flat*)

4 SB p79 Look at the pictures. Ask and answer.

Aim: to practise talking about two different types of home
- Talk about the diagrams and make sure students realise they show two different homes seen from above.
- Ask the first question and elicit which type of home each picture shows.
- In pairs, students ask and answer about each home, taking turns.

5 Project SB p79 Design a house.

Aim: to enable students to apply their knowledge about homes
- Tell students they are going to design their own home. It can be a home of one of the types in the unit, or their own idea.
- Refer students to the model design. Ask what type of home it is and which rooms and other features there are. Ask, e.g. *Is there a garden? Why not? Are there any stairs?*
- Give each student a piece of paper. They choose a type of home and design a floorplan. They can look back through the unit to decide what kind of home they would like.
- Ask students to write a list of the rooms they would like to have and to think about other features. Encourage students to use their imagination. Provide new vocabulary, as necessary.
- Students then draw their plans and label the rooms and extra features. They add a title and decorate the design.
- Finally, students can present their house designs to a partner and tell them about the house.
- Take photos of the plans and save them to students' digital portfolios.

3 WB p79 Read, match and circle.

Aim: to enable students to practise reading and applying knowledge

Key: 2 a five, 3 b kitchen, 4 c cellar

4 WB p79 Read. Write a poem puzzle. Decorate.

Aim: to enable students to personalise the unit language

Lesson review

Aim: to review what students have learnt in the lesson
- Write on the board: *Today I've …*
- Elicit what students did today, e.g. *designed a home.*
- Write it on the board. Students copy it into their notebooks.

Extension activity

Aim: to give further practice talking about homes
- In small groups, students take turns to present their home designs from SB Activity 5. They say as much as they can about their picture. Encourage the students who are listening to ask questions, e.g. *Is the bedroom big or small? Is there a dining room?*

4 Look at the pictures. Ask and answer.

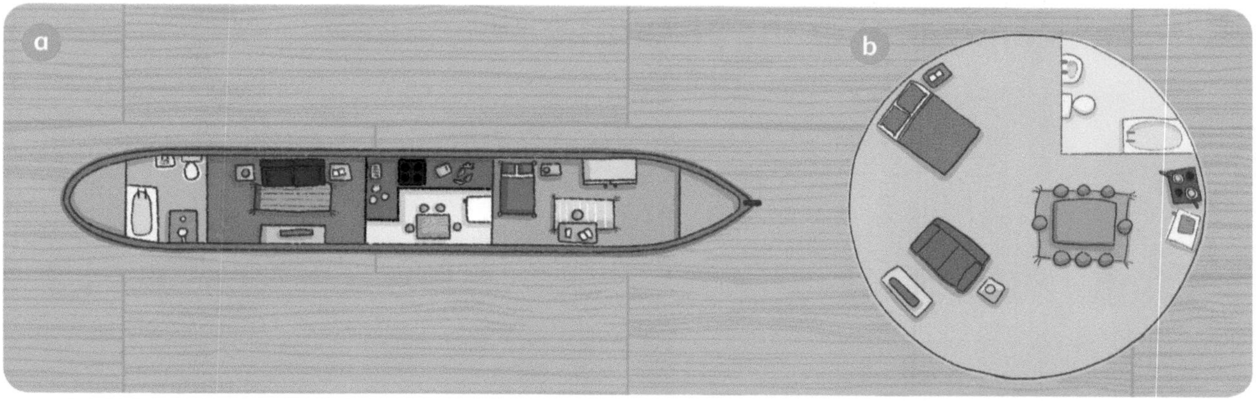

1 What homes are they?

2 How many rooms are there?

3 Which rooms are there?

4 What haven't they got?

This is a house boat. It's got … . It hasn't got … .

5 Project Design a house.

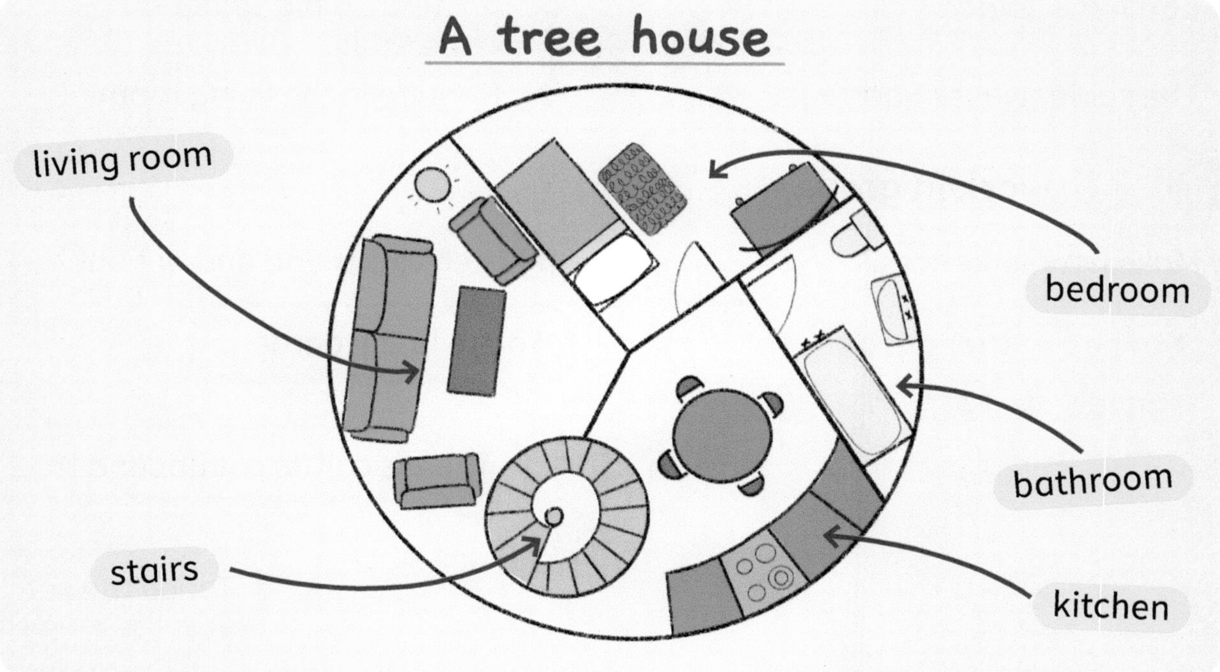

Do that!

1 (90) **Listen and act out with your teacher. Then listen again and number the pictures.**

2 **Read the sentences from the story and draw lines.**

a Open the window.

b Put the spider outside.

c Catch the spider.

d There's a big spider on the table.

e The spider waves goodbye.

f You're in the living room.

3 **Work in groups.**

a Make new sentences.

You're in the garden.
There's a ...
...

b Listen to a friend and act out.

You're in the garden.

There's a little cat under a tree.

Touch the cat.

Learning outcomes:
- to practise the language through listening and responding physically
- to practise giving instructions

New language: *window, catch, put outside, wave goodbye*

Recycled language: the home, animals, prepositions, imperatives, colours, *there's, spider, big, table*

Creative thinking: Participates in investigative, exploratory, open-ended tasks

Creative thinking (WB): Uses different media to make and describe his/her own designs

Materials: card, pencils, rulers, scissors, coloured pens or pencils

Warm-up

Aim: to review vocabulary

- Draw the outline of a house, seen from above. Ask students to tell you what rooms to put in the house and what to put in the garden, as you draw it on the board.
- Prompt with questions, if necessary, e.g. *Is there a cellar? Is the garden big or small? Are there any trees or flowers?*
- When the picture is finished, ask students *Do you want to live there?*

1 90 SB p80 Listen and act out with your teacher. Then listen again and number the pictures.

Aim: to practise listening and following instructions

- Tell students to look at the pictures and say what they can see. Elicit, e.g. *a spider, a living room*. Teach *window* and *catch*.
- Remind students that the pictures are not in the correct order, but they make a short story about the girl and the spider.
- Say *Listen and act out.* Play the recording. Mime each action and encourage students to copy you.

For script see TB p124.

- Play the recording again and repeat.
- Say *Now listen and number.* Remind students that they have to write numbers in the small boxes next to the pictures. Ask them to guess which is the first picture before they listen.
- Play the recording again for students to check their answers. Then elicit answers.

Key: 4, 2, 6, 5, 1, 3

2 SB p80 Read the sentences from the story and draw lines.

Aim: to give students practice in reading

- Look at the example and make sure students remember that they have to link the dots in the correct order.
- Check they recognise the written forms of the words *catch* and *waves goodbye.*
- Students read and draw lines between the dots individually. Check answers by eliciting the story in the correct order.

Key: f, d, c, a, b, e

3 SB p80 Work in groups.

Aim: to give students practice in creating and giving instructions

- Students work individually to make their own sequence of sentences telling a story. Monitor and help as necessary.
- In pairs, students take turns to read their sentences. The student who is listening mimes the story.
- Choose volunteer pairs to show one or both of their 'stories'.

1 WB p80 Make a pop-up house.

Aim: to enable students to follow a set of instructions to make a pop-up house

- Students work in pairs. Make sure students have all the items they need by reading the list and saying, e.g. *Show me a ruler.*
- Read the instructions, helping students make their pop-up house, step by step.

Ending the lesson

Aim: to review language from the lesson

- Give instructions from the lesson, but miss out the last word, e.g. *Put the spider …* Students say the last word in chorus (e.g. *outside*) and do the action.

Extension activity

Aim: to enable students to compare houses

- Review *door* and *window* and teach *roof.*
- Put students into groups of four. They take turns to talk about the features and colours of their pop-up houses, e.g. *This is my house. The roof is blue, the door is white and the windows are green.*

Learning outcomes:
- to review language from Units 5 and 6
- to collaborate and reflect on learning

BIG QUESTION to think about how the unit has helped them talk about the Big Question *How are houses different?*

Recycled language: vocabulary and grammar from Units 5 and 6

Creative thinking: Substitutes words and phrases to create new texts

Cognitive control functions: Working memory

Creative thinking (WB): Creates texts that express personal interests, emotions, or identity

Cognitive control functions (WB): Cognitive flexibility

Materials: flashcards 72–80 (home), coloured pens or pencils

Warm-up

Aim: to review the home
- Display the flashcards on the board. Write a number between *1* and *9* under each one. Students write the number and then the word in their notebooks.
- They compare answers in pairs and then check in their Student's Book.

1 SB p81 How many words can you remember? Draw pictures or write words.

Aim: to review vocabulary and spelling
- Write the headings *Days of the week* and *The home* on the board.
- Students copy the category headings in their notebooks and draw more items in each group, with a space below each picture. Students share their pictures in small groups.

2 SB p81 Write and say the words.

Aim: to review vocabulary for the home
- Students write labels below the pictures they drew for Activity 1. Check spelling.
- In pairs, students take turns to point to one of their pictures and say the word.

3 91 SB p81 Listen and number.

Aim: to practise listening and revise unit language
- Elicit the toy in the picture (a board game). Remind students that the speech bubbles next to the picture are in the wrong order. Read the instructions.
- Play the recording for students to listen only.

For script see TB p124.

- Play it again, pausing so they can write numbers. Check answers.
- Play the recording again for students to listen and repeat. They can practise the dialogue in pairs, swapping roles.

Key: 2, 5, 4, 1, 3

4 SB p81 Write a new dialogue. Act it out.

Aim: to review grammar and practise writing
- Remind students how to make a new dialogue by completing the gaps, e.g. *Do you go swimming at the weekends? Yes, I do. Where do you go swimming? In the swimming pool. That's great!*
- In pairs, students write a new dialogue. Help with vocabulary.
- Students practise in pairs.

1 WB p81 Write and circle.

Aim: to enable students to assess their own learning

2 WB p81 Write the words.

BIG QUESTION Aim: to enable students to revisit the Big Question and consolidate learning
- Check and ask students for more examples of homes. Encourage them to look through the unit and think about how homes vary (e.g. age, size, shape, where they are).

Key: 2 house boat, 3 yurt, 4 tree house

3 WB p81 Read. Then draw and write.

Aim: to enable students to personalise the topic

Picture dictionary

Aim: to review vocabulary for the home
- Students complete the Picture dictionary page for The home (WB p125).

Key: bedroom, cellar, dining room, hall, kitchen, living room, stairs

Ending the lesson

Aim: to enable students to express their preferences
- Have a class vote and repeat the most popular activity.

Extension activity

Aim: to enable students to share what they have learnt
- In groups, students take turns to read aloud what they have written for WB Activity 3 and say something about their pictures.

1 How many words can you remember? Draw pictures or write words.

Days of the week

MONDAY

TUESDAY

The home

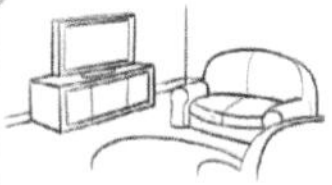

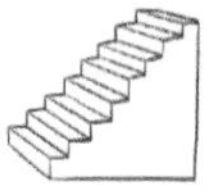

2 Write and say the words.

3 91 Listen and number.

- Yes, I do. ☐
- That's great! ☐
- In my living room. ☐
- Do you play board games at the weekend? ☐
- Where do you play them? ☐

4 Write a new dialogue. Act it out.

Do you ______________________ at the weekend?

Yes, I do.

Where ______________________?

In ______________________.

That's great!

7 Get dressed

1 (92) **Listen and look. Then listen and say the words.**

BIG QUESTION How do clothes look different?

2 (93) **Listen and chant.**

Put on your trousers,
Put on your skirt,
Put on your sweater,
Put on your T-shirt.
Put on your shoes,
And your baseball cap.
Now let's rap!

Trousers, T-shirt,
Shoes and cap.
Sweater, skirt,
Now let's rap.

Come on Whisper,
It's time for school.

Learning outcomes:
- to name and talk about clothes
- to say a chant

BIG QUESTION to start to think about the Big Question *How do clothes look different?*

New language: *clothes, sweater, skirt, shorts, trousers, jacket, socks, jeans, shoes, baseball cap, T-shirt, You look great, Hurry up, Ready, Put on (your trousers), Let's rap, time for school*

Cognitive control functions: Working memory

Materials: flashcards 81–90 (clothes), clothing made from different materials and with different patterns and colours (optional)

Warm-up

Aim: to activate vocabulary
- Point to some of your clothes or students' clothes and elicit any words they know.
- Write *Clothes* in a circle on the board and write the words.

Presentation

Aim: to present clothes vocabulary
- Hold up each flashcard in turn. Say the word for the class to repeat in chorus.
- Do this three or four times.
- Hold up each flashcard for the class to say the word without your help. They point to the item if they or their friends are wearing it.
- Stick the flashcards on the board with *Clothes* in the centre, to make a word map. Students can refer to this throughout the lesson.

1 92 SB p82 **Listen and look. Then listen and say the words.**

Aim: to practise clothes vocabulary
- Students look at the picture in their Student's Books. Elicit who they can see (*Whisper, his brother and his mum*) and where they are (*in his bedroom*).
- Play the recording. Students point to the clothes when they hear them.

For script see TB p124.

- Play the recording again. Students repeat the clothes words.
- Students practise pointing and naming the clothes in pairs.

BIG QUESTION **How do clothes look different?**

Aim: to encourage students to find out how colours and patterns make clothes look different
- Read the Big Question. Show or point to two items of clothing which are the same (e.g. a pair of socks) and ask *Do they look different?* (*No*) Say *They look the same.* Repeat with different items, some the same, some different. Students say *Same* or *Different*.
- Draw attention to two different items of clothing (e.g. two socks of different colours). Ask *How are they different?*
- Pass around clothing made of different materials and with different patterns, if possible. Discuss ways that clothes can look different.

2 93 SB p82 **Listen and chant.**

Aim: to give students further practice with clothes vocabulary
- Play the recording. Students listen and follow the chant in their books.

For chant script see SB p82.

- Check understanding of new vocabulary.
- Play the recording again, pausing after each verse for students to repeat.
- Do the chant as a class and in groups. Students mime putting on the clothing as they chant.

1 WB p82 **Find the clothes. Look → and ↓. Circle.**

Aim: to give practice recognising clothes vocabulary

Key: T-shirt (row 2), baseball cap (row 3), skirt (row 4), shorts (row 6), sweater (row 7), trousers (row 8), shoes (column 1), jacket (column 9), jeans (column 10)

2 WB p82 **Look and write the words from Activity 1.**

Aim: to give practice spelling clothes vocabulary

Key: 2 baseball cap, 3 skirt, 4 sweater, 5 shorts, 6 trousers, 7 jacket, 8 T-shirt, 9 shoes, 10 jeans

Ending the lesson

Aim: to review key language from the lesson
- Say the clothes words one after another.
- If students are wearing the item you say, they point to it. If not, they shake their heads.

Extension activity

Aim: to enable students to talk about their clothes
- In pairs, students talk about their favourite clothes, using *I've got* and colours.
- Students can also draw and write about their favourite clothes.

Learning outcomes:
- to ask and answer about preferences using *like*
- to identify clothes using *this* and *these*

New language: *Do you like …? Yes, I do, No, I don't, this, these*

Recycled language: clothes, *I like, I don't like*

Materials: flashcards 81–90 (clothes), real items of clothing, e.g. trousers, skirts, T-shirts, shorts, shoes (optional)

Warm-up

Aim: to review clothes
- Give instructions with clothes, e.g. *Put on your (socks).* Students listen and do the action.
- Students repeat the activity in pairs.

Presentation

Aim: to present *this* and *these*
- Pick up a book and say *This is a book*. Repeat for other singular objects.
- Introduce *these* by picking up more than one object.
- Point to objects and clothes items and elicit sentences with *This is …* and *These are …*

1 94 SB p83 Listen, look and draw lines.

Aim: to present and practise *Do you like …? Yes, I do. / No, I don't.*
- Present *Do you like …?* by showing clothes flashcards and asking, e.g. *Do you like these socks?*
- Students look at the pictures in the Student's Book and read the sentences.
- Play the recording. Students match the questions and answers with the pictures. They then compare answers in pairs.

For script see TB p124.

- Play the recording again. Check with the class.
- Say each question and answer for students to repeat.

Key: Picture a: 1, 2; picture b: 3, 4

2 95 SB p83 Watch, listen and say.

Aim: to focus students on grammatical form
- Play the *Penny the penguin* video. Students watch and listen, then watch and read. Check understanding of the grammar.
- Play the audio. Students follow in their Student's Book and join in.

For script see SB p83.

- Students practise the sentences in pairs (gesturing to their feet for *shoes* and their heads for *hat*).

3 SB p83 Look around the classroom. Ask and answer.

Aim: to give students further practice with the new language
- Show students clothes items you have brought in, asking, e.g. *Do you like these trousers?* Different students reply *Yes, I do. / No, I don't.*
- Students walk around in pairs, taking turns to ask and answer about objects or items of clothing they see. Ensure students are sensitive and kind to their classmates.
- Elicit a question and answer from each pair.

1 WB p83 Read and write the numbers.

Aim: to give students practice with *like* and *don't like*

Key: b 1, c 2, d 4

2 WB p83 Circle the words.

Aim: to give students further practice with the language

Key: 2 this, 3 this, 4 these, 5 don't, 6 do

3 WB p83 Write the words.

Aim: to give students writing practice

Key: 2 do, 3 these, 4 don't

Ending the lesson

Aim: to review new language from the lesson
- Write two questions from the lesson on the board, with jumbled word order, for students to unjumble, e.g. *these / shoes / you / Do / like / ?*

Extension activity

Aim: to give students further practice with the new language
- In pairs, students make a role play in a clothes shop, acting as shopkeeper and customer, e.g. *Do you like this jacket, sir? No, I don't. Do you like these trousers, madam? Yes, I do.*
- They swap roles.

1 (94) Listen, look and draw lines.

1 Do you like this T-shirt?

2 No, I don't.

3 Do you like these shoes?

4 Yes, I do.

2 (95) Watch, listen and say.

Language focus

Do you like these shoes?	Yes, **I do**.
Do you like this hat?	No, **I don't**.

3 Look around the classroom. Ask and answer.

1 Listen and sing. Then tick ☑ the clothes in the song.

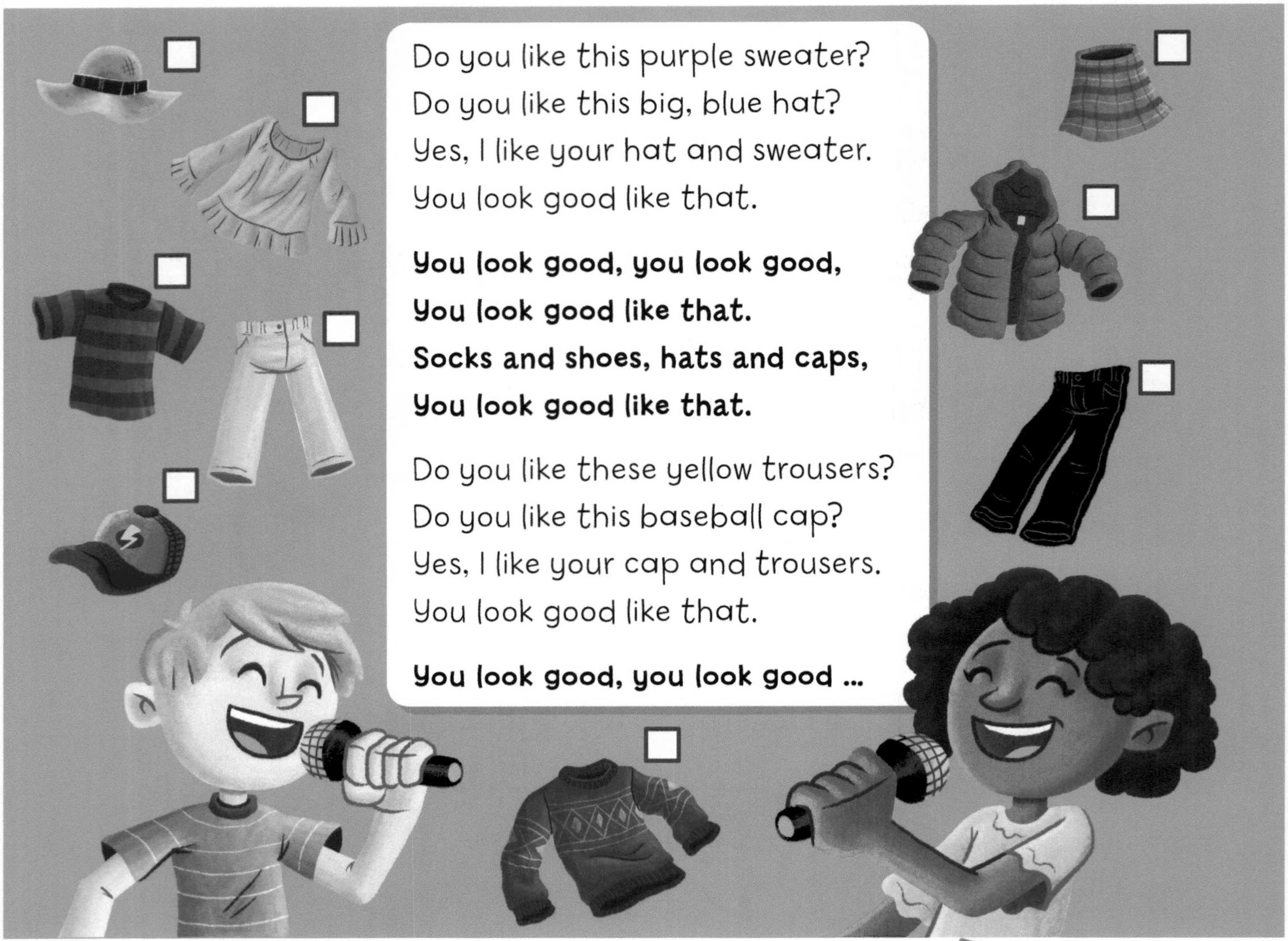

Do you like this purple sweater?
Do you like this big, blue hat?
Yes, I like your hat and sweater.
You look good like that.

You look good, you look good,
You look good like that.
Socks and shoes, hats and caps,
You look good like that.

Do you like these yellow trousers?
Do you like this baseball cap?
Yes, I like your cap and trousers.
You look good like that.

You look good, you look good ...

2 Write a new verse for the song.

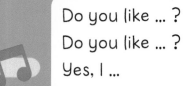

Do you like ... ?
Do you like ... ?
Yes, I ...
You look good like that.

Learning outcomes:
- to sing a song
- to practise *Do you like …?* with *this* and *these*

New language: *You look good, like that*

Recycled language: clothes, colours, *big, I like (your hat and sweater).*

Creative thinking: Substitutes words and lines to a song or poem

Cognitive control functions (WB): Working memory

Materials: flashcards 81–90 (clothes), coloured pens or pencils

Warm-up

Aim: to review clothes
- Stick the clothes flashcards on the board.
- Volunteers write a word under the appropriate flashcard, in turn.

Extra support: The rest of the class help, by calling out letters.

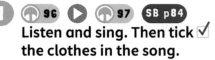

1 96 97 SB p84 Listen and sing. Then tick ✓ the clothes in the song.

Aim: to sing a song with the class
- Students look at the pictures. Say, e.g. *Point to the yellow trousers. Point to the baseball cap. What colour is it?* Ask different students, e.g. *Do you like these black trousers? Do you like this orange skirt?*
- Pre-teach *You look good like that.*
- Play the audio (96). Students follow the song in their Student's Books.

For song lyrics see SB p84.

- Read the second part of the instructions. Play the audio again, pausing for students to tick the clothes they hear in the song.
- Students compare answers in pairs before the class check. Ask which clothes in the song are not in the pictures (*socks and shoes*).
- Play the song video, pausing after each verse for students to repeat.
- When students have learnt the song, use the karaoke version of the audio (97) or video to practise the song with the whole class and then in groups.

Key: Students tick the purple sweater, the blue hat, the yellow trousers and the purple baseball cap.

2 SB p84 Write a new verse for the song.

Aim: to enable students to personalise the language
- Students make their verse with two questions and a positive answer. They use *this* for singular words (*hat, skirt, sweater, T-shirt, baseball cap, jacket*) and *these* for plural words (*trousers, shoes, socks, shorts, jeans*).

Extra support: Write the words on the board in two groups, if necessary.
- Monitor and help as students write their verse.
- Volunteers read or sing their verse to the class.

1 27 WB p84 Can you remember? Listen and write.

Aim: to practise listening for specific information

For song lyrics see SB p84.

Key: 2 blue hat, 3 yellow trousers, 4 baseball cap

2 WB p84 Read, draw and colour.

Aim: to give further practice with reading for specific information

Key: Students draw and colour clothes following the instructions.

Ending the lesson

Aim: to review key language from the lesson
- Ask students to stand in a circle. Hand out the clothes flashcards. Play some music (e.g. the song from the lesson). Students pass the flashcards around. Pause the music. Choose a student who is holding a flashcard. He/She makes a question about the clothes item on the flashcard, e.g. *Do you like these trousers?* and chooses someone to answer.
- Start the music again and repeat the activity. Continue until most students have asked and/or answered a question.

Extension activity

Aim: to consolidate understanding of the vocabulary
- In their notebooks, students draw and colour a picture of themselves in their favourite outfit.
- They add labels, e.g. *my red T-shirt, my blue shorts.*

Stronger students: Students write a caption: *I look good like that!*

Learning outcomes:
- to use the present continuous to talk about what people are wearing

New language: *He's/She's/(Jim)'s wearing …, Is he/she wearing …? Yes, he/she is, No, he/she isn't.*

Recycled language: clothes, colours, *wave, girl*

Materials: flashcards 81–90 (clothes), clothing in different colours (optional)

Warm-up

Aim: to review clothes and colours

- Show different items of clothing and say *This is a …* Students say, e.g. *green jacket.* Alternatively use the clothes flashcards. Then ask *Do you like this (green jacket)? Do you like these (blue shoes)?*

Presentation

Aim: to present *He's/She's/(Jim)'s wearing …*

- Call several students to the front, some boys and some girls.
- Make sentences about what each student is wearing, e.g. *Alicia's wearing a yellow skirt. She's wearing white socks.* Give examples with *he* and *she*. Write example sentences on the board.
- Ask questions, e.g. *Is Alicia wearing a yellow skirt? Is she wearing yellow socks?* Students answer *Yes, he/she is* or *No, he/she isn't.*

1 98 SB p85 Listen and draw lines. Exam skills

Aim: to practise the new language

- Students look at the three pictures and think about what the children are wearing. Make sentences, e.g. *He's wearing a green T-shirt.* Students point to the correct child.
- Play the recording, pausing for students to draw a line from the names to the children.

For script see TB p124.

- Students compare answers in pairs. Play the recording again.
- Check with the class.

Key: David – green T-shirt, James – blue T-shirt, Emily – green cap, Gemma – red cap, Katy – watching TV, Oliver – red T-shirt

Stronger students: Ask, e.g. *What's James doing? (He's playing a board game.)*

- Elicit sentences about clothing from the recording in the present continuous and write them on the board, e.g. *Oliver is wearing a red T-shirt.*

2 99 SB p85 Watch, listen and say.

Aim: to focus students on grammatical form

- Play the *Penny the penguin* video. Students watch and listen, then watch and read.
- Play the audio. Students follow in their Student's Book and join in.

For script see SB p85.

- Students practise the sentences in pairs.
- Ask questions about the pictures in Activity 1, e.g. *Is David wearing a red T-shirt? (No, he isn't.) Is Gemma wearing blue shorts? (Yes, she is.)*

3 SB p85 Look at Activity 1. Play the guessing game.

Aim: to give students practice asking questions

- Demonstrate the game. Student A chooses a child from the pictures in Activity 1 without telling Student B who it is. Student B asks questions to find out who it is. Then they swap roles.
- Students play the game in pairs.

1 WB p85 Read and look. Point to Sam.

Aim: to practise reading

Key: Picture 4

2 WB p85 Read and write the names under the pictures in Activity 1.

Aim: to give students further practice with the new language

Key: 1 Tim, 2 Jo, 3 Kim

3 WB p85 Look at the pictures in Activity 1. Read and circle *yes* or *no*.

Aim: to give students further practice with the new language

Key: 2 no, 3 yes, 4 no

Ending the lesson

Aim: to review present continuous questions

- Ask questions about students in the class, e.g. *Is* (name) *wearing a sweater?*
- Students ask and answer in open pairs.

Extension activity

Aim: to personalise the new language and unit theme

- Students write about what their friend is wearing.

1 98 Listen and draw lines.

David | James | Emily | Gemma | Katy | Oliver

2 99 Watch, listen and say.

Language focus

Look, that's Jim!
Is he wear**ing** a red hat?
No, he **isn't**.
Is he wear**ing** a blue hat?
Yes, he **is**. Jim's wear**ing** a blue hat.
Wave to him!

3 Look at Activity 1. Play the guessing game.

It's a girl.

Is she wearing a yellow T-shirt?

Yes, she is.

Is she … ?

The cap

1 100 Where's Whisper's cap?

Whisper: My cap isn't here.
Flash: Oh, no!

Whisper: Look! Gary's wearing my cap.
Flash: Are you sure?
Misty: Maybe Gary has got the same cap.

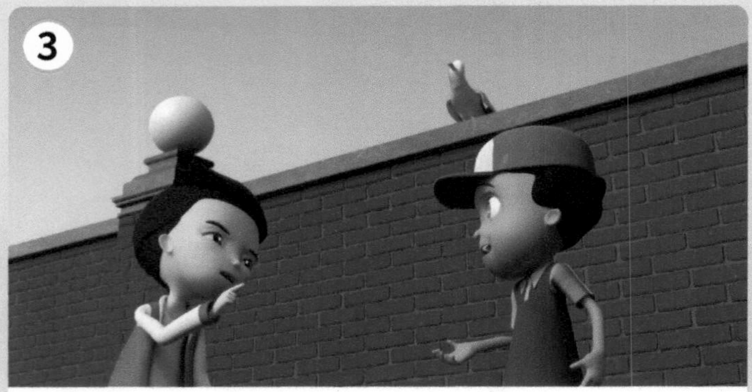

Whisper: Stop! That's my cap, Gary.
Gary: No, it's my cap.

Whisper: Get my cap, please.
Bird: No problem.

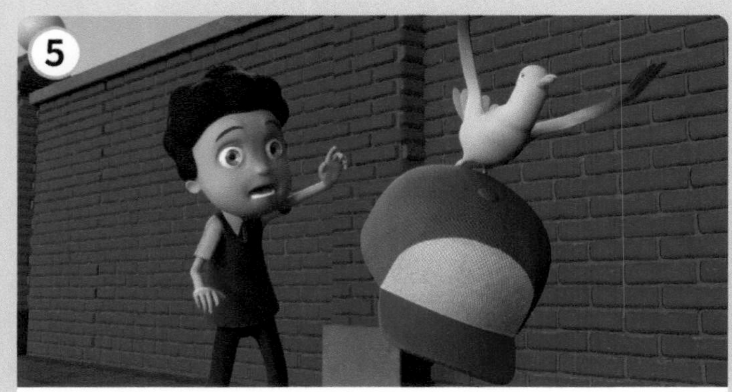

Gary: Hey!

Whisper: Thanks.

Learning outcomes:
- to listen to, read, watch and act out a picture story
- to review language from the unit

New language: *Are you sure? maybe, that, no problem, I'm very sorry.*

Recycled language: clothes, character names, present continuous, *has got, same, please, thanks*

Value: saying sorry

Critical thinking (WB):
Draws conclusions from given information
Identifies characters, setting, plots and theme in a story

Materials: two baseball caps (optional)

Warm-up

Aim: to review the characters and the story
- Write key phrases from the last episode of the story on the board, e.g. *old house, Careful, Misty! stairs, cold, Spiders! Rats! You can come in, Here I am.*
- Using the phrases, gesture and mime, students help you retell the last episode of the story. Remind them of the value (Misty looked after her friends).

The cap

1 100 SB pp86–87 Where's Whisper's cap?

Aim: to present a picture story
- Give students time to look at the pictures. Point to the first picture and ask *Where are the Super Friends?* (*At school*) Elicit the name of the boy in picture 2 (*Gary*). Ask *What colour is his baseball cap?* (*Blue and white*)
- Ask *Where's Whisper's cap?*
- Play the audio. Students listen and find out the answer.

For script see SB pp86–87.

- Play the whole *Super Friends* video. Then play the video again, pausing to check comprehension. Ask *Has Whisper got his cap?* (*No, it isn't there*), and *What does Whisper think about Gary?* (*He's wearing his cap*). Check students understand that Misty tries to give a different explanation (that they have the same cap – review the meaning of *same*). Ask *What does Gary say?* (*'No, it's my cap.'*) Then ask *Who helps Whisper get the cap?* (*A bird*) and *Why does Whisper say 'Oh no!'?* (*He made a mistake – his cap is in his bedroom and he's got Gary's cap.*) Ask what Whisper does at the end of the story. Make sure students realise that he goes to Gary's house and gives him back his cap.
- Talk with the class about the value (saying sorry). Ask who says sorry in the story (*Whisper*).

Key: It's in his bedroom.

1 28 WB p86 Who says it? Listen and tick ☑.

Aim: to review the story

For script see TB p124.

Key: 1 Whisper (2nd picture), 2 Flash (1st picture), 3 Whisper (1st picture)

2 WB p86 Write the names. Who's wearing …?

Aim: to check understanding of the story

Key: 1 Whisper, 2 Whisper, 3 Misty

3 WB p86 Who says it? Match.

Aim: to review short dialogues

Key: 2 a (Bird), 3 b (Whisper), 4 c (Misty)

Ending the lesson

Aim: to practise the story
- Put students in groups of five. They each take a role of one of the characters.
- Play the recording. Students repeat in role.
- Students practise the role play in groups.
- Volunteer groups role play for the class. If possible, give them two caps to use as props.

Extension activity

Aim: to discuss the value of saying sorry
- Focus on the end of the story, when Whisper said sorry.
- Ask why this value is important and elicit examples of when students have said sorry to their friends, or when someone has said sorry to them.
  Note: This discussion will probably need to take place in L1.

Learning outcomes:
- to interpret deeper meaning from a story
- to practise consonant clusters starting with *s*
- to review language from the story and the unit

Recycled language: language from the story, clothes, animals, toys, food, the home

Phonics focus: Your students will be able to read and say consonant clusters starting with the letter sound *s*.

Value: saying sorry

Critical thinking (WB): Demonstrates understanding of links between new ideas

Warm-up

Aim: to review the story
- Write some key phrases from the story on the board and elicit who says them.
- Play the recording of the story for students to listen and spot the key phrases.

2 SB p87 Look at the picture and tick ☑ the correct sentence.

Aim: to check comprehension of the story
- Students find the expression which best matches the picture. They compare their ideas in pairs.
- Elicit the answer.

Key: 3 Can you get my ball?

3 SB p87 Find who says ...

Aim: to present consonant clusters starting with *s*
- Write *stop* on the board, using a red pen for the letters *st*. Say the consonant clusters *st* and *sp* so that students can hear that there are no vowel sounds before or between the two letters.
- Students repeat *Stop!* after you.
- Students find the word in the story (frame 3).

Key: Whisper

4 101 SB p87 Listen and say.

Aim: to practise and identify consonant clusters at the beginning of words
- Play the recording. Students look at the picture, read and repeat. Review *spots* and *stripes* using the picture.

For script see TB p124.

- Repeat the sentence as a class without the recording. Say it loudly, slowly, quickly, whisper it, etc.
- Students take turns to repeat in pairs.

1 WB p87 Look and write.

Aim: to focus students on the value of saying sorry

Key: 1 I'm very sorry. 2 It's OK.

2 29 WB p87 Write the letters. Listen and say.

Aim: to practise reading, writing and saying words with consonant clusters starting with *s*

For script see TB p124.

Key: 2 spider, 3 steak, 4 sweater, 5 skirt, 6 stairs, 7 school, 8 snake

Ending the lesson

Aim: to write decodable words with consonant clusters starting with *s*, and to review clothes, colours and numbers
- Students close their Student's Books.
- Dictate the sound sentence while students write. They compare their sentences with a partner before checking in the Student's Book.
- Play the 'Big step, small step race'. Students line up in a row at one side of the classroom. Say *Students wearing T-shirts, take one big step. Girls wearing skirts, take three small steps. Boys wearing red socks, take five big steps*, etc. until a student reaches the other side of the classroom and you have a winner.

Extension activity

Aim: to give practice in writing descriptions
- Write a short description of a student. Don't give his/her name, e.g. *This student's wearing a blue T-shirt, black trousers, grey socks and white shoes.*
- Students look around the room and guess who it is.
- Students write their own description of a student in the class, without the name. Monitor and help, as appropriate.
- Volunteers read their descriptions aloud for the class to guess.

7

Whisper: Oh, no! That's my cap!

8

Whisper: I'm very sorry, Gary.
Gary: It's OK.

2 Look at the picture and tick ✓ the correct sentence.

1 Oh no! ☐
2 My coat isn't here. ☐
3 Can you get my ball? ☐
4 She's wearing my T-shirt! ☐

Phonics

3 Find who says … Stop!

4 101 Listen and say.

There are **st**ripes and **sp**ots on the socks on the **st**airs.

1 Read and write the numbers on the T-shirts.

1 May is wearing a yellow baseball cap, a blue T-shirt and white socks.

2 Hugo is wearing a red baseball cap, a blue T-shirt and white socks.

3 Lucy is wearing a yellow baseball cap, an orange T-shirt and black socks.

4 Mike is wearing a red baseball cap, a green T-shirt and purple socks.

5 Dan is wearing a white baseball cap, a green T-shirt and black socks.

6 Jen is wearing a white baseball cap, an orange T-shirt and purple socks.

Learning outcomes:
- to read for specific information
- to listen for specific information
- to describe what people are wearing

Recycled language: clothes, colours, free time activities, *He's/She's wearing …*

Flashcards: 81–90 (clothes)

Warm-up

Aim: to review clothes vocabulary

- Play a chain game. Say *My friend is wearing a pink T-shirt.* Choose a volunteer. He/She says *My friend is wearing a pink T-shirt* and adds another item of clothing and colour, e.g. *and blue jeans.* The next student repeats the two items and adds another piece of clothing, and so on.
- When there are six or seven pieces of clothing in the chain, the class say the chain together from memory. Put the clothes flashcards on the board as prompts, if necessary.

1 SB p88 Read and write the numbers on the T-shirts.

Aim: to practise reading for specific information

- Give students time to look at the picture. Ask *How many girls?* (*Three*) *How many boys?* (*Three*) *What are they doing?* (*Playing baseball*)
- Read the activity instruction and then go through the names in the sentences asking *Girl or boy?*
- Students read silently and write numbers on the T-shirts in pencil.
- They compare their answers in pairs.
- Check with the class by asking, e.g. *Who's number 1? Who's Lucy?* A volunteer points to the correct person in the picture. Ask *What's Lucy wearing?*
- In pairs, students take turns to make sentences about the picture, e.g. Student A: *She's wearing white socks.* Student B: *May.*

Key: Clockwise from top left (the boy in the blue T-shirt): 2, 3, 5, 4, 1, 6

1 30 WB p88 Listen and colour. Exam skills

Aim: to give students practice in listening for following instructions

For script see TB p124.

Key: Students colour the clothes in the picture: T-shirt (held up) – red, socks (on the floor) – orange, sweater (in the box) – yellow, shoes (on the floor) – green

2 WB p88 Read and write the numbers.

Aim: to give students practice in reading for specific information

Extra support: Before students read, revise free time activities using mime (e.g. *dance, go swimming, ride my bike, sing, play tennis, play piano, play football*).

Key: a 3, b 4

3 WB p88 Write about pictures one and two in Activity 2.

Aim: to give students writing practice

Extra support: Before students write, review the present continuous by miming and saying what you are doing, e.g. *I'm dancing. I'm swimming.* Write example sentences on the board and circle *ing*.

Key: 1 singing (a song), 2 wearing a red sweater, eating an apple

Ending the lesson

Aim: to practise memory skills

- Students look at the picture in SB Activity 1 for 30 seconds and then close their Student's Books.
- Say sentences about the picture. Students stand up (or stay standing) if they are true, and sit (or stay sitting) if they are false, e.g. *One boy is wearing a red baseball cap.* (*False*) *Two girls are wearing orange T-shirts.* (*True*)

Extension activity

Aim: to practise listening and speaking

- Call a volunteer to the front of the class and ask them to close their eyes. Describe someone in the class for the volunteer to guess, e.g. *This person is wearing black jeans and a white T-shirt. He likes football. He's got a red bag. He's sitting next to the door.*
- If the volunteer doesn't guess, start to spell the person's name aloud, with the class.
- Repeat the game with different volunteers.

Learning outcomes:
- to listen for specific information
- to use the present continuous in a game and a written description

New language: *riding, Are you (eating a hot dog)? Yes, I am, No, I'm not.*

Recycled language: clothes, free time activities, colours, animals, present continuous, *horse, bike*

Critical thinking: Formulates and verifies hypotheses

Creative thinking: Creates texts that express personal interests, emotions, or identity

Materials: Unit 7 stickers, soft ball for each group of eight students (optional)

Warm-up

Aim: to review free time activities
- Students take turns to mime free time activities. The class guess (*He's/She's …ing …*) Prompt by asking, e.g. *Is she playing baseball?*
- Write the free time activities on the board.

1 SB p89 Ask and answer.

Aim: to give students practice in interactive speaking and making choices
- Students look at the pictures carefully. Two students read the speech bubbles aloud. Explain that *riding* is from *ride* (the 'e' is removed and the 'ing' is added).
- In pairs, students ask and answer about the pictures.
- Elicit ideas, but don't confirm answers.

Extra support: Students ask and answer about the pictures in open pairs around the class until they are confident with the language.

2 102 SB p89 Listen, check and stick.

Aim: to enable students to check their answers by listening
- Students find their stickers.
- Play the recording. Students check their ideas from SB Activity 1 and put their stickers in the correct places.

For script see TB p124.

- Students compare answers in pairs.
- Play the recording again if necessary.
- Check answers by eliciting complete sentences.

Key: Tom is riding a bike. Emma is playing the piano. Kylie is eating an apple. Fred is playing football.

3 SB p89 Choose an object and play the mime game.

Aim: to give students further practice through a game
- Demonstrate the game by asking a volunteer to choose an item and mime. Guess unlikely things by asking *Are you …ing?* The student replies *No, I'm not* each time. Write the short answer on the board. The rest of the class guess using *Are you …?* When someone guesses, teach *Yes, I am* and write it on the board.
- Students play in pairs.

4 SB p89 Find a photo of your friend and write.

Aim: to give students practice with writing descriptions
- Read the description with the class.
- Students choose a friend and write a first draft in their notebooks, using the model.
- Go around the class to check their work.

Stronger students: Students write more sentences about their friend, e.g. *She's got a pet cat* or *She likes ice cream.*
- Students write a final draft of their descriptions.

1 WB p89 Look at the pictures and read the questions. Write one-word answers. Exam skills

Aim: to give students practice with reading for specific information and following instructions

Key: 1 eating, 2 kitchen, 3 games, 4 TV, 5 two, 6 sweater

Ending the lesson

Aim: to review clothes vocabulary
- Make circles of seven or eight students and give each group a soft ball (or a paper ball).
- The student holding the ball says an item of clothing, e.g. *jacket*, and throws the ball to another student who says a different item, and so on.

Extension activity

Aim: to practise listening for detail
- Read a description, similar to the one in SB Activity 4. Students listen only.
- Read the description again in short sections for students to draw and colour.

1 Ask and answer.

Is Tom riding a horse?

No, I think he's riding a bike.

Tom: ride | Emma: play | Kylie: eat | Fred: play

2 102 Listen, check and stick.

3 Choose an object and play the mime game.

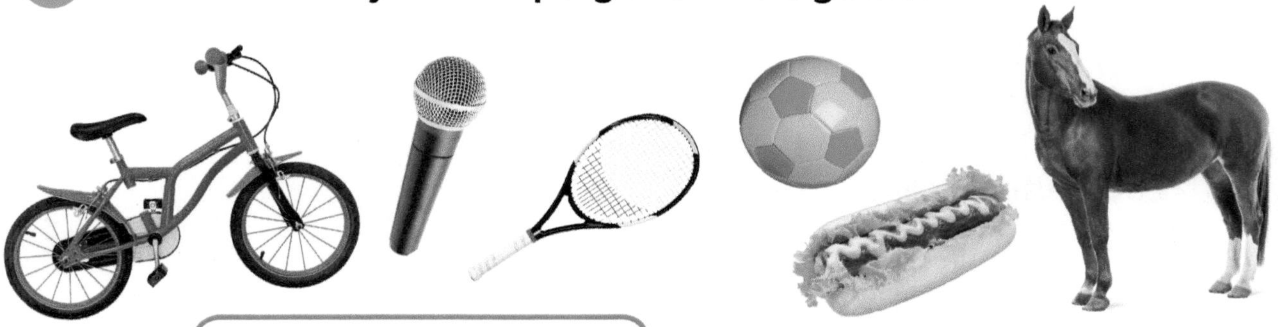

Are you eating a hot dog?

Yes, I am.

4 Find a photo of your friend and write.

This is my friend Tom.
He's wearing a blue
sweater and blue trousers.

Think and learn

Patterns

What patterns do you know?

1 103 **Listen and point.**

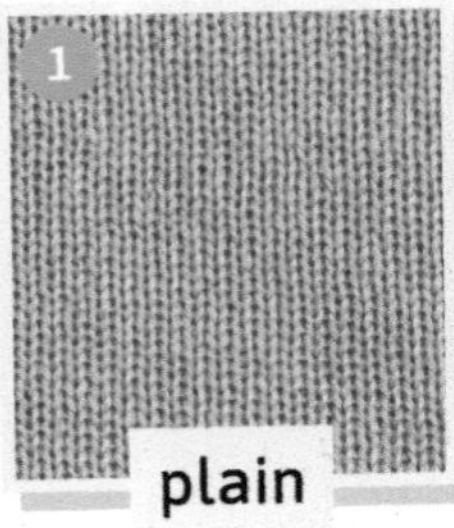
1 plain

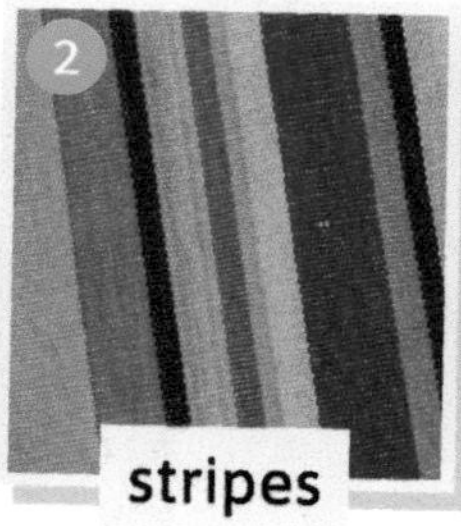
2 stripes

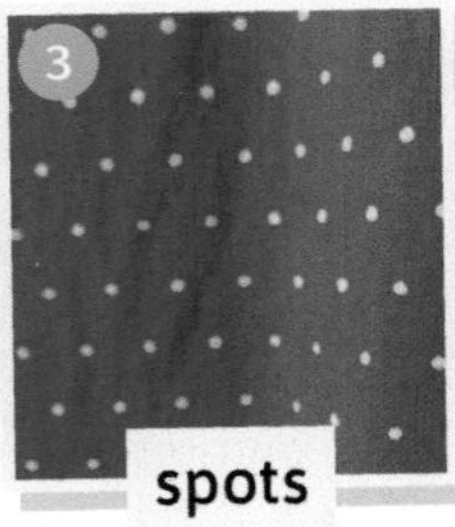
3 spots

4 zigzags

5 flowers

2 **Cover the photos in Activity 1. Ask and answer.**

What number are the spots?

They're number …

3 **Look and circle *yes* or *no*.**

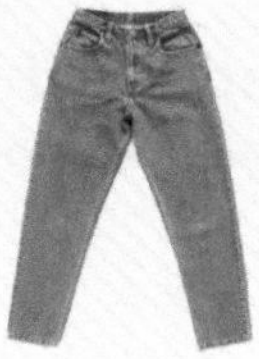

1 Has the jacket got spots? yes / no

2 Have the jeans got flowers? yes / no

3 Have the shoes got spots? yes / no

4 Has the T-shirt got zigzags? yes / no

5 Has the skirt got flowers? yes / no

Learning outcomes:
- to integrate other areas of the curriculum through English: Art and design
- to identify and describe different patterns

BIG QUESTION to explore the Big Question *How do clothes look different?*

New language: *pattern, plain, stripes, spots, zigzags, flowers, a (jacket) with (spots), (jeans) with (flowers)*

Recycled language: clothes, colours, numbers

Materials: clothes and other objects with the target patterns (optional)

Warm-up

Aim: to review clothes
- Write the Big Question *How do clothes look different?* on the board.
- Play a guessing game. Say, e.g. *I'm thinking of some clothes. They're black.*
- Students guess, e.g. *Are they your socks?*

Stronger students: Play the same game in pairs. Write the first sentence *I'm thinking of some clothes* on the board as a prompt.

SB p90 What patterns do you know?

Aim: to raise students' awareness of different patterns
- With Student's Books closed, play the video.

For videoscript see TB p124.

- Ask students what they remember. They can use L1 to tell you what the children were wearing (*school uniform*) and the different patterns they saw. Ask students if they like dressing up and what their favourite dressing up outfit is.
- Ask students to watch again and answer *What patterns do you know?* Play the video again and elicit answers in English or L1.

1 103 SB p90 Listen and point.

Aim: to present words to describe patterns
- Play the recording. Students listen and point to the different fabrics.

For script see SB p90.

- Play the recording again. Students repeat the words.

2 SB p90 Cover the photos in Activity 1. Ask and answer.

Aim: to practise words to describe patterns
- Students look at and memorise the order of the patterns. With books closed, ask different students *What number is plain? / What number are the (zigzags)?* Check that students know when to use the singular and plural forms of *be*.
- Students work in pairs. Student A closes their book. Student B looks at the book and asks, e.g. *What number are the (flowers)?* Student A replies, e.g. *They're number (five).* Students swap roles.
- Volunteers say the patterns in order from memory.

3 SB p90 Look and circle *yes* or *no*.

Aim: to practise reading and identifying clothes and patterns
- Read the first question aloud and elicit the answer. Show students how to circle the correct word.
- Students read the questions and circle *yes* or *no*. They compare answers in pairs.
- Check as a class.

Stronger students: Volunteers make sentences for the 'no' answers, e.g. *1 No, the jacket has got stripes. 2 No, the jeans are plain. 4 No, the T-shirt has got stripes.*

Key: 1 no, 2 no, 3 yes, 4 no, 5 yes

1 WB p90 Look and write.

Aim: to practise pattern words

Key: 2 flowers, 3 stripes, 4 plain, 5 zigzags

2 WB p90 Read and match.

Aim: to enable students to evidence their understanding by reading and matching

Key: 2 b, 3 f, 4 d, 5 e, 6 a

Lesson review

- Elicit what students learnt today and write it on the board, e.g. *Today I've learnt how to describe patterns*. Students copy in their notebooks.

Extension activity

Aim: to review language from the lesson
- Ask the Big Question *How do clothes look different?*
- Show students patterned and non-patterned items and ask, e.g. *Is it plain? Can you see spots or zigzags? What colour are the stripes?*
- Students point and describe patterned clothing they can see, e.g. *They're socks with black and white stripes.*

Learning outcomes:
- to extend the focus on Art and design in English
- to complete a project

New language: *What patterns can you see? What colours are they? It's a (white T-shirt) with (zigzags).*

Recycled language: clothes, colours, patterns

Creative thinking: Uses different media to make and describe his/her own designs

Cognitive control functions: Cognitive flexibility

Creative thinking (WB): Based on a model, develops new games, dishes, clothes, etc. Participates in investigative, exploratory, open-ended tasks

Materials: paper, coloured pens or pencils (or white T-shirts and fabric pens, card), pictures of decorative art from the past, e.g. plates, instruments and furniture (optional), digital or print portfolios

Warm-up

Aim: to review patterns
- Draw on the board a simple figure wearing different items of clothing, e.g. a white hat with red stripes, green trousers with black zigzags, a T-shirt with flowers and plain blue shoes.
- Ask *What clothes can you see?* Elicit words and label the picture.
- Ask *What patterns can you see?* Students say, e.g. *Flowers / A T-shirt with flowers.*
- Ask about colours in the same way.

4 SB p91 Ask and answer.

Aim: to practise talking about what clothes look like
- Practise pronunciation of the questions.
- Two volunteers demonstrate the activity.
- Then students ask and answer about the pictures in pairs.
- Students can draw their own pictures of clothing with different patterns. They ask and answer about their pictures in new pairs.

5 Project SB p91 Design a T-shirt.

Aim: to enable students to apply their knowledge in a creative task
- Read the instruction.
- Hand out paper and ask students to think about a design for their T-shirt before they begin. Say *Think about your T-shirt. What patterns can you use? What colours?*
- Students draw three or four T-shirt outlines and design the decoration. Circulate and ask *What pattern is this? What colours are these?*
- Students compare their designs in pairs and choose their favourite from their own designs.
- Hand out clean paper for students to copy and finalise their favourite design. Alternatively, students can transfer their design to a T-shirt using fabric pens. They need to put a piece of card inside to stop the design coming through to the back of the shirt.
- Students show their finished design to the class and describe it, e.g. *It's a white T-shirt with blue and yellow spots and flowers.*
- Students' presentations could be recorded (audio or video) and saved to their digital portfolios.

3 WB p91 Design some trousers. Then write.

Aim: to enable students to personalise the topic and practise writing

4 WB p91 Find out about your clothes. Complete the chart.

Aim: to enable students to personalise the topic and practise note-taking

Lesson review

- Elicit what students learnt today, e.g. *Today I've designed a T-shirt.*
- Write it on the board. Students copy it into their notebooks.

Extension activity

Aim: to think about decorative art in everyday life
- Ask students to think about other everyday items which are patterned. Make a list on the board and help with new vocabulary, e.g. *pencil cases, skateboards, curtains.*
- Encourage students to think about how this type of decoration is different from art we see in paintings or sculptures. If possible, show students pictures of decorative art from the past, e.g. plates with patterns, inlaid musical instruments, carved wooden furniture. Ask *What can you see? What patterns can you see? What colours are they?*
- Students can research decorative art from their area or a particular period in history, printing or drawing pictures and labelling the patterns and colours.

4 Ask and answer.

What patterns can you see?

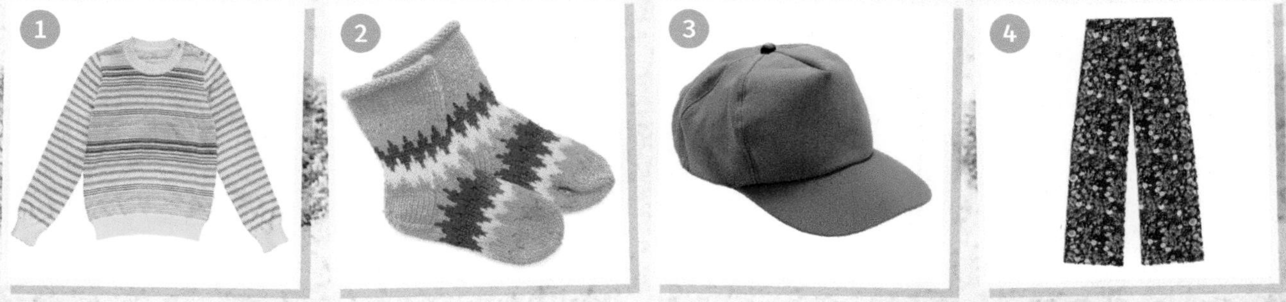

What clothes can you see?

What colours are they?

5 Project Design a T-shirt.

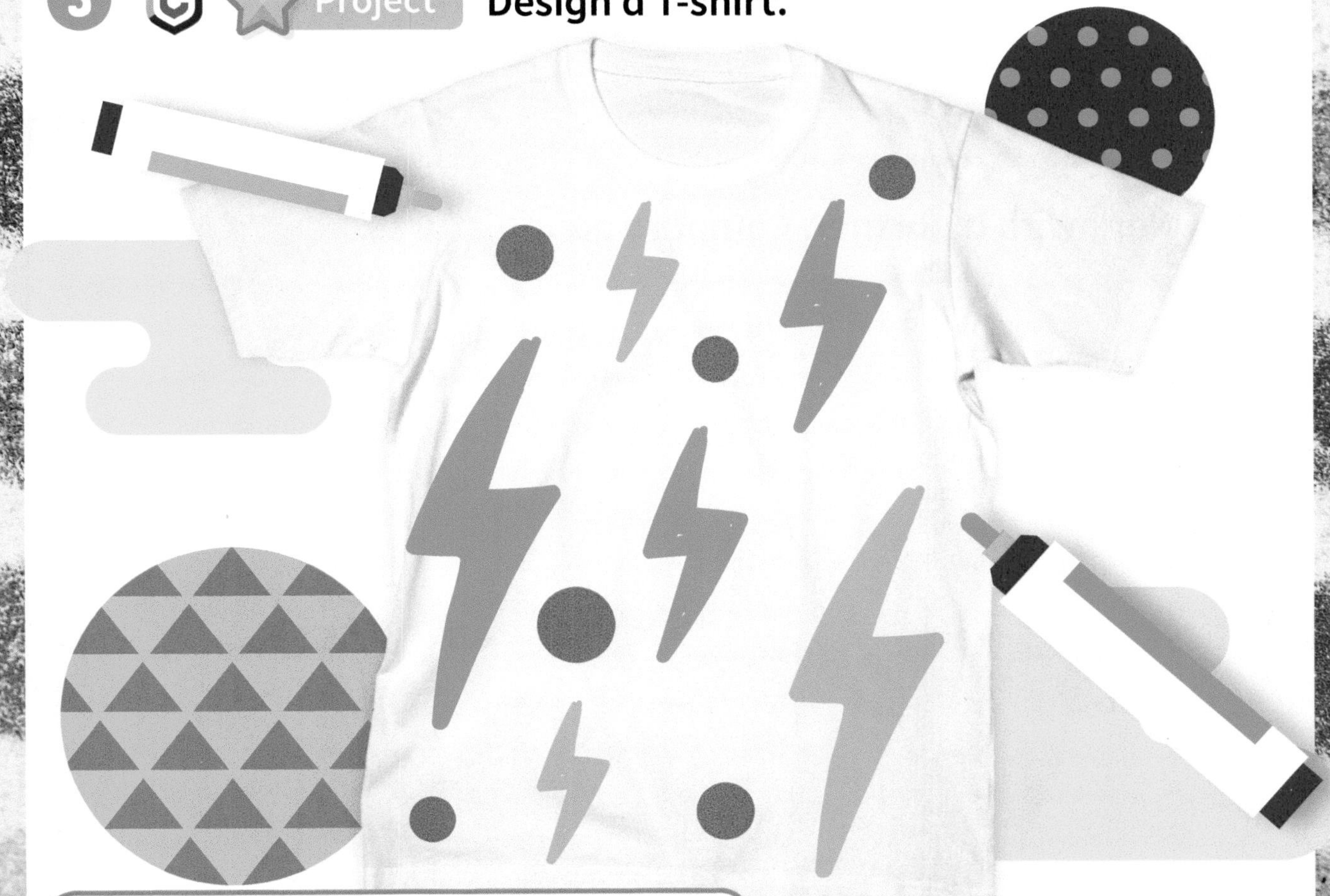

It's a white T-shirt with zigzags and spots.

Create that!

1 104 **Listen and imagine. Then draw your picture.**

2 **Work with a partner. Compare your pictures.**

She's wearing …

He's wearing …

Learning outcomes:
- to listen, imagine and draw to demonstrate meaning
- to describe what someone is wearing

Recycled language: imperatives, clothes, colours, patterns, *You are wearing, Are you wearing …? What colour are …? Are they …? Are there …? He's/She's wearing …*

Creative thinking: Chooses options to create something new

Cognitive control functions: Inhibitory control

Creative thinking (WB): Uses different media to make and describe his/her own designs

Materials: flashcards 81–90 (clothes), triumphant music (optional), coloured pens or pencils, paper (optional); For the WB making activity: coloured card and paper, stapler, coloured pens or pencils, scissors, glue

Warm-up

Aim: to review instructions
- Stick the clothes flashcards on the board in a line.
- Elicit what each item is and the colour. Ask about the pattern, if there is one. Take one away. Elicit all the clothes words, including the missing one.
- Repeat until there are no flashcards on the board.
- Put the flashcards back, one at a time, until they are all on the board again.

1 104 SB p92 Listen and imagine. Then draw your picture.

Aim: to give students practice in listening and following instructions
- Remind students how to do the activity.
- Play the recording for students to follow instructions.

For script see TB p124.

- Play the recording again before students draw, if necessary.
- Circulate as they draw, asking *What are you wearing in your picture? Are these trousers or shorts? Are they plain? What colour are your socks?*
- Praise students for using their imagination and for their originality.

2 SB p92 Work with a partner. Compare your pictures.

Aim: to practise speaking

Stronger students: Ask volunteer students to describe the two pictures in SB Activity 2, e.g. *She's wearing an orange sweater and a skirt. It's a skirt with red and blue stripes. She's wearing orange shoes. She isn't wearing socks.*

Extra support: Describe the pictures in SB Activity 2 yourself, pausing and encouraging the class to help you to complete sentences.
- Students work in pairs. They show each other their pictures and take turns to talk about them.

1 WB p92 Make a party hat.

Aim: to enable students to follow a set of instructions to make a party hat
- Read the list of items students need and show each thing in turn. Students check they have what they need on their desk.
- Work through the instructions before students begin, showing them at the front of the class how to make a hat.
- Students make their hats. Circulate and help with the stapling at stage 2.

Ending the lesson

Aim: to enable students to use their paper hats
- Play some triumphant music or the unit song.
- Students walk proudly around the room in their paper hats.
- Give instructions, e.g. *You are walking past the Queen / the King. Wave to her/him. You are running. Hold on to your hat!*

Extension activity

Aim: to enable students to further practise using the present continuous
- Give students two pieces of paper. Ask them to draw a boy and a girl on the first piece of paper, wearing different outfits. Monitor and encourage them to use different colours and patterns. Set a time limit.
- Put students into pairs with someone who hasn't seen their picture. Student A describes his/her picture (e.g. *The boy is wearing black trousers. He's wearing a T-shirt with zigzags. He's wearing blue shoes.*) while Student B draws. Then they swap.
- Students compare their pictures to see if they listened well.

Learning outcomes:
- to review language from the unit by doing a quiz
- to reflect on learning

BIG QUESTION to think about how the unit has helped them talk about the Big Question *How do clothes look different?*

Recycled language: vocabulary and grammar from the unit

Creative thinking (WB): Creates texts that express personal interests, emotions, or identity

Cognitive control functions (WB): Cognitive flexibility

Materials: flashcards 81–90 (clothes), blindfold (optional)

Warm-up

Aim: to review clothes
- Use the clothes flashcards to review the vocabulary.
- When students say the word, they point to the item of clothing if they are wearing it.
- Ask different students who are wearing the item *What colour is your (skirt)? Is it plain or has it got a pattern? / What colour are your (socks)? Have they got (stripes)?*

Stronger students: Ask two volunteers to stand at the front of the class (A and B). Student A looks at what Student B is wearing for one minute and tries to remember everything. Blindfold Student A or ask him/her to turn around so he/she can't see Student B. Ask five questions about Student B's clothes, e.g. *What colour are* (name)*'s trousers? Has* (name)*'s T-shirt got a pattern?* Student A scores a point for each correct answer.

1 SB p93 Read and circle.

Aim: to enable students to review language from the unit by doing a quiz
- Remind students that they answer by circling one option for each sentence, using the picture clues.
- Do the first item in the quiz as an example, if necessary.
- Students do the quiz in pairs. The first time, they do it without looking back through the unit.
- Pairs check their work with other pairs.
- Students then look back to check questions they did not know.
- Check answers with the class.

Key: 1 b, 2 b, 3 a, 4 b, 5 a, 6 b, 7 b, 8 a

1 WB p93 Write and circle.

Aim: to enable students to assess their own learning

2 WB p93 Draw patterns and write.

BIG QUESTION **Aim:** to enable students to revisit the Big Question and consolidate learning
- Check and ask students to give more examples of the ways that clothes look different (e.g. colour, material, style).

Key: 2 flowers, 3 plain, 4 spots, 5 zigzags

3 WB p93 Read. Then draw and write.

Aim: to enable students to personalise the topic

Picture dictionary

Aim: to review vocabulary for clothes
- Students look at the Picture dictionary page for clothes (WB p126).
- In pairs, they take turns to point to one of the pictures and say/spell the word.
- Then students write the words under the pictures.

Key: jacket, jeans, shoes, shorts, skirt, socks, sweater, jeans, T-shirt

Ending the lesson

Aim: to enable students to express their preferences
- Ask students what their favourite activity is from the unit (e.g. the song, chant or one of the games) and have a class vote.
- Repeat the most popular activity with the class.

Extension activity

Aim: to enable students to share what they have learnt
- Put students into groups of four.
- They take turns to show the picture they drew for WB Activity 3 and read their description.
- Students can copy their pictures and descriptions onto a piece of paper. The pages can be put together to make a class book, called 'Our favourite clothes'.

1 Read and circle.

1 **This is a …**

a shirt. b skirt. c sweater.

2 **These are …**

a shorts. b socks. c trousers.

3 **Do you like my baseball cap?**

a Yes, I do. b No, I don't.

4 **Do you like these trousers?**

a Yes, I do. b No, I don't.

5 **Is Olivia wearing a red skirt?**

a Yes, she is. b No, she isn't.

6 **Is Tim wearing a blue sweater?**

a Yes, he is. b No, he isn't.

7 **In the story, Whisper's cap is …**

a orange. b blue. c red.

8 **This T-shirt has got …**

a spots. b stripes. c zigzags.

8 The robot

1 105 Listen and look. Then listen and say the words.

BIG QUESTION How can we move?

2 106 **Listen and chant.**

Let's make a robot.	Here's an arm.	Here are the hands.
You and me.	Here's a leg.	Here are the toes.
Here's a foot.	Here are the fingers.	Let's make a robot.
Here's a knee.	Here's the head.	Off it goes!

Learning outcomes:
- to name and talk about parts of the body
- to say a chant

BIG QUESTION to start to think about the Big Question *How can we move?*

New language: *arm, hand, knee, fingers, leg, foot, toes, head, move, make, robot, Here's a …, Here are the …, Off it goes!*

Recycled language: *Let's …*

Cognitive control functions: Working memory

Flashcards: 91–98 (the body)

Warm-up

Aim: to activate vocabulary
- Use the flashcard of *head* to teach *robot*, or mime being a robot.
- Tell the class that this unit is about a robot.

Presentation

Aim: to present body vocabulary
- Hold up each flashcard in turn and point to the part of your body. Say the word for the class to repeat. Do this three or four times.
- Hold up each flashcard for students to say the word and point to the part of their body without your help.
- Stick the flashcards on the board to make a word map, with the title *My body* at the centre.

1 105 SB p94 Listen and look. Then listen and say the words.

Aim: to practise parts of the body
- Students look at the picture in their Student's Books. Elicit the names of the Super Friends and where they are (*in the garden*). Ask students what they think Thunder is carrying. Pre-teach *(robot) kit*.
- Play the recording. Students point to the parts of the body when they hear them.

For script see TB p125.

- Check comprehension of *Let's make a robot*.
- Play the recording again. Students repeat the words.
- Students point to parts of their body and name them in pairs.

BIG QUESTION How can we move?

Aim: to encourage students to find out about how we can move
- Read the Big Question. Students think about the different ways we can move. They can stand up and move around.
- Accept any reasonable suggestions.
- Ask students if they know any words for movements in English, e.g. *run, jump, hop, wave.*

Note: Some of the discussion will need to be in your students' first language (L1).

2 106 SB p94 Listen and chant.

Aim: to give students further practice saying parts of the body
- Play the recording. Students listen and follow the chant in their Student's Books. Check comprehension of *Here's / Here are* and *Off it goes!*

For chant script see SB p94.

- Play the recording again, pausing after each verse for students to repeat. Do the chant as a class and then in groups.
- Students do the chant again, standing up and pointing to the parts of the body when they chant them.

1 WB p94 Make parts of the body. Write the letters.

Aim: to give students practice in recognising and spelling parts of the body

Key: 2 hand, 3 arm, 4 head, 5 toes, 6 leg, 7 foot, 8 finger

2 WB p94 Look and write.

Aim: to give students practice in recognising and writing parts of the body

Key: 2 arm, 3 knee, 4 head, 5 foot, 6 hand, 7 toes, 8 fingers

Ending the lesson

Aim: to review key language from the lesson
- Students stand up. Say the parts of the body one after another. Students repeat each word and touch the relevant body part.
- Repeat the activity, faster and with the words in a different order.

Extension activity

Aim: to enable students to personalise the chant
- Students copy the chant into their notebooks, leaving space between lines.
- They draw the relevant body part of the robot next to the lines.
- They can draw the complete robot under the chant.

Learning outcomes:
- to talk about ability using *can/can't*

New language: *can/can't* for ability, *touch, skip, stand, Go on, have a try, walk, A (penguin) can/ can't (walk).*

Recycled language: the body, *Wow! swim, sing, fly, penguin, duck, fish*

Critical thinking: Uses pre-defined categories to analyse familiar concepts

Cognitive control functions: Cognitive flexibility

Materials: flashcards 91–98 (the body), Unit 8 stickers, scissors

Warm-up

Aim: to review the body
- Review parts of the body with the flashcards.
- Play 'Simon says', e.g. *Simon says 'Wave your hand.' Simon says 'Stand on one leg.' Touch your head.*

Presentation

Aim: to present *can* and *can't*
- Bend down and pretend to try to touch your toes (without reaching them). Say *I can't touch my toes.*
- Touch your head. Say *I can touch my head.*
- Prompt students to do the actions (some will be able to touch their toes). Elicit *I can* ... or *I can't* ...
- Check students say the weak form of *can* in the positive sentence.

1 107 SB p95 Look and listen. What can Misty do?

Aim: to practise *can* and *can't* for ability
- Pre-teach *skip.*
- Students look at the picture and read the speech bubbles.
- Play the recording. Students listen for the answer.

For script see TB p125.

- Play the recording again. Check with the class.
- Say each sentence for students to repeat. Ask students to demonstrate the actions.

Key: Misty can touch her toes, skip and stand on one leg.

2 SB p95 Read and stick. Help the Super Friends see Misty.

Aim: to give students practice reading the new language
- Students find their stickers and cut them out together with the backing paper.
- Students read and place the stickers in the correct shapes. They compare in pairs.
- Check with the class. Students stick in the stickers.

3 108 SB p95 Watch, listen and say.

Aim: to focus students on grammatical form
- Play the *Penny the penguin* video. Students watch and listen, then watch and read. Check understanding of the grammar and *Go on* and *have a try*.
- Play the audio. Students follow in their Student's Book. They join in and mime each activity.

For script see SB p95.

- Students practise the sentences in pairs.

4 SB p95 Tick ✓ or cross ✗ and say.

Aim: to give students further practice with the new language
- Elicit the names of the animals in the pictures. Pre-teach *walk.*
- Read the speech bubbles and check comprehension.
- Copy the table on the board and complete the row about penguins with students' help.
- In pairs, students make sentences and complete the table.
- Check answers and complete the table on the board.

Stronger students: Students write the sentences in their notebooks after the class check.

Key: a penguin: swim ✓ fly ✗ walk ✓; a fish: swim ✓ fly ✗ walk ✗; a duck: swim ✓ fly ✓ walk ✓

1 WB p95 Read and write the numbers.

Aim: to give students further practice reading the new language

Key: 2 d, 3 f, 4 a, 5 c, 6 e

2 WB p95 What can Penny do? Write *can* or *can't*.

Aim: to give students practice writing the new language

Key: 2 can, 3 can, 4 can, 5 can't

Ending the lesson

Aim: to review new language from the lesson
- In small groups, students tell each other which actions they can and can't do.
- Take them to a large space so they can demonstrate.

Extension activity

Aim: to give students further practice with the new language
- Students write about their friends. Provide a model, e.g. (Name) *can skip, swim and sing. He can't stand on one leg. He can't touch his toes.*

1 107 Look and listen. What can Misty do?

I can't touch my toes.
I can't skip.
I can't stand on one leg.

2 Read and stick. Help the Super Friends see Misty.

I can touch my toes.

I can skip.

I can stand on one leg.

3 108 Watch, listen and say.

Language focus

I **can** stand on one leg.
Go on – have a try.
I **can** skip.

I **can** swim.
I **can** sing.
But I **can't** fly.

4 Tick ✓ or cross ✗ and say.

A penguin can swim.

A penguin can't fly.

	swim	fly	walk
a penguin			
a fish			
a duck			

1 🎧 109 ▶ **Listen and sing. Then look and draw lines.**

I can take my foot
And put it on my head. ●
I can take my arm
And put it on my leg. ●

I can put my tongue out
And I can touch my nose. ●
I can take my right hand
And touch all of my toes. ●

I can cross my fingers
And I can cross my knees. ●
But now I'm stuck. Oh dear!
Can you help me, please? ●

2 🛡 **Read, think and say. How are you the same as the boy in the song? What can you do?**

I can take my arm and put it on my leg.

Learning outcomes:
- to sing a song
- to practise *can/can't* for ability

New language: *take my (foot), put it on (my head), put my tongue out, nose, right (hand), all (of my toes), cross my (fingers), I'm stuck, Can you help me?*

Recycled language: the body, *I can …, Oh dear!*

Critical thinking: Responds to songs, rhymes and poems in a variety of ways.

Creative thinking (WB): Creates texts that express personal interests, emotions, or identity

Cognitive control functions (WB): Working memory

Materials: coloured pens or pencils

Warm-up

Aim: to review parts of the body and *can*
- Make sentences with *I can*, e.g. *I can wave my hands.* Students who can do this repeat the sentence and do the action. Possible sentences: *I can touch my toes. I can jump. I can stand on one foot. I can swim.*

1 109 110 SB p96 Listen and sing. Then look and draw lines.

Aim: to sing a song with the class
- Use gesture to teach *touch my nose, put my tongue out, cross my fingers* and *cross my knees.* Write the phrases on the board. Students say them and do the actions in pairs.

Note: If it is considered rude for your students to show their tongue, use the picture to teach the word.
- Students look at the pictures to find *put my tongue out, cross my fingers* and *cross my knees*.
- Play the audio (109). Students follow the song in their Student's Books.

For song lyrics see SB p96.

- Teach *I'm stuck* and *right hand.*
- Read the second part of the instructions and show students that each dot in the lyrics relates to two lines.
- Play the audio again for students to read and match. They compare their answers in pairs. Check answers.
- Play the song video, pausing after each verse for students to repeat.
- When students have learnt the song, use the karaoke version of the audio (110) or video to practise the song with the whole class and then in groups.

Key: d, e, b, f, c, a

2 SB p96 Read, think and say. How are you the same as the boy in the song? What can you do?

Aim: to give students practice with the new language
- In pairs, students tell each other which of the things in the song they can do.
- Ask different students to say what they can do and demonstrate to the class.

Extra support: Say *I can* sentences using actions from the song. Students raise their hands if they can do the action and demonstrate as a group.

1 31 WB p96 Can you remember? Listen and write.

Aim: to give further practice with reading and listening

For song lyrics see SB p96.

Key: 1 foot, 2 arm, 3 hand, 4 toes, 5 fingers, 6 knees

2 WB p96 What can you do? Draw and write.

Aim: to personalise the new language

Ending the lesson

Aim: to review key language from the lesson
- Do one of the actions from the song, but say a false sentence, e.g. cross your fingers, but say *I can cross my knees*. Students say *No!* and correct the sentence.
- Repeat with different actions. Students can play the game in pairs.

Extension activity

Aim: to encourage students' creativity
- Students work in pairs or small groups and write a new verse for the song about things they can do.
- Monitor and help with new language. Students share their ideas with the class.

Learning outcomes:
- to use *can* to talk about abilities

New language: question forms and short answers using *can*: *Can you/he/she swim? Yes, I/he/she can, No, I/he/she can't, cook*

Recycled language: free time activities, action verbs

Warm-up

Aim: to review free time activities and introduce *Can you …?*
- Write *Free time* in the middle of the board.
- Brainstorm free time activities to create a word map. Review *play football, play tennis, play the piano, ride my bike, ride my pony, run, swim, dance* and *sing*.
- Ask *Can you (play football)?* for each activity. Students put their hands up if they can do it.

1 111 SB p97 Look and say. Then listen and tick ✓ or cross ☒.

Aim: to practise comprehension of *Can you …?*
- Students look at the first picture. A student reads out the example.
- In pairs, students say what is in the other pictures.
- Students look at the table. Explain that they tick the square if the person pictured on the left can do the activity, or put a cross if he/she can't.
- Play the recording. Students listen and tick or cross.

For script see TB p125.

- Students compare answers. Play the recording again.
- Check with the class. Elicit full sentences, e.g. *Sophie can't play tennis. She can play the piano.*

Key: 2 play the piano, 3 ride a horse, 4 ride a bike, 5 swim, 6 dance
Sophie: 1 play tennis ☒ 2 play the piano ✓ 3 ride a horse ✓ 4 ride a bike ✓ 5 swim ✓ 6 dance ☒;
Tom: 1 play tennis ☒ 2 play the piano ☒ 3 ride a horse ☒ 4 ride a bike ✓ 5 swim ✓ 6 dance ✓

2 ▶ 112 SB p97 Watch, listen and say.

Aim: to focus students on grammatical form
- Play the *Penny the penguin* video. Students watch and listen, then watch and read. Check understanding of *cook* and *draw*.
- Play the audio. Students follow in their Student's Book. They join in and mime each activity.

For script see SB p97.

- Students practise the sentences in pairs.

3 SB p97 Ask and answer.

Aim: to give students practice asking questions
- Practise the question and short answers *Yes, I can* and *No, I can't* in open pairs. Then put students in pairs to practise.
- Student A thinks of a free time activity and asks, e.g. *Can you play the piano?*
- Student B mimes the activity and answers.

1 WB p97 Look, write and tick ✓.

Aim: to give students practice writing the new language

Key: 2 Can she, Yes, she can. 3 Can he, Yes, he can. 4 Can she, No, she can't.

2 WB p97 Look and write the answer for you.

Aim: to give students further practice with the new language

Ending the lesson

Aim: to review pronunciation of *can* and *can't*
- Ask students to write numbers *1* to *6* in their notebooks.
- Say six statements using *can* or *can't*, e.g. *1 Jill can't swim.* Students write a tick next to the number if the sentence is positive and a cross if it is negative.
- Check with the class.

Extension activity

Aim: to encourage students to practise the new language
- Students sit in a circle, with you at the centre. They ask you as many questions as they can with *Can you …?*
- When they have finished asking you questions, see if they can remember all your answers by making sentences, e.g. *You can cook. You can't play tennis.*

1 (111) Look and say. Then listen and tick ☑ or cross ☒.

Number 1 is play tennis.

play the piano swim ride a horse
ride a bike play tennis dance

Sophie

Tom

Sophie						
Tom						

2 (112) Watch, listen and say.

Language focus

Can you cook?
Yes, I **can**.
Can you draw?
No, I **can't**.

Can you fly?
No, I **can't**.
No, I **can't**.
But I **can** dance!

3 Ask and answer.

The problem

1 113 When does Thunder touch his head?

1

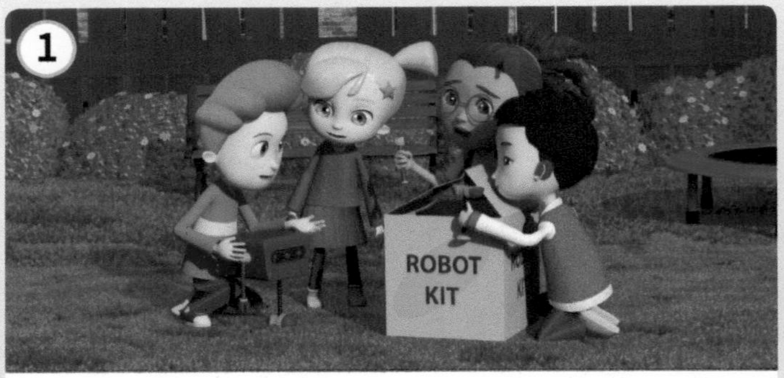

Thunder: Give me the right leg and the left arm.
Whisper: Here's the right leg.
Flash: Here's the left arm.

2

Thunder: And now the head, please.
Whisper: Here's the head.

3

Thunder: Batteries! We haven't got batteries.
Flash: No problem.

4

Flash: Here you are.
Thunder: Thank you.

5

Thunder: Robot, can you speak?
Robot: nac I sey.

6

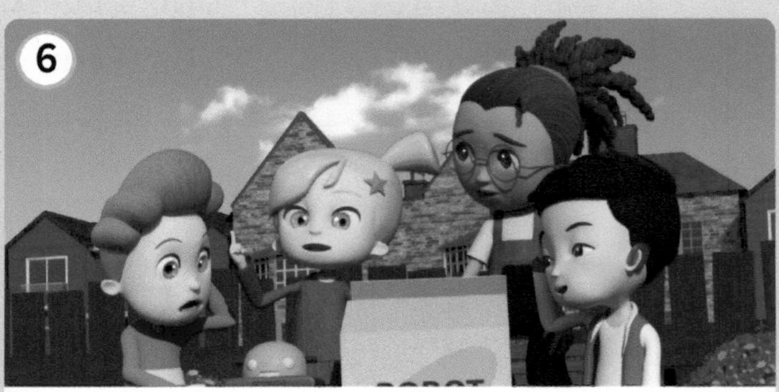

Whisper: We've got a problem.
Thunder: It can't speak.
Misty: Let me try something.

Learning outcomes:
- to listen to, read, watch and act out a picture story
- to review language from the unit

New language: *Give (me), left (leg), batteries, speak, It can't (speak), try, something, What are you doing? Well done*

Recycled language: parts of the body, *right (leg), Here's …, No problem, Here you are, Thank you, Can you …?*

Value: teamwork

Critical thinking (WB): Identifies characters, setting, plots and theme in a story

Materials: some boxes (optional)

Warm-up

Aim: to review the story
- Elicit what happened in the last episode of the story (in L1: Whisper thought another boy, Gary, had taken his cap).
- Write lines from the story on the board and ask who said them, e.g. *My cap isn't here.* (*Whisper*) *Stop! That's my cap!* (*Whisper*) *No, it's my cap.* (*Gary*) *No problem.* (*Bird*) *Oh, no! That's my cap!* (*Whisper*)
- Ask *Who said sorry?* (*Whisper*)

The problem

1 113 SB pp98–99 When does Thunder touch his head?

Aim: to present a picture story
- Elicit where the Super Friends are in picture 1 (*In the garden*). Ask *What have they got?* (*The robot kit from the beginning of the unit*) and which parts of the robot's body they can see.
- Play the audio. Students listen and read to find out when Thunder touches his head (picture 6).

For script see SB pp98–99.

- Explain the meaning of *batteries*. Ask which toys need batteries.
- Play the whole *Super Friends* video. Then play the video again, pausing to check comprehension. Ask *Who has got the robot's leg?* (*Whisper*) Make sure students know what *left* and *right* mean. Ask *Who says 'No problem'?* (*Flash*) and ask why (*Because she's going to fetch batteries very quickly*). Teach *speak* and ask *Can the robot speak?* (*Yes, it can*) See if any students know what the robot says (the words are backwards). Explain *Let me try something* and clarify that Misty solves the problem by turning the robot's head around and then it can speak. Explain *Well done* at the end.
- Talk with the class about the value (teamwork) and where each person helps (pictures 1, 2, 3, 4 and 7) and what they do.

1 32 WB p98 Who says it? Listen and tick ☑.

Aim: to review the story

For script see TB p125.

Key: 1 Flash (1st picture), 2 Flash (1st picture), 3 Robot (2nd picture)

2 WB p98 Write the words.

Aim: to check understanding of the story

Key: 3 Here, 6 try, 8 done

3 WB p98 Look at the pictures in Activity 2. Write the numbers.

Aim: to review short dialogues

Key: b 1, c 5, d 4

Ending the lesson

Aim: to practise the story
- Put students in groups of five. They take a role of a character or the robot.
- Play the recording. Students repeat in role.
- Students practise the role play in groups. They can use a box. Encourage the 'robot' to move and talk like a robot.
- Volunteer groups role play for the class.

Extension activity

Aim: to stimulate students' creativity
- Students each choose one of the short dialogues from WB Activity 3. They make up a role play with their short dialogue.
- Help with vocabulary. They can change words, e.g. *Food! We haven't got food!*
- Students perform their dialogues for the class.

Learning outcomes:
- to interpret deeper meaning from a story
- to identify the sound /g/ as in *green* and *bag*
- to review language from the story and the unit

Recycled language: language from the story, *big, green, bag*

Phonics focus: Your students will be able to identify and say the sound /g/ at the beginning, in the middle and at the end of words.

Value: teamwork

Critical thinking: Solves simple puzzles (e.g. word puzzles)

Critical thinking (WB): Identifies characters, setting, plots and theme in a story

Warm-up

Aim: to review the story
- Write phrases from the story on the board (e.g. *Here's the right leg. We haven't got batteries. No problem. We've got a problem. It can't speak. Let me try something. Robot, can you speak now? Yes, I can.*) Say them for students to repeat.
- Elicit who says each phrase and recap the story.

2 SB p99 What does the robot say?

Aim: to check comprehension of the story
- In pairs, students work out what the words say.
- Check with the class.
- Elicit what the robot said in picture 5 of the story (*Yes, I can backwards*).

Key: book, arms, foot, bike, swim

3 SB p99 Find who says …

Aim: to present the sound /g/ at the beginning and end of a word
- Write *give* and *leg* on the board, using a red pen for the *g*. Make the hard /g/ sound and explain that in English we can use this sound at the beginning, in the middle and at the end of words.
  Note: If students ask, explain that the letters *igh* in *right* make a long vowel sound /ai/ as in *eye*.
- Students repeat *Give me the right leg* after you and find the sentence in the story (picture 1).

Key: Thunder

4 114 SB p99 Listen and say.

Aim: to practise the sound /g/ at the beginning, in the middle and at the end of words
- Students look at the cartoon picture. Elicit what they can see (*a big green bag*). Ask *Where are his fingers?* (*In the bag*)
- Play the recording. Students look at the picture, read and repeat.

For script see TB p125.

- Repeat the sentence as a class without the recording. Say it loudly, slowly, quickly, whisper it, etc.
- Students take turns to repeat in pairs.

1 WB p99 Which picture shows good teamwork? Tick ☑.

Aim: to focus students on the value of teamwork

Key: Picture 1

2 33 WB p99 Write and match. Listen and say.

Aim: to practise reading, writing and saying words containing the sound /g/

For script see WB p99 and Key.

Key: 2 b frog, 3 e computer game, 4 a garden, 5 f fingers, 6 c leg, 7 d dog

Ending the lesson

Aim: to review and write words containing the sound /g/
- Students close their Student's Books.
- Dictate the sound sentence while students write. They compare before checking in the Student's Book.
- Make flashcards of words with the hard consonant sound /g/. Show them for students to read, e.g. *good, bag, big, great, green, grey, go, get, got, game, give, frog, dog, leg, fingers, ugly.*

Extension activity

Aim: to discuss the value of teamwork
- Elicit examples of teamwork in class. Ask why it is important and how students can improve their teamwork.
  Note: This discussion will probably need to take place in L1.

Whisper: What are you doing?
Misty: Robot, can you speak now?
Robot: Yes, I can.

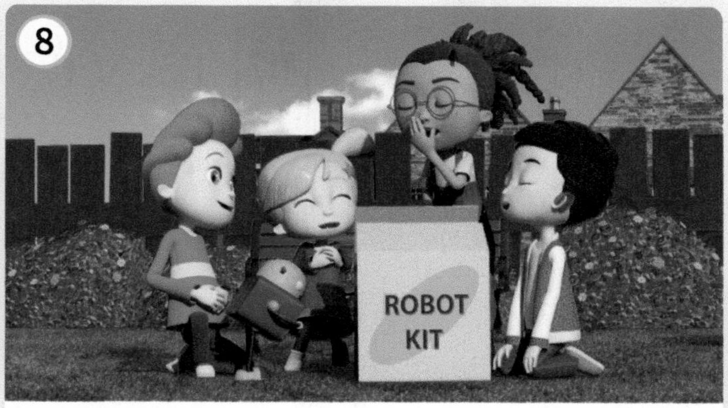

Robot: Thank you, Misty.
Thunder: Well done, Misty.

2 **What does the robot say?**

koob

smra

ekib

toof

miws

Phonics

3 **Find who says …** Give me the right leg.

4 114 **Listen and say.**

Greg's got his fingers in a big green bag.

Skills

1 (115) Listen and tick ✓ the correct picture.

1 Can Patch swim?

a 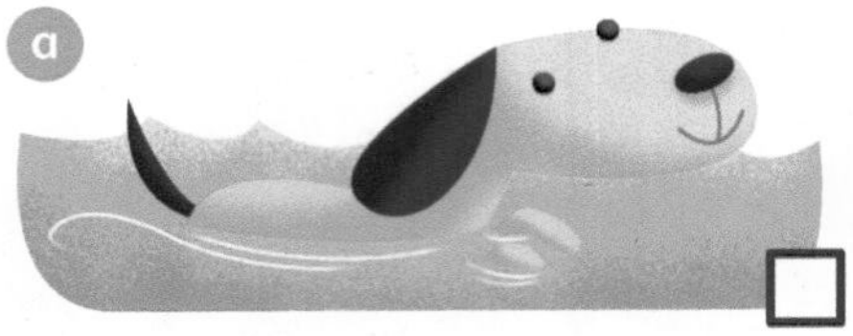

b 

2 Can Sue ride a bike?

a 

b 

3 Can Coco stand on one leg?

a 

b 

2 Play the find someone game.

Can you ...		**Name**
	play chess?	
	fly a kite?	
	ride a horse?	
	play the piano?	

Learning outcomes:
- to listen for specific information
- to read for specific information
- to exchange information

New language: *play chess, fly a kite*

Recycled language: actions (*swim, ride a bike, stand on one leg, ride a horse, play the piano*)

Critical thinking (WB): Uses tables, charts, mind maps etc. to evaluate ideas or options Draws conclusions from given information

Warm-up

Aim: to review actions
- Ask *What can I do?* and mime an action from the unit (e.g. *cook*).
- Students take turns to guess.
- The student who guesses correctly comes to the front and mimes another action. Prompt by writing or whispering an action for the student, if necessary (e.g. *dance, draw, play the piano, swim, play tennis, skip*).

1 115 SB p100 Listen and tick ✓ the correct picture.

Aim: to practise listening for specific information
- Read the activity instruction and check students know what to do. Read the questions, point to the pictures and ask *What's the dog's name?* (Patch) *What's her name?* (Sue) *What's his name?* (Coco)
- Play the recording. Students tick the pictures in pencil.

For script see TB p125.

- Students compare their answers in pairs. Play the recording again if necessary.
- Check with the class using open pairs.

Key: 1 b, 2 a, 3 b

2 SB p100 Play the find someone game.

Aim: to give students practice with interactive speaking
- Use the pictures to review *ride a horse* and *play the piano*. Teach *play chess* and *fly a kite*.
- Demonstrate the activity and make sure students know what to do.
- They can do the survey either in small groups or as a mingling activity around the class. They ask different students, e.g. *Can you play chess?* and when someone answers *Yes, I can* they write their name in the second column of the table.
- Elicit what individual students found out, asking, e.g. *Who can play chess?*

1 WB p100 Read and tick ✓ or cross ✗.

Aim: to give students practice reading for specific information and transferring information

Key:

Ben: ✓ ✗ ✓ ✓ ✗ ✓ ✗

Anna: ✗ ✓ ✓ ✗ ✓ ✓ ✓

Tom: ✓ ✓ ✗ ✓ ✓ ✓ ✗

2 WB p100 Look at Activity 1. Write.

Aim: to give students practice in writing and transferring information

Key: 3 No, I can't. 4 Yes, I can. 5 Yes, I can. 6 No, I can't.

Ending the lesson

Aim: to practise interpreting tabular information
- Draw a simple table on the board, similar to the one in WB Activity 1, but with five activities and different names. Complete the table with ticks and crosses.
- Ask students questions about the table, e.g. *Can Stacey skip?*
- Students take turns to ask and answer questions about the table in open pairs.

Extension activity

Aim: to practise writing skills
- Students write sentences using the information they found out in SB Activity 2.
- Write a model on the board, e.g. (Name), (name) *and* (name) *can play the piano, but* (name) *can't play the piano. I can play the piano.*
- Go around the class and help as necessary.

Learning outcomes:
- to read for specific information
- to write a description from a model

New language: *What am I? climb (trees), well, shark, bee, bear*

Recycled language: actions, the body, numbers, colours, *can* for ability, *spots, web, spider, penguin*

Creative thinking: Creates content for peers to use in class activities

Materials: flashcards 91–98 (the body), coloured pens or pencils, blank card for each student (optional)

Warm-up

Aim: to review the body
- Show each flashcard quickly. Students say the word together.
- Tell students to pretend to be robots. Give them instructions to follow, e.g. *Robots! Stand on one leg. Wave your left hand. Touch your head. Cross your fingers.* Encourage them to move like robots in response.
- Students repeat the same activity in pairs, taking turns to give instructions.

1 SB p101 Read and match. Say the animal.

Aim: to give students practice in reading for specific information (scanning)
- Students look at the pictures carefully. Pre-teach *Who am I?, climb trees* and *well.*
- Students do the matching task individually and then compare ideas in pairs.
- Check with the class.
- Ask four students to read the short texts aloud and teach any new words.

Key: a 3, b 1, c 4, d 2

2 SB p101 Draw and write about an animal.

Aim: to enable students to write a description from a model
- Check students know what to do and read through the model. Encourage students to refer to the texts in SB Activity 1, too.
- Students write a rough draft in their notebooks first. Go around the class to help with language and new vocabulary.
- When you have checked their work, students write a final draft on a piece of card and draw a picture of the animal on the other side.
- Collect in the cards and hand them out around the class, picture side down.
- Students read the card they have and guess the animal, before turning it over to check the picture. They turn the card over and pass it to someone else in the class.
- Continue in this way so students read as many cards as possible.

1 34 WB p101 Read the questions. Listen and write a name or a number. Exam skills

Aim: to practise listening for specific information

For script see TB p125.

Key: 2 six/6, 3 Bruno, 4 three/3, 5 Spotty

Ending the lesson

Aim: to practise memory skills
- Students look at WB Activity 1 for 30 seconds and then close their Workbooks.
- Say sentences about the picture. Students stand up (or stay standing) if they are true, and they sit (or stay sitting) if they are false.

Extension activity

Aim: to play a guessing game
- Put students into groups of four or five. Each group chooses an animal (not on SB p101) without telling the rest of the class what it is. They write a short description of it in four or five sentences, as if they were the animal, e.g. *We've got four legs. We're big. We're yellow with brown spots. We can walk and run. We can't fly.*
- Monitor and check all the sentences.
- Groups take turns to stand up and say their sentences (each student says a sentence). The rest of the class guess the animal. Students might need to use L1, but write the answers in English on the board.

1 Read and match. Say the animal.

a I've got eight legs. I'm black with red spots. I can make webs. What am I?

b I haven't got arms or legs. I can't walk or run but I can swim. What am I?

c I've got four legs. I'm big and brown. I can climb trees. What am I?

d I've got six legs and I can fly. I can't walk well. What am I?

2 Draw and write about an animal.

My animal project

I've got two legs.
I'm black and white
and I can't fly.
What am I?

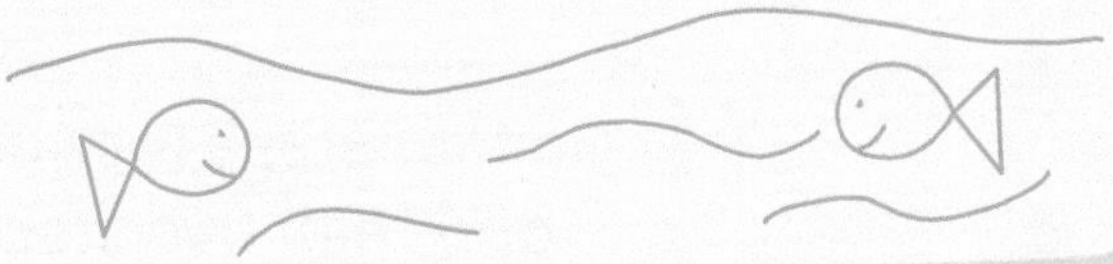

Think and learn

Movements

How do you move?

1 116 Listen and point.

2 117 Listen and do the movements.

3 Look and say.

go forwards ↑ go backwards ↓
go sideways to the left ← go sideways to the right → steps

1	↑	4	steps	and then	→	5	steps
2	↓	3	steps	and then	←	2	steps
3	↑	1	steps	and then	↓	1	steps
4	←	2	steps	and then	↑	6	steps

Go four steps forwards and then five steps sideways to your right.

Learning outcomes:

- to integrate other areas of the curriculum through English: Physical education
- to talk about moving in different directions

BIG QUESTION to explore the Big Question *How can we move?*

New language: *movements, (go) forwards, backwards, sideways, step* (n), *jump, to the left/right, then*

Recycled language: actions, parts of the body

Critical thinking (WB): Solves simple puzzles (e.g. word puzzles)

Flashcards: 91–98 (the body)

Warm-up

Aim: to review parts of the body

- Take a flashcard without showing the class what it is. Say *I'm thinking of a body part. What is it?*
- Students guess, e.g. *Is it a hand?*
- The student who guesses correctly chooses the next flashcard for the class to guess.

SB p102 How do you move?

Aim: to raise students' awareness of directions of movement

- Write *movement* on the board and elicit what it means. Tell students they're going to watch a video about the different ways we move. Elicit examples of movements students already know in English (e.g. *walk, run, climb*). Pre-teach *step* and *babies*.
- With Student's Books closed, play the video.

For videoscript see TB p125.

- Ask what students remember.
- Students watch again and answer *How do you move?* Ask them to look out for words to describe movement. Elicit ideas, e.g. *walk, jump, dance, do sport, swim*. They may also mention yoga and gymnastics. Ask what animals they saw and how they move (e.g. *monkey – climbing, kangaroo – jumping, bird – flying*).

1 116 SB p102 Listen and point.

Aim: to present ways of moving

- Play the recording. Students listen and point. Demonstrate each movement at the same time.

For script see SB p102.

- Play the recording again. Students stand up, say the words and move.

2 117 SB p102 Listen and do the movements.

Aim: to practise the new language

- Give some instructions using the directions from Activity 1, showing students which way to move, e.g. *Go one step forwards. Go two steps sideways. Jump!* Continue until students get the idea and are able to follow directions without your help.
- Play the recording. Students listen and move according to the directions.

For script see TB p126.

3 SB p102 Look and say.

Aim: to practise the new language and interpret symbols, using a key

- Check students understand the key. Read the example speech bubble and help them work out the second instruction.
- In pairs, students read the symbols. Elicit instructions for each row of symbols.

Extra support: Say one of the instructions. Students point to the correct row of symbols. Say the instructions again. Students repeat, following the symbols in their books.

Key: 2 Go three steps backwards and then two steps sideways to your left. 3 Go one step forwards and then one step backwards. 4 Go two steps sideways to your left and then six steps forwards.

1 WB p102 Look and write.

Aim: to practise writing the new language

Key: 2 jump, 3 backwards, 4 forwards, 5 sideways, 6 stretch

2 WB p102 Read and draw lines. Write.

Aim: to practise reading the new language and following written instructions

Key: rectangle

Lesson review

- Elicit what students learnt today and write it on the board, e.g. *Today I've learnt about different ways of moving.* Students copy in their notebooks.

Extension activity

Aim: to personalise language from the lesson

- In pairs, students write their own instructions with two stages, using the same symbols as SB Activity 3.
- Pairs swap instructions and do the actions.

Learning outcomes:
- to extend the focus on Physical education through English
- to complete a project

New language: *stretch (your arms), stretches*

Recycled language: the body

Creative thinking: Interprets characters in games, drama and dance

Creative thinking: Creates and shares new content

Cognitive control functions: Cognitive flexibility

Critical thinking (WB): Demonstrates understanding of links between new ideas

Creative thinking (WB): Chooses options to create something new

Materials: A4 paper (one piece for each pair), coloured pens or pencils, musical instruments for each pair of students (if available), instrumental music with a strong beat for dancing (optional), digital or print portfolios

Warm-up

Aim: to review ways of moving
- Give instructions for students to follow, e.g. *Go three steps forwards. Go three steps sideways to the left. Jump. Go three steps sideways to the right. Go three steps backwards. Jump.*

4 SB p103 Read and write the numbers.

Aim: to extend vocabulary for describing movement, and review the body
- Teach *stretch* by demonstrating. Give students instructions, e.g. *Stretch your legs. Stretch your fingers.*
- Students read the sentences and match them with the pictures by numbering.

Key: 1 She stretches her arms forwards. 2 She stretches her legs. 3 She jumps. 4 She stretches backwards.

5 Project SB p103 Make a dance. Show your friends.

Aim: to enable students to creatively engage with what they have learnt about movement
- Read the instructions and ask some volunteers to do the dance in the example.
- Give each pair or group of students a piece of A4 paper and ask them to divide it into four sections.
- Each pair/group chooses movements for the four parts of their own dance, draws a picture and writes a text for each part of their dance. Tell students they can draw stick pictures like the ones in the SB.
- Pairs or groups do their dances for the class (students take turns to describe the movements while the others dance). Play a recording of instrumental music, if available.
- The dances could be filmed and saved to students' digital portfolios.

Stronger students: Groups chant or rap their dances to a beat, as they do the movements. Give them time to rehearse before they perform it for the class.

Extra support: The teacher reads out the instructions for a dance, while the class do the movements.
- If time, have a class vote for the best dance and then all do that dance together. Students can also perform their dances for other students at school.

3 WB p103 Read and write the numbers.

Aim: to give practice reading and interpreting instructions

Key: b 1, c 2, d 3, e 6, f 5

4 WB p103 What can you do? Make sentences, and tick ✓.

Aim: to enable students to personalise the new language

Lesson review

- Write on the board: *Today I've …*
- Elicit what students did today, e.g. *made a dance.*
- Write it on the board. Students copy it into their notebooks.

Extension activity

Aim: to give further practice with language for instructions
- Play 'Simon says' with instructions from the last two lessons.

4 Read and write the numbers.

1 
2 
3 
4 

☐ She stretches her legs.

☐ She jumps.

☐ She stretches backwards.

☐ She stretches her arms forwards.

5 Project Make a dance. Show your friends.

Stretch your arms.

Stretch your legs.

Go sideways.

Jump.

Do that!

1 118 **Listen and act out with your teacher. Then listen again and number the pictures.**

2 **Read the sentences from the story and draw lines.**

a Bounce your ball. — b The ball is in a tree.

c Throw your ball in the sky. — d Where is the ball?

e You've got a big ball. — f Oh dear!

3 **Work in groups.**

a Make new sentences.

You've got a small plane.
Throw ... in the sky.
... is ...

b Listen to a friend and act out.

You've got a small plane.

Throw your plane in the sky.

Your plane is in the water.

Learning outcomes:
- to practise the language through listening and responding physically
- to practise giving instructions

New language: *bounce, (in the) sky*

Recycled language: instructions, toys, *ball, big, throw, tree, You've got, in (the tree), Where is the (ball)? Oh dear! plane, water*

Creative thinking: Participates in investigative, exploratory, open-ended tasks

Creative thinking (WB): Uses different media to make and describe his/her own designs

Materials: flashcards 25–34 (toys), soft balls (optional), cardboard, scissors, coloured pens or pencils

Warm-up

Aim: to review toys

- Revise toys using the flashcards or mime.
- Give out soft balls or tell students to imagine they are holding balls. Teach *bounce* by demonstrating (*Bounce the ball!*) Students repeat and do the action (either with a real ball or miming). Repeat with *throw*.
- Students stand in a circle with a soft ball. Give instructions, e.g. *Throw the ball to* (name). *Bounce the ball! Hold the ball in your left hand.*

1 118 SB p104 Listen and act out with your teacher. Then listen again and number the pictures.

Aim: to practise listening and following instructions

- Students look at the pictures and say what they can see, e.g. *a tree, a big ball*. Teach *sky*.
- Remind students that the pictures are not in the correct order, but they make a short story.
- Say *Listen and act out.* Play the recording. Mime each action and encourage students to copy.

For script see TB p126.

- Play the recording again and repeat.
- Say *Now listen and number.* Remind students what to do. Ask them to guess which is the first picture before they listen.
- Play the recording again for students to check their answers. Then elicit answers.

Key: 5, 2, 4, 1, 3, 6

2 SB p104 Read the sentences from the story and draw lines.

Aim: to give students practice in reading

- Look at the example and make sure students remember that they have to link the dots in the correct order.
- Students read and draw lines between the dots individually.
- Check answers by eliciting the story in the correct order.

Key: e, a, c, d, b, f

3 SB p104 Work in groups.

Aim: to give students practice in creating and giving instructions

- Students work in groups to make their own sequence of sentences, by adding their own words, as shown in the model. Monitor and help as necessary. Make sure each student in the group writes the sentences.
- Put students in pairs to work with someone from a different group. They take turns to read out their sentences. The one who is listening mimes the story.
- Volunteer pairs show one or both of their 'stories'.

1 WB p104 Make a robot mask.

Aim: to enable students to follow a set of instructions to make a robot mask

- Students work in pairs. Make sure students have all the items they need, saying, e.g. *Show me the scissors.*
- Read the instructions step by step. Help with the cutting out stage (2).

Ending the lesson

Aim: to review language from the lesson

- Give incomplete instructions from the lesson, e.g. *Bounce your …* Students say the word (e.g. *ball!*) and do the action.

Extension activity

Aim: to enable students to share ideas

- Students make up a name for their robot from WB Activity 1 and decide what it can and can't do.
- Students put their robot masks on. Say actions, e.g. *Swim*. Students mime swimming if their robot can do it, or stay still if not.

Learning outcomes:
- to review language from Units 7 and 8
- to collaborate and reflect on learning

BIG QUESTION to think about how the unit has helped them talk about the Big Question *How can we move?*

Recycled language: vocabulary and grammar from Units 7 and 8

Creative thinking: Substitutes words and phrases to create new texts

Cognitive control functions: Working memory

Creative thinking (WB): Creates texts that express personal interests, emotions, or identity

Cognitive control functions (WB): Cognitive flexibility

Materials: poster paper, magazines or the Internet, scissors, coloured pens or pencils, glue

Warm-up

Aim: to review the body
- Write the parts of the body on the board with the letters jumbled.
- In pairs, students write each word correctly.
- Check answers with the class.

1 SB p105 How many words can you remember? Draw pictures.

Aim: to review vocabulary and spelling
- Write the headings *Clothes* and *The body* on the board.
- Students copy the category headings in their notebooks and draw more items in each group, with a space below each picture. Elicit ideas and encourage students to share their pictures in small groups.

2 SB p105 Write and say the words.

Aim: to review vocabulary for clothes and the body
- Students write labels below the pictures they drew for Activity 1. Monitor and check spelling.
- In pairs, students take turns to point to one of their pictures and say the word.

3 119 SB p105 Listen and number.

Aim: to practise listening and revise unit language
- Students look at the picture. Explain that the speech bubbles are in the wrong order. Read the instructions.
- Play the recording for students to listen only.

For script see TB p126.

- Play it again, pausing so they can write numbers. Check answers. Teach *over there*.
- Play the recording again for students to listen and repeat. They can practise the dialogue in pairs, swapping roles.

Key: 5, 3, 1, 4, 2

4 SB p105 Write a new dialogue. Act it out.

Aim: to review grammar and practise writing
- Students make a new dialogue by completing the gaps, e.g. *Can you see Clara? No, I can't. Which girl is she? She's over there. Is she wearing a green skirt? Yes, she is.*

1 WB p105 Write and circle.

Aim: to enable students to assess their own learning

2 WB p105 Write the movement words.

BIG QUESTION Aim: to enable students to revisit the Big Question and consolidate learning
- Check and ask students to give more examples of ways we move (e.g. *run, stretch, jump, throw, walk, climb, swim, skip*). Encourage them to look through the unit.

Key: 2 backwards, 3 sideways, 4 jump, 5 step

3 WB p105 Read. Then draw and write.

Aim: to enable students to personalise the topic

Picture dictionary

Aim: to review vocabulary for the body
- Students complete the Picture dictionary pages for the body (WB p127).

Key: fingers, foot, hand, head, knee, leg, toes

Ending the lesson

Aim: to enable students to express their preferences
- Have a class vote and repeat the most popular activity.

Extension activity

Aim: to enable students to share what they have learnt
- In groups, students share their texts and pictures from WB Activity 3.

Group check units 7 and 8

1 How many words can you remember? Draw pictures.

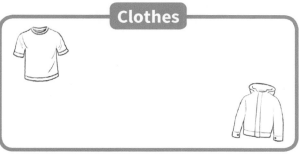

Clothes

The body

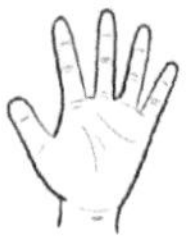

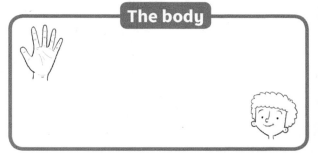

2 Write and say the words.

3 119 Listen and number.

Yes, he is. ☐

He's over there. ☐

Can you see Luke? ☐

Is he wearing blue jeans? ☐

No, I can't. Which boy is he? ☐

4 Write a new dialogue. Act it out.

Can you see ________________________________?

No, I can't. Which ________________________________?

________________________________ over there.

Is ________________________________?

Yes, ________________________________ is.

9 At the beach

1 120 **Listen and look. Then listen and say the words.**

BIG QUESTION Where can we go on holiday?

2 121 **Listen and chant.**

Eat ice cream,
Yum, yum.
Take a photo,
Click, click.
Catch a fish,
Splash, splish.

Make a sandcastle,
Dig, dig.
Look for shells,
Look, look.
Play in the sun.
It's lots of fun!

Learning outcomes:
- to name and talk about holiday and leisure activities
- to say a chant

BIG QUESTION to start to think about the Big Question *How can we go on holiday?*

New language: *at the beach, paint a picture, listen to music, catch a fish, take a photo, eat ice cream, play the guitar, read a book, make a sandcastle, look for shells, Where can we go on holiday? click, splash, dig, (in the) sun*

Recycled language: activities, *lots of, fun*

Cognitive control functions: Working memory

Cognitive control functions (WB): Cognitive flexibility

Flashcards: 99–107 (holidays)

Warm-up

Aim: to activate vocabulary
- Write *Holidays* on the board and elicit/explain what it means.
- Elicit words to do with holidays: action verbs, adjectives and nouns. Write them around *Holidays* to create a word map.

Presentation

Aim: to present holiday vocabulary
- Hold up each flashcard in turn. Say the words for students to repeat in chorus.
- Do this three or four times.
- Hold up each flashcard for students to say the words in chorus.
- Add the flashcards to the word map on the board.

1 120 SB p106 **Listen and look. Then listen and say the words.**

Aim: to practise holiday and leisure vocabulary
- Students look at the picture in their Student's Books. Elicit who they can see and where they are (teach *at the beach*).
- Play the recording. Students point to the different activities when they hear the phrases.

Stronger students: Ask what Flash says (*We can have a race.*)

For script see TB p126.

- Play the recording again. Students repeat the words.
- Students practise pointing to the holiday activities and naming them in pairs.

BIG QUESTION Where can we go on holiday?

Aim: to encourage students to find out about where we can go on holiday
- Read the Big Question and check comprehension.
- In pairs, students think about as many different types of holiday as they can, e.g. beach, camping in a forest, skiing in the mountains, staying on a canal boat.
  Note: Some of the discussion will need to be in your students' first language (L1).

2 121 SB p106 **Listen and chant.**

Aim: to give students further practice saying holiday vocabulary
- Students look at the chant.
- Play the recording. Students listen and follow in their Student's Books.

For chant script see SB p106.

- Check comprehension of *play in the sun, it's lots of fun, dig, yum, click* and *splash*.
- Play the recording again, pausing after each verse for students to repeat. Do the chant as a class and then in groups.
- Students help you invent actions for the activities in the chant. Students do the chant again, including the actions.

1 WB p106 **Write the words.**

Aim: to give students practice in recognising and spelling holiday activities

Key: 2 photo, 3 fish, 4 picture, 5 music, 6 ice cream, 7 book, 8 sandcastle, 9 guitar

2 WB p106 **Read. Then write and draw.**

Aim: to enable students to personalise the language

Ending the lesson

Aim: to review key language from the lesson
- Mime a holiday activity, e.g. *making a sandcastle*. Students say the activity.

Stronger students: Students use the present continuous to guess (*Are you making a sandcastle?*)
- Students take turns to mime for the rest of the class to guess.

Extension activity

Aim: to enable students to personalise the holiday activities
- Say, e.g. *On holiday I like eating ice cream. I don't like looking for shells.*
- Write the example sentences on the board and underline the *-ing* forms.
- In groups of four, students take turns to say what they like and don't like doing on holiday.

Learning outcomes:
- to make suggestions and respond using *Let's*
- to review holiday activities

New language: *Let's (listen to music), Good idea, I'm not sure, Sorry, I don't want to.*

Recycled language: holiday activities, free time activities

Flashcards: 99–107 (holidays)

Warm-up

Aim: to review holiday and free time activities
- Make two teams. A student from each team sits at the front of the class with his/her back to the board.
- Write a holiday activity on the board. The teams mime this activity for their representative at the front to guess. The students at the front can't look at the board and the teams can't say the words on the board.
- Whichever student at the front guesses first gets a point for his/her team.
- Two more students come and sit at the front (one from each team).
- Continue with different activities.

Presentation

Aim: to present *Let's ...*
- Students look at SB p74 and the first frame of the story. Misty says *Let's go in*. Use this example to elicit/teach the meaning and use of *Let's ...*
- Make sure students notice that it is followed by a simple verb, e.g. *go/paint*.
- Suggest activities using *Let's*, e.g. *Let's play tennis*. Students do the correct mime with you.

Stronger students: Volunteers suggest different activities for the class to mime.

1 122 SB p107 Listen and number the pictures. Then write.

Aim: to present and practise *Let's* for suggestions
- Students look at the pictures in the Student's Book and read the sentences.
- Tell students to number the pictures. Play the recording. Students listen for the correct order and write numbers in the boxes in pencil.

For script see TB p126.

- Students compare answers in pairs. Then they write the missing words in the sentences from the box at the top of the activity.
- Play the recording again. Check with the class.
- Say each suggestion and response for students to repeat. Check understanding.

Key: 3 listen, 1 paint, 4 look, 2 take

2 123 SB p107 Watch, listen and say.

Aim: to focus students on grammatical form
- Play the *Penny the penguin* video. Students watch and listen, then watch and read. Check understanding of the grammar.
- Play the audio again. Students follow in their Student's Book and join in.

For script see SB p107.

- Students practise the sentences in pairs.

3 SB p107 Look and act out.

Aim: to give students further practice with the new language
- Demonstrate the activity for the class and then give practice in open pairs.
- Students take turns to act out and respond in closed pairs, e.g. Student A: *Let's play football.* Student B: *Sorry, I don't want to.*

1 WB p107 Write the words.

Aim: to give students practice writing the new language

Key: 2 catch, 3 take, 4 read, 5 look, 6 make

2 WB p107 Look and match with Activity 1. Write the numbers.

Aim: to give students further practice with the meaning of the new language

Key: b 5, c 3, d 6, e 1, f 2

Ending the lesson

Aim: to review new language from the lesson
- Make some suggestions, e.g. *Let's say a chant. Let's read a story.*
- Elicit responses and do the most popular activity with the class.

Extension activity

Aim: to give students further practice with the new language
- Students draw a simple two-column table. They write two holiday activities in the left column.
- Students do a mingling activity, making suggestions from their table, e.g. *Let's play the guitar.*
- They write the names of the classmates who respond *Good idea* in the right column.

1 🎧 122 Listen and number the pictures. Then write.

paint take look listen

2 ▶ 🎧 123 Watch, listen and say.

Language focus

Let's eat ice cream.
I'm not sure.
Let's listen to music.
Sorry, I don't want to.

Let's play the guitar.
Good idea.
Let's listen to music
and **play** the guitar.

3 Look and act out.

Let's …

Good idea.

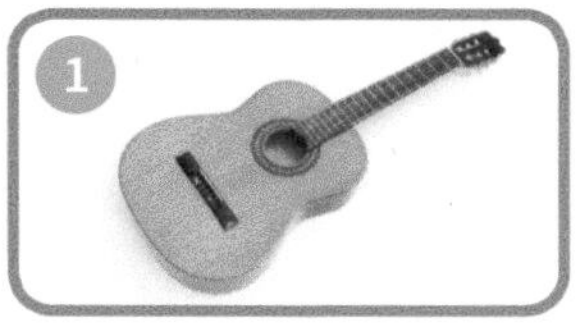

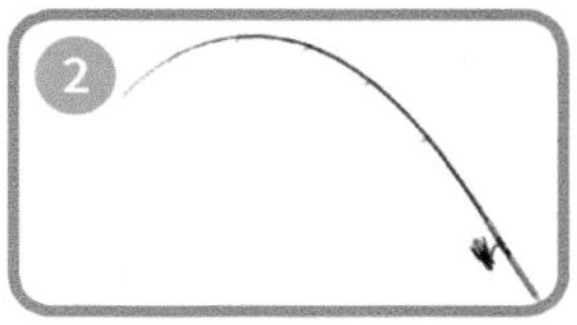

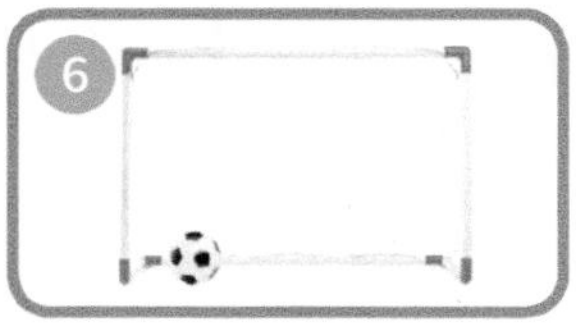

1 🎧 124 ▶ Listen and sing. Then number the pictures.

Let's go to the mountains
And climb a tree.
Let's take some photos,
You and me.

The holidays, the holidays,
The holidays are near.
The holidays, the holidays,
The end of the year!

Let's go to the beach
And swim in the sea.
Let's catch a fish,
You and me.

The holidays, the holidays …

No! Let's stay at home
And watch TV.
Let's play and talk,
Just you and me.

The holidays, the holidays …

2 Plan a perfect holiday.

Let's go to the mountains.

No, let's stay at home. It's too cold.

Learning outcomes:
- to sing a song
- to practise *Let's* for suggestions and responses

New language: *near, the end of the year, mountains, stay at home, just you and me*

Recycled language: holiday activities, *holidays, climb a tree, watch TV, talk, play a board game, Let's (go to the …)*

Critical thinking: Makes a choice of activity

Creative thinking (WB): Substitutes words and lines to a song or poem

Cognitive control functions (WB): Working memory

Flashcards: 99–107 (holidays)

Warm-up

Aim: to review *Let's* and holiday activities
- Draw a beach on the board. Say *We're on holiday at the beach. Hooray! What shall we do? Let's …*
- Volunteers suggest activities. Elicit complete sentences, e.g. *Let's make a sandcastle.* Say *Good idea!* (Students repeat.) Draw something to represent the activity in your picture (e.g. a bucket and spade). Then ask *What shall we do?*
- Build up a picture on the board. Use the holiday flashcards as prompts.
- When the picture is complete, point to the items you have drawn and elicit the suggestions (e.g. point to the bucket and spade – students say *Let's make a sandcastle!*)

1 124 ▶ 125 SB p108 **Listen and sing. Then number the pictures.**

Aim: to sing a song with the class and practise reading
- Elicit the activities in the pictures. Use picture c to teach *mountain* and picture d to teach *stay at home*.
- Play the audio (124). Students follow the song in their Student's Books. Explain the meaning of *the holidays are near, the end of the year* and *just you and me*.

For song lyrics see SB p108.

- Read the second part of the instructions. Play the audio again for students to read the song lyrics and number the pictures according to the activities in the song.
- Students compare answers in pairs before the class check.
- Play the song video, pausing after each verse for students to repeat.
- When students have learnt the song, use the karaoke version of the audio (125) or video to practise the song with the whole class and then in groups.

Key: a 3 (go to the beach and swim in the sea), b 6 (play and talk), c 2 (take some photos), d 5 (stay at home and watch TV), e 1 (go to the mountains and climb a tree), f 4 (catch a fish)

2 SB p108 **Plan a perfect holiday.**

Aim: to personalise the new language
- In pairs, students practise making suggestions for a perfect holiday, using the speech bubbles as models.

Extra support: Stick the holiday flashcards on the board, with the phrases written below, for students to refer to.

Stronger students: Students make up exchanges with different responses, e.g. *Good idea* or *Sorry, I don't want to.*

1 35 WB p108 **Can you remember? Listen and write.**

Aim: to practise listening for specific information

For song lyrics see SB p108.

Key: 2 take some photos, 3 swim in the sea, 4 catch a fish, 5 watch TV, 6 play and talk

2 WB p108 **Write two more sentences for the song. Draw pictures.**

Aim: to encourage creativity and personalisation

Ending the lesson

Aim: to review key language from the lesson
- Sing the song again, adding the new verses from WB Activity 2.

Extension activity

Aim: to focus students on spelling
- Write the following words in jumbled letter order on the board: *sandcastle, shells, fish, music, book, photo, picture, ice cream, guitar.*
- Students work in pairs to unjumble them and to add the correct verbs.

Learning outcomes:
- to use *Where's …?* and *Where are …?* to talk about where things are

New language: *Where's …? Where are …? It's, They're … It isn't …, They aren't …, sunglasses, rocks, toy box*

Recycled language: *in, on, box, bag, hat*, holiday items and toys, colours

Critical thinking (WB): Compares different types of information

Materials: soft toy animal or animal flashcard (optional)

Warm-up

Aim: to review prepositions (*in, on, under*)
- Hide a soft toy animal or animal flashcard before the lesson (inside something).
- Say *There's an animal in the classroom. Where is it? Stand up and look!* Students walk around looking. Give clues using prepositions, e.g. *It's not under the chair. It's not on my desk.* Students ask, e.g. *Is it in the bin?*
- When a student finds the animal, he/she says, e.g. *It's in your bag!*

1 126 SB p109 Listen and read. Tick ✓ the correct picture.

Aim: to present *Where's / Where are the …? It's/They're …*
- Play the recording. Students listen and read.

For script see TB p126.

- In pairs, students choose the correct picture to match the questions and answers.
- Check, using open pairs.

Key: 1 a, 2 d

2 127 SB p109 Watch, listen and say.

Aim: to focus students on grammatical form
- Use the picture to teach *sunglasses.*
- Play the *Penny the penguin* video. Students watch and listen, then watch and read. Point out that to say 'no' we use *it isn't* or *they aren't*. Explain that the apostrophe represents the 'o' (*not*). Teach *rocks*.
- Play the audio. Students follow in their Student's Book and join in.

For script see SB p109.

- Students practise the sentences in pairs.

3 SB p109 Play the question game.

Aim: to give students practice asking and answering questions and playing a game
- Give students time to look at the pictures. Ask them questions with *Where's* and *Where are*, e.g. *Where's the red book?* (*It's in the orange bag.*) *Where are the green books?* (*They're in the pink bag.*)
- Tell students that they are going to play a memory game.
- Give them one minute to study the pictures.
- Student A then closes their book. Student B asks questions about the pictures using *Where's / Where are …?* Student A responds *It's / They're in the* (colour) *bag.* Monitor and check use of singular/plural forms. You can make the game competitive (students score a point for each correct answer).
- Repeat the game, swapping roles.

1 WB p109 Write the words.

Aim: to give students practice writing the new language

Key: 2 They're, 3 Where's, 4 It's

2 WB p109 Look and match.

Aim: to give students further practice with the new language

Key: 2 h, 3 b, 4 c, 5 g, 6 f, 7 a, 8 d

Ending the lesson

Aim: to review the new language
- Students take out classroom objects and take turns to place them in/on things on their desks and to ask each other questions, e.g. *Where's the blue pencil? It's on your book.*

Extension activity

Aim: to give further practice with the language
- Choose a picture from the Student's Book.
- Each student writes a *Where is/are …?* question about the picture and the answer on a strip of paper. Collect the strips of paper.
- Make four teams.
- Choose a question at random and ask one team. If they answer correctly, they get a point.
- Repeat for all the teams. The team with the most points wins.

1 (126) Listen and read. Tick ✓ the correct picture.

1 Where's the shell?

2 Where are the kites?

2 (127) Watch, listen and say.

Language focus

Where **are** my sunglasses?	Where**'s** my hat?
They aren't in my bag.	**It isn't** in my bag.
They aren't in the box.	**It isn't** in the box.
They aren't on the rocks.	**It isn't** on the rocks.
They're on my head!	**It's** on my head!

3 Play the question game.

Where's … ?

It's …

The top of the hill

1 128 What has Thunder got in picture 7?

Whisper and Misty: A race?
Flash: Yes! Let's go.

Flash: Bye. See you at the top of the hill!

Whisper: A race is not a good idea.
Misty: I can walk up the hill, but I can't run!
Thunder: Just wait and see.

Flash: What's that? … Oh, no!

Flash: This is the end of the race. We can't get to the top of the hill.

Thunder: Let me try.
Flash: Thanks, Thunder.

Learning outcomes:
- to listen to, read, watch and act out a picture story
- to review language from the unit

New language: *see you, (to the) top, hill, up (the hill), Just wait and see, end, get, Let me try, together, more, bye, race* (v), *What a good idea!*

Recycled language: character names, action verbs, *race* (n), *fun, Let's go, good idea, rock, thanks, can/can't*

Value: modesty

Critical thinking (WB): Identifies characters, setting, plots and theme in a story

Warm-up

Aim: to review the characters, *can* and the story
- Ask students what the special powers of the Super Friends are (e.g. *What can Thunder do? Who can run very fast? Can Flash talk to animals?*) Use mime to help show the meaning of the questions.
- Elicit what happened in the last episode (the friends used teamwork to put the robot kit together).

The top of the hill

1 128 SB p110–111 What has Thunder got in picture 7?

Aim: to present a picture story
- Use the first picture to teach *hill* and explain the meaning of the story title (*The top of the hill*).
- Give students time to look at the pictures and guess what the story is about.
- Ask *What has Thunder got in picture 7?*
- Play the audio. Students listen, look and read.

For script see SB pp110–111.

- Play the whole *Super Friends* video. Then play the video again, pausing to check comprehension. Ask *Do all the Super Friends want to race?* (*They are not sure – only Flash really wants to*). Check comprehension of *See you at the top of the hill!* and ask why Flash says it (*She is sure she'll win the race*). Ask *Who can't run?* (*Misty*), *What can she do?* (*She can walk*), and *What's the problem?* (*There's a big rock*). Explain the meaning of *This is the end of the race* and *Let me try*. Ask what Thunder says when he lifts the rock (*Now you can race to the top, Flash!*) Make sure students realise that the characters all decide to go to the top of the hill together. Check comprehension of *together*.
- Talk with the class about the value (modesty). Ask who is modest in the story (*Flash*) and when she shows modesty (*pictures 7 and 8, when she doesn't race to the top of the hill*).

Key: Thunder has got a rock.

1 36 WB p110 Who says it? Listen and tick ✓.

Aim: to review the story

For script see TB p126.

Key: 1 Flash (2nd picture), 2 Whisper (1st picture), 3 Flash (2nd picture)

2 WB p110 Write the words.

Aim: to check understanding of the story

Key: 2 top, hill, 3 end

3 WB p110 Look and write the numbers.

Aim: to review short dialogues

Key: a 3, b 1, c 2

Ending the lesson

Aim: to practise the story
- In groups of four, students each take a role of one of the characters.
- Play the recording. Students repeat in role.
- Groups practise the role play.
- Volunteer groups role play for the class.

Extension activity

Aim: to stimulate students' creativity
- In pairs, students choose one of the first two dialogues from WB Activity 3. They make up a short role play and include their short dialogue at the end.
- Pairs perform their new role plays for the class.

Learning outcomes:
- to interpret deeper meaning from a story
- to practise saying the long vowel sound /iː/, as in *see*
- to review language from the story and the unit

New language: *super, really (I really like …)*

Recycled language: language from the story, *happy, eat, ice cream, tree, beach*

Phonics focus: Your students will be able to say the sound /iː/ spelt *ee* or *ea*.

Value: modesty

Critical thinking: Interprets implicit meanings of characters in a story

Critical thinking (WB): Demonstrates understanding of links between new ideas

Warm-up

Aim: to review the story
- Write *See you at the top of the _____! I can walk up the hill, but I can't _____. This is the end of the _____. _____ me try. Let's go _____. What a _____ idea!* on the board and elicit the complete sentences (missing words: *hill, run, race, Let, together, good*).
- Use these sentences and mime to retell the story.

2 SB p111 Read, think and write the names.

Aim: to check comprehension of the story
- Tell students that the phrases in Activity 2 are not exact words from the story. Read each phrase and explain the meaning.
- In pairs, students look at the story and try to work out who would say something similar (they infer what the characters are thinking from their actions and attitudes).
- Check with the class.

Key: 1 Flash, 2 Whisper, 3 Thunder, 4 Flash

3 SB p111 Find who says …

Aim: to present the long vowel sound /iː/
- Write *see* on the board using a red pen for the letters *ee*. Show students how to smile to make the long /iː/ sound.
- Students repeat *Just wait and see* after you.
- Students find the sentence in the story (picture 3).

Key: Thunder

4 129 SB p111 Listen and say.

Aim: to practise and identify the sound /iː/ spelt *ee* or *ea*
- Play the recording. Students look at the picture, read and repeat. Point out that the letters *ee* in *tree* and *ea* in *beach* represent the same sound.

For script see TB p126.

- Repeat the sentence as a class without the recording.
- Students take turns to repeat in pairs.

1 WB p111 Who shows modesty? Look and tick ✓ the correct picture.

Aim: to focus students on the value of modesty

Key: Picture 2

2 37 WB p111 Write *ee* or *ea* and match. Listen and say.

Aim: to practise reading, writing and saying words with the sound /iː/

For script see TB p126.

Key: 3 three a, 4 cheese h, 5 eat g, 6 beach b, 7 peas d, 8 ice cream f

Ending the lesson

Aim: to discuss the value of modesty
- Elicit why modesty is important and examples of when the students or people they know have been modest.
  Note: This discussion will probably need to take place in L1.

Extension activity

Aim: to review and write words with the sound /iː/ spelt with *ee* or *ea*
- Elicit examples of more words which students know with the sound /iː/, e.g. *green, week, knee, free, please, jeans, speak, team, sea, me, he, she, we.*

7

Thunder: Now you can race to the top, Flash!
Flash: No. Let's go together. That's more fun!

8

Misty: What a good idea!
Whisper: Yes!

2 Read, think and write the names.

1 I'm super! ______________
2 A race? I'm not happy about that. ______________
3 Flash can't see it. ______________
4 I really like my friends. ______________

Phonics

3 Find who says …

Just wait and see.

4 129 Listen and say.

Jean eats an ice cream under a tree on the beach.

Skills

1 130 **Listen and stick.**

2 **Look at Activity 1 again. Make sentences.**

The ice cream is …

Learning outcomes:
- to listen for specific information
- to speak about a picture

New language: *sand*

Recycled language: holiday activities, instructions, prepositions (*in, on, under*), *boat, ball, hat, kite*

Materials: flashcards 99–107 (holidays), Unit 9 stickers, scissors

Warm-up

Aim: to review holiday activities
- Stick the holiday flashcards around the walls of the classroom.
- Make a sentence with *Let's* and one of the activities, e.g. *Let's paint a picture*. Students move to the correct flashcard as quickly as they can. (Alternatively, they mime the action.)
- Students take turns to come to the front and lead the activity by making a different sentence, e.g. *Let's look for shells.*

1 130 SB p112 Listen and stick.

Aim: to give students practice in listening for specific information and following instructions
- Students look at the picture. Review vocabulary by asking questions, e.g. *Where are they? Where's the kite? Who's taking a photo? Point to the sandcastle.*
- Students find their stickers and cut them out together with the backing paper.
- Elicit the items (*ice cream, shell, ball, boat, hat*). Teach *sand*.

Extra support: Practise prepositions *in, on, under* and get students to place the stickers in different places by giving instructions (e.g. *Put the hat under the kite.*)
- Play the recording. Students listen, look and place the stickers without sticking them.

For script see TB p126.

- Students compare answers in pairs. Play the recording again.
- Check with the class before students stick.

Key: boat on the sea, ice cream in the boy's hand, ball on the sand, hat on the sandcastle, shell under the kite

2 SB p112 Look at Activity 1 again. Make sentences.

Aim: to give students practice in productive speaking
- In pairs, students look at their pictures and say where the stickers are, e.g. *The ball is on the sand.*

Stronger students: Students make extra sentences, e.g. *He's flying a kite. She's taking a photo.*

Key: The boat is on the sea. The ice cream is in his / the boy's hand. The ball is on the sand. The hat is on the sandcastle. The shell is under the kite.

1 WB p112 Read. Choose a word from the box. Write the correct word next to numbers 1–6. Exam skills

Aim: to give students practice in reading and completing a text

Key: 2 sea, 3 sandcastle, 4 hat, 5 ice cream, 6 guitar

Ending the lesson

Aim: to practise memory skills
- Students look at the picture in SB Activity 1 for 30 seconds and then close their books.
- Say sentences about the picture. Students stand up if they are true and sit if they are false.

Suggested sentences: *There are five birds in the sky.* (*False*) *The boy and girl are wearing blue T-shirts.* (*True*) *The camera is red.* (*False*) *The woman has got a kite.* (*False*) *The kite is red and yellow.* (*True*) *The woman is wearing a skirt.* (*False*) *The birds are white.* (*True*) *The woman isn't wearing shoes.* (*True*)

Stronger students: Ask students to correct the false sentences.

Extension activity

Aim: to enable students to express their ideas
- Students close their eyes. Say *It's a beautiful day! You are at the beach. What can you see?*
- Give students thinking/ visualisation time and then elicit their ideas.

Stronger students: Ask students to write two or three sentences about what they can see.

Learning outcomes:
- to read for specific information
- to listen for specific information
- to write a persuasive text from a model

New language: *country, come (to), the USA, national park, South Africa, go on a safari, lion, hippo, giraffe, Mexico*

Recycled language: holiday activities, *beautiful, old, lake, sleep, tent, under the stars, penguin, great*

Creative thinking: Based on a model, develops new games, dishes, clothes, etc.

Critical thinking (WB): Solves simple puzzles (e.g. word puzzles)

Materials: world map (optional), soft ball per group of eight students (optional)

Warm-up

Aim: to review landscape features

- Teach *country*. Give examples. Say *Let's draw a country. What is there? What can you see? I can see … mountains.* Draw some mountains in the background. Elicit more features and draw as students suggest them, e.g. hills, a lake, a beach, the sea, trees, houses, birds, horses. Ask, e.g. *Are they big hills or small hills? Are the houses old or new?*
- When the picture is finished, students describe it (e.g. *There's a big lake.*)

1 SB p113 Read and write the country.

Aim: to practise reading for specific information

- Check students know what to do. Students read silently and identify the countries in the photos.
- Students compare their ideas in pairs. They re-read the texts.
- Check with the class. Teach any unknown words and explain that we use *the* before *USA* (United States of America) because the country is made up of a group of states. Show where the countries are on a world map.

Key: a South Africa, b the USA

2 131 SB p113 Listen and tick ✓ the country.

Aim: to give students practice with listening for specific information and key words

- Read the activity instruction and explain that students have to think about what they read in Activity 1 while they listen.
- Play the recording. Students compare their answers in pairs.

For script see TB p126.

- Play the recording again.
- Check answers with the class. Elicit how they know.

Key:

	1	2	3	4	5
USA		✓			✓
South Africa	✓		✓	✓	

3 SB p113 Make a poster about your country.

Aim: to give students practice in writing from a model

- Re-read the texts in Activity 1 with the class.
- Elicit the key features of students' own country/countries and write them on the board.
- Students write a draft of their texts individually.
- Students write a final version and draw a feature or their flag.

1 38 WB p113 Listen and number. Exam skills

Aim: to practise listening for specific information

For script see TB p126.

Key: 2 b, 3 e, 4 d, 5 h, 6 c, 7 a, 8 g

2 WB p113 Look at the picture in Activity 1. Write the names.

Aim: to practise working out connections between pictures

Key: b Jim, c Pip, d Sue, e Kay, f Tom, g Bob, h Mia

Ending the lesson

Aim: to practise reading and comparative skills

- Make groups of four to six.
- Students take turns to read aloud their texts from SB Activity 3. They compare texts.

Extension activity

Aim: to review vocabulary sets

- Make groups of eight and arrange each group in a circle. Make a paper ball for each group (or use a soft ball).
- The student with the ball says a holiday activity and then throws it to another student, who says another holiday activity and so on.
- Change to landscape and animal words and repeat.

1 Read and write the country.

Come to the USA

Go to a National Park. Look at the beautiful old trees. Catch a fish in a lake. Sleep in a tent under the stars.

Come to South Africa

Go on a safari. See the animals – lions, hippos and giraffes. Go to Boulder's Beach and see the penguins. Our beaches are great!

a ______________

b ______________

2 131 Listen and tick ☑ the country.

	1	2	3	4	5
USA					
South Africa					

3 Make a poster about your country.

Come to Mexico. See the beautiful beaches and swim in the sea.

Think and learn

Landscapes

What can we do on holiday?

1 132 **Listen and point.**

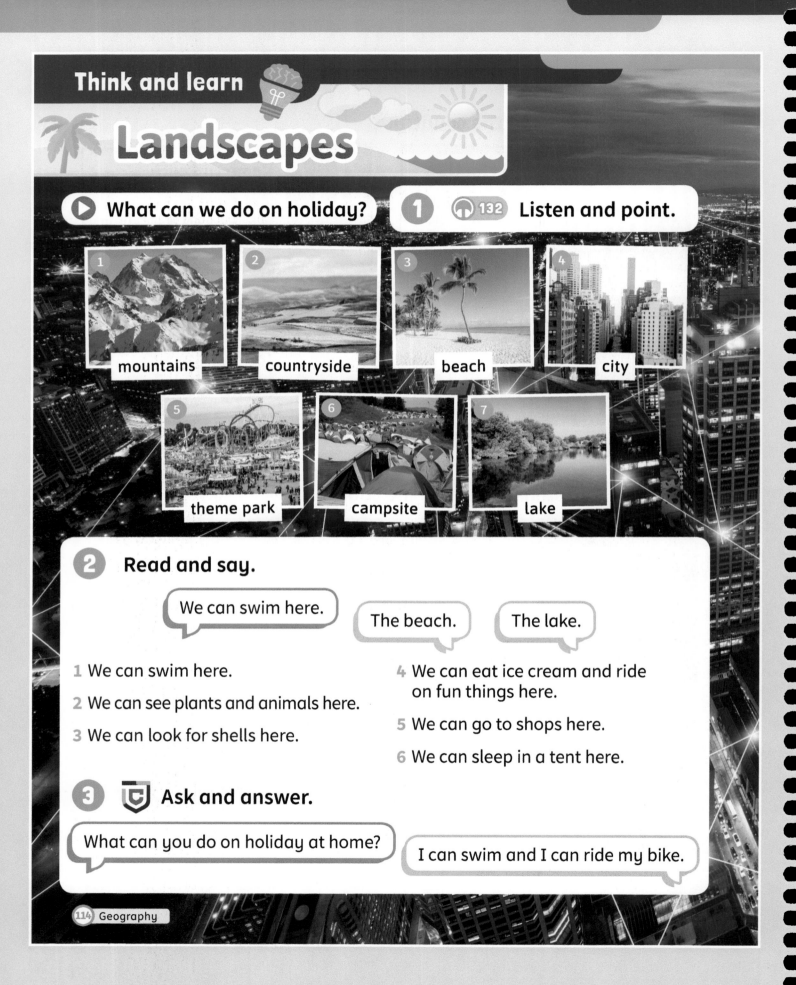

1

mountains

2

countryside

3

beach

4

city

5

theme park

6

campsite

7

lake

2 **Read and say.**

We can swim here.

The beach.

The lake.

1 We can swim here.

2 We can see plants and animals here.

3 We can look for shells here.

4 We can eat ice cream and ride on fun things here.

5 We can go to shops here.

6 We can sleep in a tent here.

3 **Ask and answer.**

What can you do on holiday at home?

I can swim and I can ride my bike.

Learning outcomes:
- to integrate other areas of the curriculum through English: Geography
- to identify and name different landscape features

BIG QUESTION to explore the Big Question *Where can we go on holiday?*

New language: *countryside, city, theme park, campsite, outdoors, fun things*

Recycled language: holiday activities, *I can …, mountains, beach, lake, plants, animals, ride, shop, sleep*

Creative thinking: Generates ideas around a topic (elaboration)

Critical thinking (WB): Draws conclusions from given information

Materials: pictures of features in the local area, e.g. a city, a beach, a mountain range (optional)

Warm-up

Aim: to review the idea of different types of holiday
- Write the Big Question *Where can we go on holiday?* on the board.
- Say *We can go to different places on holiday. Where can we go?* Elicit destinations (e.g. *beach, mountains, lake*) and write them on the board. Say *On holiday, we can stay at … (home).* Elicit things students do when they are at home and on holiday. Write them on the board.

Stronger students: Pairs make two lists of places and activities.

SB p114 What can we do on holiday?

Aim: to extend students' awareness of holiday activities
- With Student's Books closed, play the video.

For videoscript see TB p126.

- Ask students what they remember. They can use L1 to tell you about the theme park, the bus trip, etc.
- Students watch again to answer *What can we do on holiday?* Play the video again and elicit the answer.

1 132 SB p114 Listen and point.

Aim: to present words for landscape features
- Play the recording. Students listen and point to the photos.

For script see SB p114.

- Play the recording again. Students repeat. Ask students for the names of features in their area (e.g. a big city, a beautiful beach, a mountain range). Show pictures, if possible.

2 SB p114 Read and say.

Aim: to link new language to previous knowledge, and practise reading
- Read the activity instruction and the example. Explain the meaning of *fun things*.
- In pairs, students read each sentence and choose places from Activity 1.

Key (possible answers): 2 The mountains, The countryside, The beach, The lake; 3 The beach; 4 The theme park, The city, The beach; 5 The city; 6 The campsite

3 SB p114 Ask and answer.

- Read the speech bubbles.
- In pairs, students think of activities they can do on holiday at home, as well as in each of the places in Activity 1. Monitor and make sure they are taking turns to ask and answer.
- Pairs share ideas with the class.

1 WB p114 Look and write.

Aim: to practise writing the new language

Key: 2 lake, 3 countryside, 4 campsite, 5 mountains, 6 theme park, 7 beach

2 WB p114 Read. Then look at the pictures in Activity 1. Write the numbers.

Aim: to reinforce learning from the lesson

Key: b 5, c 4, d 2, e 6, f 3, g 1

Lesson review

- Elicit what students learnt today and write it on the board, e.g. *Today I've learnt about locations for holidays.* Students copy in their notebooks.

Extension activity

Aim: to further practise generating ideas around a topic
- In pairs, students choose one of the places in the pictures in SB Activity 1 and make a list of things you can see and do there.
- They make a leaflet advertising the place. Write a model text on the board, e.g. *Come to the mountains! You can go skiing. You can walk with your friends. You can see beautiful birds and animals.*

Learning outcomes:
- to extend the focus on Geography through English
- to complete a project

New language: *diary, perfect (holiday), take the train, go on a boat*

Recycled language: landscape features, holiday activities, days of the week, *tent, climb, view, go surfing, trees, have a pizza*

Creative thinking: Uses own ideas for doing creative activities like retelling stories

Cognitive control functions: Cognitive flexibility

Critical thinking (WB): Demonstrates understanding of links between new ideas

Creative thinking (WB): Chooses options to create something new

Materials: diary (optional), A3 paper, coloured pens or pencils, magazines, scissors, glue, digital or print portfolios

Warm-up

Aim: to review landscape features
- Elicit landscape words from the previous lesson (*mountain, beach, lake, countryside, city, theme park, campsite*).
- Ask *Where am I?* and mime an activity (e.g. putting up a tent). Students say, e.g. *Campsite!*

4 SB p115 Read and match.

Aim: to enable students to apply their own knowledge and experience
- Make sure students know they have to match each place to a number on the map by drawing lines (the numbers refer to the sentences). Do an example.
- Students read and match individually, and then compare answers in pairs.
- Check and discuss as a class. Accept any reasonable answers (e.g. some students might take photos and eat pizza at the beach or in the countryside, too).

Key: 1 d, 2 a, 3 b, 4 f, 5 c, 6 e

5 Project SB p115 Write a diary for a perfect holiday.

Aim: to enable students to apply what they have learnt about landscapes
- Show students a diary or draw one on the board. Briefly discuss what a diary is for (planning what to do or writing about what you have done).
- Practise the days of the week with the class.
- Look at the example diary and ask, e.g. *What does she do on Tuesday? (Go to the beach.)*
- Write *My perfect holiday* on the board and elicit/explain the meaning of *perfect*.
- Students make notes about where their perfect holiday is, how they can go there and two or three things they can do.

Extra support: Brainstorm words for transport, landscapes and appropriate activities, and write them in columns on the board.

- Give each pair a piece of A3 paper and show them how to draw a table with five columns, labelled with five days, e.g. Monday to Friday or Wednesday to Sunday.
- Pairs can then either draw a picture or find, cut out and stick pictures into their diaries for each day. They write the activity above each picture. They can use *Go home* on the last day, as in the model.
- Pairs show their diaries and tell the class their plans.
- Students' diaries could be saved to their digital portfolios.

3 WB p115 Read and match.

Aim: to practise reading the new language

Key: 2 e, 3 d, 4 c, 5 b

4 WB p115 Choose, write and draw.

Aim: to practise writing the new language

Lesson review

- Write on the board: *Today I've …*
- Elicit what students did today, e.g. *written a diary.*
- Write it on the board. Students copy it into their notebooks.

Extension activity

Aim: to give further practice with writing about holiday places
- Students share what they wrote for WB Activity 4.
- Have a class vote on the favourite place for a holiday or day trip.

4 Read and match.

a

mountains

b
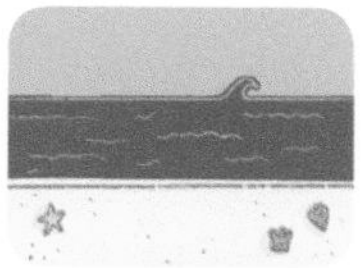
beach

c
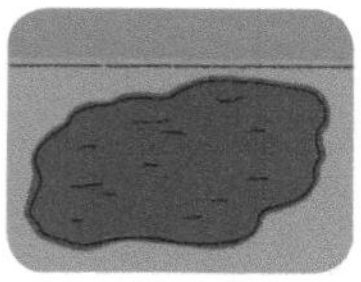
lake

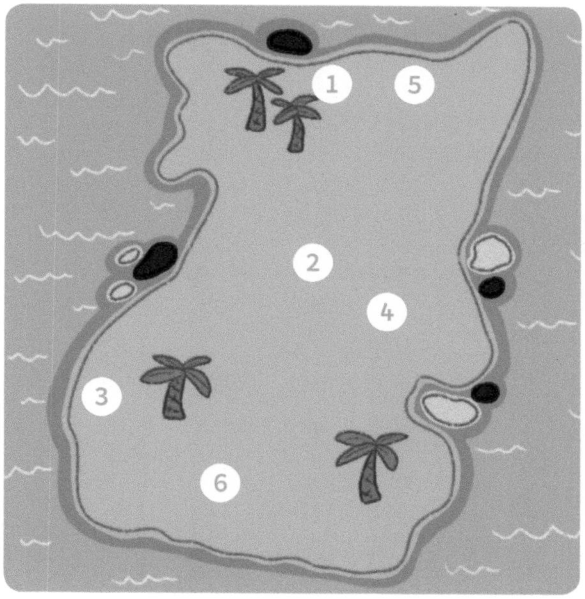

d

campsite

e

city

f

countryside

1 Take a tent and have a holiday.

2 Climb up and see the view.

3 Make a sandcastle and go surfing.

4 Ride bikes and see lots of trees.

5 Go on a boat and catch a fish.

6 Take photos and have a pizza.

5 Project Write a diary for a perfect holiday.

Monday	Tuesday	Wednesday	Thursday	Friday
Take the train.	Go to the beach.	Eat an ice cream.	Go on a boat.	Go home.
			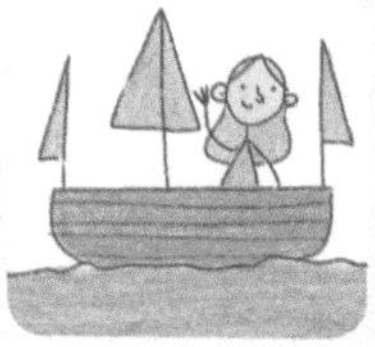	

Create that!

1 133 **Listen and imagine. Then draw your picture.**

2 **Work with a partner. Compare your pictures.**

I can ... on my holiday.

You can ... on your holiday.

Learning outcomes:
- to listen, imagine and draw to demonstrate meaning
- to describe holiday activities

Recycled language: holiday activities, imperatives

Creative thinking: Chooses options to create something new

Cognitive control functions: Inhibitory control

Creative thinking (WB): Uses different media to make and describe his/her own designs

Materials: flashcards 99–107 (holidays), coloured pens or pencils, recording of guitar music (optional); For the WB making activity: white paper, coloured paper, hole punches, string, coloured pens or pencils, students' own holiday photos

Warm-up

Aim: to review holiday activities
- Place the holiday flashcards in a row on the board. Draw an outline around each one.
- Elicit the phrase for each picture, e.g. *catch a fish.*
- Take one flashcard away.
- Elicit the phrase for each picture, working from left to right, including the missing flashcard.
- Continue in this way, removing one flashcard at a time, until there are none on the board and students are reciting the phrases from memory.
- Hand out the flashcards to nine students, who place them in the correct spaces on the board.

Extra support: Encourage students to help each other and give clues, e.g. *You can do this at the beach.*

1 133 SB p116 Listen and imagine. Then draw your picture.

Aim: to give students practice in listening and following instructions
- Remind students how to do the activity.
- Play the recording for students to follow instructions.

For script see TB p126.

- Play the recording again before students draw, if necessary.
- Circulate as they draw, asking *Are you in the countryside? Is there a lake? Who's this? Is this your family or your friends? Are you taking a photo?* Praise students for using their imagination and for their originality.

2 SB p116 Work with a partner. Compare your pictures.

Aim: to practise speaking
- Ask volunteer students to describe their picture in Activity 1, using *I can …* Encourage them to say as much as they can (e.g. *I can swim and look for shells on my holiday. There's a beach in my picture. This is my family.*)
- Students work in pairs. They show each other their pictures and take turns to talk about them.

1 WB p116 Make a holiday scrapbook.

Aim: to enable students to follow a set of instructions to make a holiday scrapbook
- Read the list of items. Students check they have what they need on their desk.
- Work through the instructions, showing students how to make the scrapbook cover.
- Students make their scrapbooks and decorate the cover. Circulate and help with stages 3 and 4.

Note: Students can stick their own photos in the scrapbook in the next lesson or draw pictures for homework.

Ending the lesson

Aim: to enable students to share their ideas
- Display the pictures from SB Activity 2 around the classroom, as if in an art gallery.
- Students walk around and look at their classmates' work.
- Monitor and ask questions, e.g. *Do you like this picture? Is this holiday in the mountains? What's this? What can you do here?*

Stronger students: Ask different students to choose a picture they liked and say something about it.

Extension activity

Aim: to enable students to show their holiday scrapbooks
- Students take turns to talk to the class about the pictures and different sections in their holiday scrapbook.

Note: They may do this in the next or subsequent lessons when they have a chance to bring in photos from home.

Learning outcomes:
- to review language from the unit by doing a quiz
- to reflect on learning

BIG QUESTION to think about how the unit has helped them talk about the Big Question *Where can we go on holiday?*

Recycled language: vocabulary and grammar from the unit

Creative thinking (WB): Creates texts that express personal interests, emotions, or identity

Cognitive control functions (WB): Cognitive flexibility

Flashcards: 99–107 (holidays)

Warm-up

Aim: to review holiday activities
- Display the flashcards on the board. Write a number between *1* and *9* under each one. Students write the numbers and then the phrases in their notebooks.
- They compare answers in pairs and then check in their Student's Book.
- In pairs, students practise the phrases. Student A closes his/her notebook. Student B says, e.g. *I can make a …* Student A says *sandcastle.*

1 SB p117 Read and circle.

Aim: to enable students to review language from the unit by doing a quiz
- Remind students that they answer by circling one option for each sentence, using the picture clues, if appropriate.
- Do the first item in the quiz as an example, if necessary.
- Students do the quiz in pairs. The first time, they do it without looking back through the unit.
- Pairs check their work with other pairs.
- Students then look back to check questions they did not know.
- Check answers with the class.

Key: 1 c, 2 a, 3 a, 4 c, 5 b, 6 a, 7 a, 8 b

1 WB p117 Write and circle.

Aim: to enable students to assess their own learning

Key: 2 Good idea. 3 Sorry, I don't want to.

2 WB p117 Draw places and write.

BIG QUESTION **Aim:** to enable students to revisit the Big Question and consolidate learning
- Check and ask students to give more examples of places we can go on holiday (e.g. *campsite, beach, stay at home*).

Key: 2 mountains, 3 lake

3 WB p117 Read. Then draw and write.

Aim: to enable students to personalise the topic

Picture dictionary

Aim: to review vocabulary for holiday activities
- Students look at the Picture dictionary page for holidays (WB p128).
- In pairs, they take turns to point to one of the pictures and say the phrase.
- Then students write the phrases under the pictures.

Key: eat an ice cream, listen to music, look for shells, make a sandcastle, paint a picture, read a book, take a photo, play the guitar

Ending the lesson

Aim: to enable students to express their preferences and review language from the course
- Ask students what their favourite song is from the whole book and have a class vote.
- Play the song with students following the lyrics in their Student's Books.
- Students practise the song (with actions, if appropriate) and then perform it in small groups or all together.

Stronger students: Make groups of four or five. Each group practises a different song and then performs it for the class, along with the karaoke audio or video.

Extension activity

Aim: to enable students to share what they have learnt
- Put students into groups of four.
- They take turns to show the picture they drew for WB Activity 3 and read their description.
- Students can copy their pictures and sentences onto a piece of paper. The pages can be put together to make a class book, called 'Our perfect holidays'.

1 Read and circle.

1 **I can … a sandcastle.**

a eat b play c make

2 **I can … a photo.**

a take b look for c read

3 **Let's …**

a catch a fish. b paint a picture. c listen to music.

4 **Let's …**

a read a book. b eat ice cream. c play the guitar.

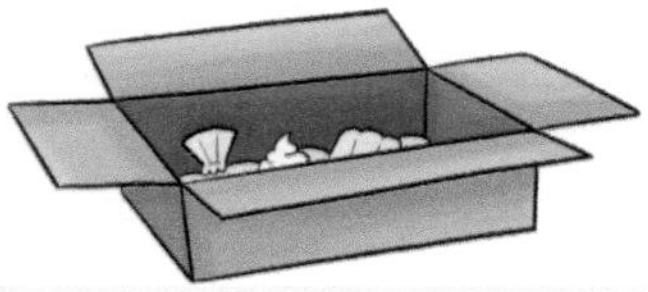

5 **Where … the shells?**

a is b are

6 **Where … the kite?**

a is b are

7 **In the story, … wants a race.**

a Flash b Thunder c Misty

8 **We are at the …**

a campsite. b lake. c theme park.

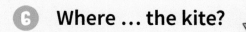

Student's Book Language Focus key

Friends

P118, Act. 1

1 7, 2 3, 3 1, 4 8, 5 5, 6 10

P118, Act. 2

1 red, 2 blue, 3 green, 4 yellow, 5 orange, 6 purple

1 At school

P119, Act. 1

1 What's this? It's a book. 2 Is it a bag? No, it isn't. 3 Is this a pencil? Yes, it is.

P119, Act. 2

1 Close, 2 Get, 3 Write, 4 Pass

2 Let's play

P120, Act. 1

1 c, 2 d, 3 b, 4 a

P120, Act. 2

1 a long blue train, 2 a new yellow kite, 3 a small green monster, 4 an old red go-kart

3 Pet show

P121, Act. 1

1 under d, 2 on a, 3 in b, 4 on c

P121, Act. 2

1 like, 2 don't like, 3 like, 4 don't like

4 Lunchtime

P122, Act. 1

1 've got / haven't got, 2 've got / haven't got, 3 've got / haven't got, 4 've got

P122, Act. 2

1 Yes, we have. 2 No, we haven't. 3 No, we haven't. 4 Yes, we have.

5 Free time

P123, Act. 1

1 play, 2 ride, 3 go, 4 play, 5 ride

P123, Act. 2

1 play / No, I don't. 2 play / Yes, I do. 3 go / Yes, I do. 4 watch / No, I don't.

6 The old house

P124, Act. 1

1 There is, 2 There is, 3 There are, 4 There is, 5 There are

P124, Act. 2

1 Are b, 2 How many c, 3 Is a

7 Get dressed

P125, Act. 1

1 this, 2 these, 3 these, 4 this, 5 don't, 6 do

P125, Act. 2

1 Tom is wearing blue jeans. 2 Is Tim wearing a jacket? 3 Are Joe and Zoe wearing shoes? 4 Dan and Ann are wearing red jackets.

8 The robot

P126, Act. 1

1 Lucy can skip. 2 Alex can't skip. 3 Lucy can't swim. 4 Alex can't swim. 5 Lucy can dance. 6 Alex can dance.

P126, Act. 2

1 Can, 2 can't, 3 But, 4 Yes

9 At the beach

P127, Act. 1

1 Let's, 2 sure, 3 build, 4 Sorry, 5 want

P127, Act. 2

1 Where are the shells? 2 They are on the beach. 3 Where is the fish? 4 It's in the sea.

Friends

01 Student's Book p4, Act. 1

Thunder: What's your name?
Whisper: I'm Whisper.
Thunder: Hi, Whisper. I'm Thunder.
Whisper: Hi, Thunder.
Misty: Hi, I'm Misty. What's your name?
Flash: I'm Flash.
Misty: Hi, Flash!
Flash: Hi, Misty!

Now say the words.
1 Thunder
2 Whisper
3 Flash
4 Misty

04 Student's Book p5, Act. 2

Teacher: How old are you, Misty?
Misty: I'm six.
Teacher: How old are you, Whisper?
Whisper: I'm eight.
Teacher: How old are you, Flash?
Flash: I'm eight.
Teacher: How old are you, Thunder?
Thunder: I'm seven.

08 Student's Book p7, Act. 2

1 Flash's bag is green.
2 Thunder's bag is blue.
3 Misty's bag is purple.
4 Whisper's bag is red.

02 Workbook p8, Act. 1

1 **Flash:** Look at me!
2 **Whisper:** I speak to animals.
3 **Cat:** I'm four.

1 At school

10 Student's Book p10, Act. 1

Flash: Oh no! My notebook!
Super Friends: Wow! Look at Flash!

Now say the words. *[numbered words on SB page]*

12 Student's Book p11, Act. 1

1 **Girl:** What's this?
Boy: Is it a rubber?
Girl: Yes, it is.

2 **Boy:** What's this?
Girl: It's a ruler.

3 **Girl:** What's this?
Boy: Is it a pencil?
Girl: No, it isn't. It's a pen.

4 **Girl 1:** What's this?
Girl 2: Is it a pencil case?
Girl 1: Yes, it is.

16 Student's Book p13, Act. 1

1 **Teacher:** Sit at your desk, please.
2 **Teacher:** Open your bag, please.
3 **Teacher:** Close your book, please.
4 **Teacher:** Pass me a pen, please.
Boy: Here you are.

04 Workbook p14, Act. 1

1 **Flash:** Mum. My notebook!
2 **Flash:** I'm sorry.
3 **Man:** It's OK.

19 Student's Book p15, Act. 4

Come back, Matt!
Here's your black bag!
Come back, Matt! Here's your black bag!

05 Workbook p15, Act. 2

a A black bag. b A cat. c A black hat. d A fat rat.

20 Student's Book p16, Act. 1

Fred: Hi, I'm Fred. This is my desk. There's a pencil case, a pencil, a rubber, a ruler and a book.
Mia: Hello, I'm Mia. This is my desk. There's a pencil case, a pencil, a rubber, a ruler and a pen.
Kim: Hi, I'm Kim. This is my desk. There's a pencil case, a pencil, a rubber, a ruler and a notebook.
Jane: Hello, I'm Jane. This is my desk. There's a pencil case, a ruler, a rubber, a pen and a book.
Sam: Hi, I'm Sam. This is my desk. There's a pencil case, a pencil, a ruler, a pen and a notebook.

06 Workbook p17, Act. 1

Woman: Can you see the pencil?
Boy: Yes.
Woman: Write a number one on the pencil.
Now find the ruler and write number two on it.
Boy: OK.
Woman: Next, find the pencil case.
Boy: What number is it?
Woman: Three.
Now find the notebook and write number four on it.
Boy: Got it.
Woman: Look for the rubber and write number five on it.
Boy: OK.
Woman: Can you see the book?
Boy: Yes.
Woman: Write the number six on it.
Boy: Number six.
Woman: And now the bag. Write number seven on it.
Boy: Yes.
Woman: The last one.
Boy: Is it the pen?
Woman: Yes, it is. Write number eight on the pen.

Student's Book p18

How do we learn?
We use our five senses to learn.
We look.
We listen.
We smell.
We taste.
And we touch.
We look at the teacher.
We listen to a story …
… and loud music!
We smell flowers …
… and old socks!
We taste our food.
We touch our toys,
our animals,
and our friends!
Which senses do you use?
Let's find out more!

22 Student's Book p20, Act. 1

Close your eyes and listen.
Imagine Penny the penguin.
Penny has got a bag for you.
Look at the bag. Touch the bag.
What colour is it?
What's in the bag? Is there a book? Is there a pencil case? Is there a notebook?
Now open your eyes and draw a picture.

2 Let's play

23 Student's Book p22, Act. 1

Thunder: Wow! Look at the go-kart!
Misty: Cool! It's my favourite toy.
Flash: It's a go-kart race. Let's join in!
Whisper: OK.

Now say the words. ***[numbered words on SB page]***

25 Student's Book p23, Act. 1

1 What's her name?
This is Sophie.
How old is she?
She's seven.
What's her favourite toy?
Her favourite toy is her bike.

2 What's his name?
This is Alex.
How old is he?
He's six.
What's his favourite toy?
His favourite toy is his train.

3 What's her name?
This is Olivia.
How old is she?
She's six.
What's her favourite toy?
Her favourite toy is her ball.

4 What's his name?
This is Mark.
How old is he?
He's seven.
What's his favourite toy?
His favourite toy is his kite.

29 Student's Book p25, Act. 1

1 It's a long yellow train.
2 It's a big blue plane.
3 It's an ugly black kite.
4 It's a new purple bike.
5 It's a small orange plane.
6 It's a short green train.
7 It's an old pink bike.
8 It's a beautiful pink kite.

08 Workbook p26, Act. 1

1 **Misty:** That isn't fair!
2 **Ben:** What an ugly old go-kart!
3 **Thunder:** Hold on, Misty!

32 Student's Book p27, Act. 4

red pens!
ten red pens!
Ken and his ten red pens!

09 Workbook p27, Act. 2

1 cat, **2** pen, **3** pencil, **4** bag, **5** desk, **6** ten, **7** black, **8** Flash

10 Workbook p28, Act. 1

Man: OK, look at the bike. Colour it grey.
Girl: OK.
Man: Now the train. Can you see it?
Girl: Yes.
Man: Colour it yellow.
Girl: OK. A yellow train. Great.
Man: Now find the plane.
Girl: The plane. Here it is.
Man: Good. Colour the plane blue.
Girl: A blue plane. That's cool.
Man: Next, colour the car.
Girl: What colour?
Man: Orange.
Girl: OK, an orange car.
Man: And now show me the computer game.
Girl: The computer game. Here it is.
Man: Good. Colour it green.
Girl: OK. A green computer game.
Man: And now look for the go-kart and colour it red.
Girl: A red go-kart. Fantastic!
Man: Very good. Thank you.

33 Student's Book p29, Act. 1

1 **Woman:** Hello, Ruby. What's your favourite colour?
Ruby: My favourite colour's orange.
Woman: What's your favourite number?
Ruby: My favourite number's ten.
Woman: And what's your favourite toy?
Ruby: My favourite toy's my yellow kite.
Woman: Thank you, Ruby.

2 **Woman:** Hello, Nathan. What's your favourite colour?
Nathan: My favourite colour's green.
Woman: What's your favourite number?
Nathan: My favourite number's three.
Woman: And what's your favourite toy?
Nathan: My favourite toy's my bike.
Woman: Thank you, Nathan.

Student's Book p30

What toys do you know?
Which shapes are in your toys? Let's see.
Look at the squares!
Look at the bicycles. Look at the triangles in the bicycles.
Look at the circles in the go-kart.
Emma's favourite toy is her favourite shape. It's a kite!
There's a rectangle in the plane …
And in the car.
And in the computer!
Which shapes are in your toys?
Let's find out more!

35 Student's Book p32, Act. 1

1 Take a piece of paper.
2 Fold the piece of paper.
3 It's a plane!
4 Fly the plane.
5 Where's the plane?
6 Ouch!

36 Student's Book p33, Act. 3

1 What's this?
2 It's a monster.
3 What's his name?
4 His name's Rory.

3 Pet show

37 Student's Book p34, Act. 1

Teacher: Welcome to the pet show.
Flash: A spider! Aagh!
Flash, Thunder, Misty, teacher: Aagh!
Spider: What's the problem?
Whisper: I don't know.

Now say the words. *[numbered words on SB page]*

39 Student's Book p35, Act. 1

1 The green frog is on the desk.
2 The yellow frog is in the desk.
3 The red frog is under the desk.

43 Student's Book p37, Act. 1

1 **Spider:** I like dogs.
2 **Spider:** I don't like cats.
3 **Spider:** I don't like lizards.
4 **Spider:** I like spiders!

12 Workbook p38, Act. 1

1 **Whisper:** Come back. He's beautiful.
2 **Spider:** I've got an idea.
3 **Flash:** He's clever.

46 Student's Book p39, Act. 4

This is Tim
and his silly sister Kim.
This is Tim and his silly sister Kim.

47 Student's Book p40, Act. 1

Take the cat.
The cat's in the tree. Stick it in the tree.

Take the duck.
The duck's under the kite. Stick it under the kite.

Take the lizard.
The lizard's in the bag. Stick it in the bag.

Take the rat.
The rat's under the ball. Stick it under the ball.

Take the dog.
The dog's on the grass. Stick it on the grass.

14 Workbook p41, Act. 1

Woman: Put the donkey under the tree.
Boy: Sorry?
Woman: Put the donkey under the tree.
Boy: OK.
Woman: Now put the duck on the pond.
Boy: Right.
Woman: Put the dog under the table.
Boy: OK.
Woman: Put the cat in the tree.
Boy: Right.
Woman: And put the spider on the chair.
Boy: Sorry?
Woman: Put the spider on the chair.
Boy: OK.

Student's Book p42

What do animals drink?
Animals need four things.
Animals need shelter.
A spider lives in a web for shelter.

Animals need water.
A bird drinks water.
And animals need food.
A lizard eats spiders.
'It's cold.
The donkey needs shelter.'

That's good!
'There's no water.
The elephant needs water.'
That's good!
All animals need four things …
air
shelter
water
and food.
Let's find out more!

49 Student's Book p44, Act. 1

Close your eyes and listen.
Imagine you can see an animal.
What animal is it? Is it a spider, a donkey or a frog?
What colour is it? Is it big, or is it small?
Where is the animal?
What does this animal need?
Does it need water? Does it need food? Does it need shelter?
Now open your eyes and draw a picture.

4 Lunchtime

50 Student's Book p46, Act. 1

Woman: Steak, chicken, sausages and pizza!
Whisper: Pizza! Yum!
Flash: Are you hungry, Thunder?
Thunder: Yes, I am.
Misty: Look at the queue!

Now say the words. *[numbered words on SB page]*

52 Student's Book p47, Act. 1

1 **Girl:** Hello! Look at my lunch today. I've got a sandwich and an apple.
2 **Girl:** Hello! Look at my lunch. I've got a sandwich and a banana.
3 **Boy:** Hi! My lunch is yummy. I've got pizza and a banana. I haven't got an apple.
4 **Boy:** Hello! Look what I've got! I've got pizza and an apple. I haven't got a banana.

16 Workbook p50, Act. 1

1 **Thunder:** Where's Misty?
2 **Flash:** Hey! That isn't fair.
3 **Woman:** Here you are.

58 Student's Book p51, Act. 4

for a hot dog.
at the shop for a hot dog.
Polly stops at the shop for a hot dog.

17 Workbook p51, Act. 2

Black: hat, bag
Red: desk, pen
Orange: doll, box
Pink: fish, six

60 Student's Book p52, Act. 2

Dad: Tom, can you look in the fridge, please? What have we got?
Tom: Just a minute, Dad. … We've got 16 carrots.
Dad: Wow! That's a lot! Have we got any apples?
Tom: Um, yes, we've got 13 apples.
Dad: Great! Have we got any steaks?
Tom: Yes, we've got one steak.
Dad: OK. And have we got any sausages?
Tom: Yes, we've got four sausages.
Dad: OK. Let's go shopping. We need lots of steaks and sausages for the party!
Tom: Yummy!

18 Workbook p53, Act. 1

Girl: Can we make a cake today, Mum?
Mum: Yes, OK. What kind of cake?
Girl: Can we make a banana cake?
Mum: Sure.

Girl: Where are the bananas? We haven't got any in the fridge.
Mum: I've got some bananas in my bag, from the shop.
Girl: Great! Can we start now?

Student's Book p54

What types of food do you know?
Some food comes from a plant.
Vegetables …
… and fruit come from plants.
Some grow under the ground.
Peas grow on a plant.
Bananas grow on a tree!
Some food comes from an animal.
Steak …
Fish …
… and cheese come from an animal.
Your food has got a story.
The apple is on the tree. The farmer picks the apple.
The apple is on a long journey.
Now, the apple is in the shop.
It's lunch time!
Where does your food come from?
Let's find out more!

62 Student's Book p56, Act. 1

1 Buy a banana.
2 Go out of the shop.
3 You are hungry.
4 Eat the banana.
5 Throw the peel down!
6 You slip on the banana peel. Ouch!

63 Student's Book p57, Act. 3

1 **Girl:** Have we got any bananas?
2 **Boy:** No, we haven't.
3 **Girl:** Oh dear. I'm very hungry.
4 **Boy:** There's an apple in my bag.
5 **Girl:** I don't like apples.

5 Free time

64 Student's Book p58, Act. 1

Misty: School on Monday, Tuesday, Wednesday, Thursday and Friday.
Thunder: Football match on Saturday!
Super Friends: Hurray!
Flash: Trip to the lake on Sunday!
Super Friends: Hurray, hurray!

Now say the words. ***[numbered words on SB page]***

66 Student's Book p59, Act. 1

Sandra: Hi, I'm Sandra. I ride my bike on Sundays.
Pat: I'm Pat. I play the piano on Mondays and Fridays.
Maria: My name's Maria. I play football on Thursdays.
Oliver: My name's Oliver. I ride my pony on Tuesdays and Saturdays.
Bill: Hi, I'm Bill. I go swimming on Wednesdays and Fridays.

70 Student's Book p61, Act. 1

Woman: Hey, Liam. Do you watch TV at the weekends?
Liam: Yes, I do. I watch a lot of TV.
Woman: And do you play board games?
Liam: Yes, I do. I play them on Saturdays and Sundays.
Woman: Do you play football?
Liam: Yes, I do. I play football.
Woman: And do you play tennis?
Liam: No, I don't.
Woman: Do you ride your bike?
Liam: No, I don't.
Woman: OK …
Liam: But I ride my horse on Sundays!
Woman: That's great! Thank you, Liam.

20 Workbook p62, Act. 1

1 **Misty:** Where's the lake?
2 **Whisper:** I've got an idea.
3 **Rabbit:** Come with me.

73 Student's Book p63, Act. 4

On Sundays Mum has fun
with the ducks in the mud.
On Sundays Mum has fun with the ducks in the mud.

74 Student's Book p64, Act. 1

1 **Woman:** Jim, do you play tennis?
Jim: Yes, I do. I play on Mondays and Wednesdays.
Woman: Really?
Jim: Yes, and I play on Fridays, too.
Woman: Do you play tennis at the weekend?
Jim: Yes, on Saturdays. But I don't play tennis on Sundays.

2 **Woman:** Emily, do you ride a bike?
Emily: No, I don't. I ride a horse.
Woman: A horse! Do you ride it on Tuesdays?
Emily: Yes, I do! And I ride on Thursdays, Saturdays and Sundays, too.
Woman: Wow! Tuesdays, Thursdays, Saturdays and Sundays! That's a lot.
Emily: I know. I love my horse!

22 Workbook p65, Act. 1

1 **Man:** James, do you play the piano on Mondays?
James: No, I don't. I play football.

2 **Man:** Emma, do you play with your friends on Wednesdays?
Emma: Yes, I do.

3 **Man:** Charles, do you watch TV on Fridays?
Charles: Yes, I do.

4 **Man:** Hannah, do you ride your bike on Saturdays?
Hannah: No, I ride my horse.

Student's Book p66

What do we do?
We do lots of different activities.
We help at home.
Some activities are fun!
We run in the sun …
And we dance in the rain!
We ride a bike in the park.
And we sing songs at home.
Children play different games around the world.
Sport is fun.
We can do lots of different sports.
We go skiing …
and sledging in the snow.
We go swimming …
and surfing in the water.
We do lots of different activities.
Let's find out more.

76 Student's Book p66, Act. 4

1 **Girl:** I go skiing and I go sledging.
2 **Boy:** I go climbing, I go running and I go swimming.
3 **Boy and girl:** We go climbing, we go running, we go surfing and we go swimming.

77 Student's Book p68, Act. 1

Close your eyes and listen.
Imagine your perfect Sunday.
You're in bed, sleeping – but it isn't much fun.
You get out of bed, but what do you do?
Do you play football with friends?
Do you ride your bike or ride a horse?
Do you play a board game or watch TV?
Do you go skiing or go surfing?
There are lots of things you can do!
Now open your eyes and draw a picture.

6 The old house

78 Student's Book p70, Act. 1

Whisper: Wow! Look at this house.
Thunder: It's old, really old.
Misty: Let's go and see it.
Whisper, Thunder, Flash: OK.

Now say the words. ***[numbered words on SB page]***

80 Student's Book p71, Act. 1

1 **Monster:** There's one frog in my bedroom.
2 **Monster:** There are four frogs in my bedroom.
3 **Monster:** There are two frogs in my bedroom.
4 **Monster:** There are five frogs in my bedroom.

84 Student's Book p73, Act. 1

Woman: Look at the picture.
Boy: OK.
Woman: Is there a park?
Boy: Yes, there is.
Woman: Are there any bikes?
Boy: Yes, there are.
Woman: Are there any dogs?
Boy: No, there aren't.
Woman: How many ducks are there?
Boy: There are seven.

24 Workbook p74, Act. 1

1 **Flash:** Go in? No way!
2 **Thunder:** Careful, Misty.
3 **Whisper:** Misty, where are you?

87 Student's Book p75, Act. 4

a hairy spider.
there's a hairy spider.
In Harry's house there's a hairy spider.

88 Student's Book p76, Act. 1

Interviewer: Mr Big, you've got a big house.
Mr Big: Yes, yes, yes! There are six living rooms.
Interviewer: Six living rooms? Really?
Mr Big: Yes, I've got a very big house.
Interviewer: How many bathrooms are there?
Mr Big: There are four bathrooms.
Interviewer: Four bathrooms?
Mr Big: Yes, there's one for me, and there are three for my friends.
Interviewer: And how many kitchens are there?
Mr Big: Ah. There are two kitchens, but they're very big.
Interviewer: OK, just a moment. Two kitchens.
Mr Big: Yes, and there are 15 bedrooms.
Interviewer: 15 bedrooms?
Mr Big: Yes, there is one for me and 14 for my friends.
Interviewer: And is there a garden?
Mr Big: Yes, there's one garden. It's very big.
Interviewer: How many dining rooms are there?
Mr Big: There are three big dining rooms.
Interviewer: Thank you, Mr Big.
Mr Big: That's OK!

26 Workbook p77, Act. 1

Boy: Here is my house. It's a big house. It's got a red door. I like the red door.
I've got two cats. One cat is black and the other cat is black and white.
In the garden there are lots of flowers. The flowers are blue and yellow. There are two big trees. The trees are orange.
My bike is in the garden. It's green. I like my bike.
And there's my football. My football is blue and yellow. Let's kick the ball. … Whoops!

Student's Book p78

What types of homes do you know?
Some people live in the countryside.
There are very big houses …

and small houses.
There are houses on wheels.
And tree houses.
There are round houses … like this yurt.
There are cave houses,
and very cold houses … like this igloo!
Some people live in the town … and the city.
There are lots of different homes in the city.
There are pretty houses …
funny houses …
and house boats on the water!
There are flats in tall towers.
Look at the view!
Homes are different in lots of ways …
Let's find out more!

90 Student's Book p80, Act. 1

1 You're in the living room.
2 There's a big spider on the table.
3 Catch the spider.
4 Open the window.
5 Put the spider outside.
6 The spider waves goodbye.

91 Student's Book p81, Act. 3

1 **Boy:** Do you play board games at the weekends?
2 **Girl:** Yes, I do.
3 **Boy:** Where do you play them?
4 **Girl:** In my living room.
5 **Boy:** That's great!

7 Get dressed

92 Student's Book p82, Act. 1

Whisper's little brother: You look great!
Whisper: Thanks, bro. It's 'Favourite clothes day' at school.
Mum: Hurry up, Whisper!
Whisper: OK, Mum. Ready!

Now say the words. ***[numbered words on SB page]***

94 Student's Book p83, Act. 1

1 **Girl 1:** Do you like this T-shirt?
Girl 2: No, I don't.

2 **Boy 1:** Do you like these shoes?
Boy 2: Yes, I do.

98 Student's Book p85, Act. 1

Girl: What are you doing, Tom?
Tom: I'm looking at some photos of my friends. David, James …
Girl: Let me see. Is that James? Is he wearing a green T-shirt?
Tom: No, he isn't. He's wearing a blue T-shirt and he's playing a board game with Emily.

Girl: Emily. Is she wearing the green cap?
Tom: Yes, she is.

Girl: And who is Oliver?
Tom: Oliver is wearing a red T-shirt. He's watching TV.

Girl: And who is watching TV with him?
Tom: That's Katy.

Girl: And what about these two with the dog? Who are they?
Tom: That's David. He's wearing the green T-shirt.

Girl: And Gemma? Is she wearing a red cap?
Tom: Yes, she is.

28 Workbook p86, Act. 1

1 **Whisper:** My cap isn't here.
2 **Flash:** Are you sure?
3 **Whisper:** I'm very sorry, Gary.

101 Student's Book p87, Act. 4

There are stripes and spots
on the socks on the stairs.
There are stripes and spots on the socks on the stairs.

29 Workbook p87, Act. 2

1 stop	3 steak	5 skirt	7 school
2 spider	4 sweater	6 stairs	8 snake

30 Workbook p88, Act. 1

Man: Look at the trousers.
Boy: The trousers. OK.
Man: Colour them blue.
Boy: Blue trousers. Great.
Man: Now the T-shirt. Can you see it?
Boy: Yes.
Man: Colour it red.
Boy: A red T-shirt. Cool.
Man: Next, find the socks. They're on the floor.
Boy: The socks. Here they are.
Man: Good. Colour them orange.
Boy: OK, orange socks.
Man: Now find the sweater. It's in the box.
Boy: The sweater. Here it is.
Man: Colour it yellow.
Boy: A yellow sweater. Great.
Man: And now the shoes. Can you see them?
Boy: Yes.
Man: Colour them green.
Boy: OK.

102 Student's Book p89, Act. 2

Tom is riding a bike.
Emma is playing the piano.
Kylie is eating an apple.
Fred is playing football.

Student's Book p90

What patterns do you know?
We all wear different clothes. Some clothes are plain.
These children are wearing white, grey and red. This is their school uniform.
These people are wearing a uniform for their job.
Some clothes have patterns: spots, stripes, flowers and zigzags.
People wear different clothes around the world.
We wear special clothes for special days. Dressing up is fun.
Our clothes look different in lots of ways. Let's find out more …

104 Student's Book p92, Act. 1

Close your eyes and listen.
Imagine you are at home. Your friends are there.
You are wearing your favourite clothes.

Are you wearing jeans and a T-shirt? Or a skirt and a sweater? Are you wearing shoes and socks?
What colour are your clothes? Are they blue? Green? Orange? Green and orange?
Are there patterns on your clothes?
What are the patterns? Spots, stripes, zigzags? Or are they plain?
Now open your eyes and draw a picture.

8 The robot

105 Student's Book p94, Act. 1

Misty: What have you got there?
Thunder: A robot kit.
Flash: Great! Let's make a robot!

Now say the words. *[numbered words on SB page]*

107 Student's Book p95, Act. 1

Thunder: I can't touch my toes.
Whisper: I can't skip.
Flash: I can't stand on one leg. Whoa!
Misty: I can touch my toes.
Thunder: Wow!
Misty: I can skip.
Whisper: Wow!
Misty: I can stand on one leg.
Flash: Wow!

111 Student's Book p97, Act. 1

Interviewer: Hello, Sophie. Can I ask you some questions?
Sophie: Yes, you can.
Interviewer: Can you play tennis?
Sophie: No, I can't.
Interviewer: Can you play the piano?
Sophie: Yes, I can.
Interviewer: Can you ride a horse?
Sophie: Yes, I can.
Interviewer: And can you ride a bike?
Sophie: Yes, I can.
Interviewer: Can you swim?
Sophie: Yes, I can.
Interviewer: Can you dance?
Sophie: No, I can't.
Interviewer: Thank you, Sophie.

Interviewer: Hello, Tom. Can I ask you some questions?
Tom: Yes, you can.
Interviewer: Can you play tennis, Tom?
Tom: No, I can't.
Interviewer: Can you play the piano?
Tom: No, I can't.
Interviewer: Can you ride a horse?
Tom: No, I can't. But I can ride a bike!
Interviewer: Can you swim?
Tom: Yes, I can and I can dance.
Interviewer: Thank you, Tom.

32 Workbook p98, Act. 1

1 **Flash:** Here's the left arm.
2 **Flash:** No problem.
3 **Robot:** Yes, I can.

114 Student's Book p99, Act. 4

in a big green bag.
his fingers in a big green bag.
Greg's got his fingers in a big green bag.

115 Student's Book p100, Act. 1

1 Can Patch swim?
A: Patch can't swim.
B: No, he can't. Look, he's in trouble.
2 Can Sue ride a bike?
A: Can you ride a bike?
B: No, I can't. But my sister, Sue, can ride a bike. Look! Here she comes now.
3 Can Coco stand on one leg?
A: Can you stand on one leg, Coco?
Coco: I don't know. Let's see. … Whoa! No, I can't.

34 Workbook p101, Act. 1

1 **Man:** Hello. Are you the little girl in the picture?
Karen: Yes, I am.
Man: What's your name?
Karen: I'm Karen.
Man: Can you spell your name?
Karen: Sure. K A R E N.

2 **Man:** Thank you. And how old are you, Karen?
Karen: I'm six.
Man: Six?
Karen: Yes.

3 **Man:** And is this your dog?
Karen: Yes. His name is Bruno.
Man: Can you spell Bruno?
Karen: Yes. It's B R U N O.
Man: Thank you.

4 **Man:** Have you got any other pets?
Karen: Yes. I've got lizards.
Man: Lizards! How many lizards have you got?
Karen: I've got three lizards.
Man: Thank you.

5 **Karen:** And I've got a horse.
Man: A horse! Can you ride him?
Karen: Yes, I can. Spotty is very friendly.
Man: Spotty. Is that his name?
Karen: Yes.
Man: Can you spell it?
Karen: S P O T T Y.

Student's Book p102

How do you move?
We can move in lots of different ways.
Babies can't walk. They crawl.
Then they take their first steps.
We can jump …
and stretch …
and stand on one leg!
We can dance to our favourite music.
People doing sport can move in amazing ways.
They can jump forwards a long way.
And they can swim backwards.

Animals can move in incredible ways.
Forwards …
Backwards …
And sideways!
We can move in lots of different ways.
Let's find out more!

117 Student's Book p102, Act. 2

Go two steps forwards.
Go three steps sideways to your left.
Jump.
Go three steps backwards.
Go two steps to your right.
Jump.

118 Student's Book p104, Act. 1

1 You've got a big ball!
2 Bounce your ball.
3 Throw your ball in the sky.
4 Where is the ball?
5 The ball is in a tree!
6 Oh dear!

119 Student's Book p105, Act. 3

1 Can you see Luke?
2 No, I can't. Which boy is he?
3 He's over there.
4 Is he wearing blue jeans?
5 Yes, he is.

9 At the beach

120 Student's Book p106, Act. 1

Thunder: Look at that hill.
Flash: We can have a race.
Thunder: OK.

Now say the words. ***[numbered words on SB page]***

122 Student's Book p107, Act. 1

1 **Boy:** Let's paint a picture.
Girl: I'm not sure.
2 **Woman:** Let's take a photo.
Man: Good idea.
3 **Girl 1:** Let's listen to music.
Girl 2: Good idea.
4 **Man:** Let's look for shells.
Boy: Sorry, I don't want to.

126 Student's Book p109, Act. 1

1 **A:** Where's the shell?
B: It's on the sandcastle.
2 **A:** Where are the kites?
B: They're in the blue and yellow toy box.

36 Workbook p110, Act. 1

1 **Flash:** Bye. See you at the top of the hill!
2 **Whisper:** A race is not a good idea.
3 **Flash:** This is the end of the race. We can't get to the top of the hill.

129 Student's Book p111, Act. 4

Jean eats an ice cream
under a tree on the beach.
Jean eats an ice cream under a tree on the beach.

37 Workbook p111, Act. 2

1 see
2 read
3 three
4 cheese
5 eat
6 beach
7 peas
8 ice cream

130 Student's Book p112, Act. 1

1 Take the boat. Put the boat on the sea.
2 Take the ice cream. Put the ice cream in the boy's hand.
3 Take the ball. Put the ball on the sand.
4 Take the hat. Put the hat on the sandcastle.
5 Take the shell. Put the shell under the kite.

131 Student's Book p113, Act. 2

1 You can see penguins at the beach here.
2 You can go fishing here.
3 You can see a lot of animals here.
4 The beaches here are very good.
5 You can sleep in a tent outside here.

38 Workbook p113, Act. 1

Boy: What a lot of people on the beach!
Girl: Jim's in the sea. He's swimming. He's a good swimmer.
Boy: And who's that eating an ice cream? It's Pip. That's a nice ice cream.
Girl: Hmm. Pip loves chocolate ice cream!
Boy: Hello, Sue.
Girl: Sue can't hear you. She's listening to music. And Liz is reading a book.
Boy: Liz likes books. There's Bob. He's taking a photo of his friends. Smile, everyone!
Girl: Mia's making a sandcastle. It's really big. There are lots of shells on it.
Boy: Look, there's Tom. Tom's looking for shells.
Girl: And don't forget Kay. Kay's painting a beautiful picture. The picture is of the beach.

Student's Book p114

What can we do on holiday?
We can stay at home and have a great holiday.
We can ride bikes in the park.
And read a book in the garden.
We can go to the beach on holiday.
It's a great place to make sandcastles
and eat ice cream.
We can go to the countryside.
This campsite has got a great view of the mountains.
We can visit a farm.
Or go to a lake.
We can go to a theme park on holiday.
We can ride on fun things!
Or we can go to a city.
We can go on a bus trip and take lots of photos.
We can go to different places on holiday.
Let's find out more!

133 Student's Book p116, Act. 1

Close your eyes and listen.
Imagine you're on a holiday. It's a beautiful day.
Where are you? Are you at the beach? Are you at a campsite?
Are you in a big city, in the countryside or at a lake? Or are you in the mountains?
What do you do? Do you go swimming? Do you catch a fish?
Do you climb mountains? Do you play with friends? Do you like your holiday?
Now open your eyes and draw a picture.